D1106158

Robert Drew
and the Development
of Cinema Verite
in America

P.J. O'Connell

Southern
Illinois
University
Press

Carbondale
and
Edwardsville

Copyright © 1992 by the Board of Trustees,
Southern Illinois University
All rights reserved
Printed in the United States of America
Edited by Annmarie Allen
Designed by Mary Rohrer
Production supervised by Natalia Nadraga
95 94 93 92 4 3 2 1

Library of Congress Cataloging-in-Publication Data

O'Connell, P. J., 1935–
    Robert Drew and the development of cinema verite in America / P.J.
O'Connell.
        p.   cm.
    Includes bibliographical references and index.
    1. Drew, Robert, 1924–   —Criticism and interpretation.
    2. Documentary films—United States—Criticism and interpretation.
    I. Title.
    PN1998.3.D73025 1992
    070.1'8—dc20   91-39992
    ISBN 0-8093-1779-6   CIP

The paper used in this publication meets the minimum requirements
of American National Standard for Information Sciences
—Permanence of Paper for Printed Library Materials, ANSI Z39.48-1984. ∞

Bob's background as a young man was as a fighter pilot.
And a fighter pilot's different from a bomber pilot.
A fighter pilot flies alone.
And makes the decisions to do whatever he does.
He's a fighter pilot.
He wanted to run his own show.

—Gregory Shuker, on his former boss Robert Drew

Contents

CONTENTS

viii

Preface

John Kennedy and Eddie Sachs, in the vernacular of the present, "blew me away."

More accurately, it was *Primary*, a documentary film on the 1960 Wisconsin presidential primary election, and *On the Pole*, a documentary on the 1960 Indianapolis 500 auto race, that accomplished the task.

In August of 1962, I was a local television news and documentary cameraman-editor, attending the Robert Flaherty Film Seminar at the University of Minnesota, watching the most advanced documentary films of the time: *Seaward the Great Ships* by Hillary Harris, *Grassroots* and *Ed and Frank* by Denis Mitchell, *Wasn't That a Time* by Michael and Phillip Burton, *The Hunters* and *Women under the Baobab* by John Marshall, *The Language of Faces* by John Korty, and *Lonely Boy* by Wolf Koenig and Roman Kroitor. But the informal observations of John Kennedy patiently having his portrait taken by an overly chatty small-town photo studio operator and Eddie Sachs praying quietly to himself in the midst of the noisy confusion surrounding the start of the world's most prestigious auto race are sequences that have remained nearly as fresh in my mind as on that day in Minneapolis.

It is hard now to communicate how fresh, how unusual, how unique were the unvarnished human behaviors those films captured. Some of us in television news had tried, awkwardly, to do the same; had sensed that closely observed actions of real people in real, unrehearsed, uncontrolled situations might be possible. But we couldn't do it. Marshall, Korty, the Burtons, Koenig and Kroitor, and Richard Leacock had.

Especially Leacock. *Primary* and *On the Pole* were listed in the Flaherty

ix

program as "by Richard Leacock." An accompanying list of films carried the notation "Courtesy: Drew Associates" in a form suggesting that this was the distribution company for the films. Documentary film was changing dramatically from the practices of Flaherty, Lorentz, Grierson and company, Van Dyke, and other directors of the 1930s, 1940s, and 1950s. It seemed clear in our screenings that an important watershed boundary had been crossed. The medium would soon be primarily television rather than the movie screen; the material natural and alive rather than staged and/or stilted. The transition from the strictures of the old to the possibilities of the new was under way, but if there were any connection between the onrushing development of cinema verite and Robert Drew, my notes do not show it.

As cinema verite grew and spread, as a new generation of equipment—and filmmakers with the initiative and imagination to use it—developed, film journals erratically traced the changes. Robert Drew remained, in these accounts, an occasionally mentioned "producer" rather than a "filmmaker," inaccurately credentialed in the eyes of a distant reader. Only with the publication of A. William Bluem's *Documentary in American Television* in 1965 did Drew's role in cinema verite begin to emerge. Bluem attacked Drew's journalistic innovations and extolled the conservatism of the television networks' documentary units; Drew became more important to me as a result.

And then he disappeared. Cinema verite was changing, rapidly. Leacock was making only an occasional film. The Maysles brothers were on a divergent course. Donn Pennebaker was moving into music. Frederick Wiseman began producing annually for public television; cinema verite moved in his direction, and then beyond, to independents and advocacy and docudrama and whatever. And Robert Drew was largely unmentioned, an incidental reference in the literature of a period of profound cinematic and journalistic change.

Then, a decade and more later, he resurfaced, or at least came back into my field of view. He presented a day-long screening and discussion at the Conference on Visual Anthropology in 1980, and a similar afternoon session at the Flaherty Seminar later that year. An autobiographical article by Drew appeared in the journal *Studies in Visual Communication* in 1982, and he released a major documentary titled *Fire Season* on public television in 1983. Critic Richard Lacayo wrote a lengthy *New York Times* article on the program—and on the reemergence of Robert Drew.

When the opportunity came to me, in 1983, to begin a major research and writing project, Robert Drew and cinema verite were among the possible topics. Both were too big, frankly, and too complex to trace accurately. There were too many important characters to talk with and too many contradictions and uncertainties to resolve. But other topics would not be as much fun. A study limited to Drew's contributions to the initial development of cinema verite was the compromise: manageable—barely— and, as a pleasant initial interview revealed, Drew was accessible. The literature search, the too-limited review of Drew's films and files, the interviews with Leacock, Pennebaker, and Gregory Shuker—all fun. The details of the origins of Drew's brand of cinema verite were fascinating: the accounts of professional and personal experiences and expectations; the tensions between people of different backgrounds, purposes, and goals; the slow, perhaps predictable, unraveling of an elegant and ambitious plan. Synthesizing the diverse—and divergent—materials into an accurate and readable recounting was a difficult experience—and an undeserved privilege.

Cinema verite, a distinctive approach to documentary filmmaking that developed in the United States, France, Canada, and England in the early 1960s, was quite different from previous forms of documentary production because it sought to record human events more directly and with less intrusion into those events by the production process than had formerly been thought possible—or felt necessary. The development of cinema verite resulted both from conceptual changes in how documentary film materials could be originated and presented, and from technological advances in filmmaking equipment and methods.

Robert Drew was a major innovator and organizer of both the conceptual and technological developments that were fundamental to cinema verite. Taking part of his inspiration from the photojournalism of *Life* magazine, where he served as writer and correspondent, Drew set out to "revolutionize television journalism." He faced difficult technological problems in his efforts to adapt *Life*'s methods of obtaining dramatic-but-not-intrusive photographs of human events to the demands of film and television. There were the conceptual problems of how to accurately observe personal human events with a camera, recorder, and two filmmakers present, and there was also the major problem of how to present such unconventional material to television audiences of the period in a form that they would find understandable and interesting.

In the end, Drew failed to reach the large national audiences he sought on a regular basis with his numerous documentaries; he failed to induce Time, Inc. to buy or create a television network for the display of his film journalism; and he failed to persuade television journalists of the value of his production philosophy. He succeeded, however, in innovating conceptual approaches and technological methods that, in fact, clearly revolutionized documentary filmmaking, if not television journalism. Drew's impact on the documentary was so fundamental that almost all later developments owe some debt to his pioneering efforts.

But while this study is an honest attempt to recall those efforts, there are important limitations that need to be called to the attention of the reader. Most important is the fact that this study relies heavily on interviews, by myself and others, with Richard Leacock, Donn Pennebaker, Gregory Shuker, and Robert Drew. The interviews with Drew and Pennebaker conducted by Barbara Hogenson between 1979 and 1981 for the Oral History Research Office of Columbia University were especially helpful and important. While I have documented most direct quotations from the interviews, I have chosen, in the interest of readability, to allow several short quotations from the interivews to appear without formal documentation. The detail of those interviews, and the opportunity to compare them with my own for consistency, added a great deal to my understanding of Drew's actions and to the overall accuracy of this account. The recall by these individuals of events that happened thirty years ago is likely to be uncertain and contradictory, in varying degrees and for varying reasons: poor recall, confusion, the influence of hindsight, or perhaps the wish to put the best face on events. It has not been possible to resolve all the contradictions; indeed, that is not a purpose of this study. The recollections included here illustrate the complexity of Drew's efforts at innovation. Each of the principal participants saw, and judged, the enterprise differently, and those differences in viewpoint are an important part of the developmental record of cinema verite. The contradictions in the testimonies serve to illustrate the difficulties that any documentary innovator would face in trying to introduce a markedly different conceptual approach and a new technology into a conservative, highly competitive industry. Drew's self-assigned task was never an easy one, but the record of his efforts provides valuable insights for both future innovators and those who would simply understand more fully the complexities of high-level documentary production.

There is another, and particularly regrettable, limitation to be noted: there are only four primary voices in this account. There should be more. Others at Drew Associates, especially James Lipscomb and Hope Ryden, would have added different perspectives on the development of the Drew organization. The voices of Time, Inc. are also underrepresented; personal accounts from Drew's supervisors would likely have provided a more practical assessment of why Drew's experiment was allowed to proceed and why it was terminated. The reactions of Drew's contemporaries in television network journalism are also unfortunately missing. (One, when contacted briefly at a very early point in the research, demanded to know why anyone would want to write about "that son-of-a-bitch!" Regrettably, that opening could not be followed up.) But there is only so much time and energy, and choices had to be made; these are mine.

A final caution: the placement of Drew's efforts within the broader development of cinema verite is skimpy at best. The Maysles brothers and Frederick Wiseman are treated briefly, along with introductory references to the work of ethnographic filmmakers and some important critics of cinema verite. The work of Jean Rouch and others in France as well as parallel developments at the National Film Board of Canada have been omitted; readers must turn to other sources for that information. This study focuses, narrowly and necessarily, on the actions of Robert Drew and his principal associates.

It is useful to recall, perhaps, that Drew's chosen field was not an uncomplicated one. The documentary was called by Richard Barsam "the most familiar, but most abused and most misunderstood term in the film lexicon." Barsam, in *Nonfiction Film: A Critical History*, gathers the best definitions of documentary by Grierson, Lorentz, Van Dyke, Sarris, and others in arguing for a new term, "nonfiction film." It is an instructive attempt; the terminological confusion that Barsam displays for his readers reflects the variety of purposes and philosophies that have uncritically—and misleadingly—been heaped under the umbrella of "documentary." It is a confusion no scholar, critic, or filmmaker has yet been able to successfully dispel. Even the terms "filmmaker" and "filmmaking" are subject to a variety of spellings, including "filmaker," "film-maker," and "film maker." "Filmmaking" is used throughout this study in the interests of consistency, both in text and in quotations.[1]

And the definitions of the key critical terms "*cinéma vérité*" and "direct cinema" have been the subject of continuing confusion since their introduction thirty years ago. The definitions that follow are offered for the purposes of this study only and do not constitute an effort to resolve the critical debate:

> —*Cinéma Vérité*: a method of documentary filmmaking based on the use of highly portable equipment and characterized by a *high* level of filmmaker involvement in the activities of the subjects, in the form of questions and requests for introspective reflections on events. The method and the name are generally attributed to French anthropologist Jean Rouch and sociologist Edgar Morin.
> —Direct Cinema: a method of documentary filmmaking based on the

use of highly portable equipment and characterized by a *low* level of filmmaker involvement in the activities of the subjects, in that the filmmakers act principally as observers of events. The method was developed by Robert Drew and Richard Leacock, and others; the name was applied by Drew after it became clear that the term "*cinéma vérité*" did not adequately describe his filmmaking intentions.

To compound the confusion, the term "cinema verite," without italics or accent marks, has come to be widely applied to all forms of filming of the spontaneous activities of subjects, while the term "direct cinema" has not been widely accepted, and "*cinéma vérité*" seems to be poorly understood. This study uses "cinema verite" to describe both "*cinéma vérité*" and "direct cinema" since that corresponds to the most common usage in the film literature.[2]

I am especially indebted to Tom Benson, my advisor and friend, for his guidance and encouragement in the research and writing of this manuscript; to the helpful questioning of Dick Barton, Gene Goodwin, Dennis Gouran, and Dorn Hetzel; to the Department of Speech Communication and the School of Communication at the Pennsylvania State University; and to Marlowe Froke and my colleagues at WPSX-TV, who were patient and supportive during the research and writing process. I would like to thank Robert Drew, Richard Leacock, Donn Alan Pennebaker, and Gregory Shukar for permission to reprint excerpts from their interviews.

Finally, as all writers do, I have an obligation to thank my family— Carolyn, Kathleen, Ellen, Mike, Dan, Joe, and Shannon—for what sometimes seemed like unending support. Only they will understand how much it has cost us all. I do appreciate it.

Robert Drew
and the Development
of Cinema Verite
in America

Background

A picture of a man in a flight suit is frozen on the nine-inch video screen. Then, at an abrupt "Okay," a control is pushed and the man lurches into a normally paced walk toward the camera.

"One—two—three—. Okay, this is our opening shot." Producer Robert Drew straightens up, makes a quick note on a legal-sized yellow pad, then bends over the shoulder of editor Marty Lucas to follow the action on the screen.

Marty: "Shall we lay it down here?"

Drew: "No. Let's plan it, then you lay it down. It'll be faster that way."

It is 10:00 A.M. on Saturday. By Tuesday morning, when Drew leaves for a client meeting in Los Angeles, a ten-minute "film" must be completed outlining a proposal to make the first unpowered aircraft ascent of Mt. Everest. It is an improbable idea—until Drew explains it.

The planning has been imaginative and carefully direct. The chief pilot will be Prince Alvero de Orleans Bourbon, the world mountain-gliding champion. "He's a member of the royal family of the King of Spain. And through his contacts, he contacted the King of Nepal and got permission for this. Nepal doesn't allow this kind of flying inside its country, but we got permission to do it." The second pilot will be actor Cliff Robertson. Robertson is an experienced pilot, but he is also "known by the public and would help people enter that experience." Drew understands the importance of that fact.

The short videotape of the two pilots simulating their adventure will be shown to network executives and potential sponsors. Drew is aiming for a movie-of-the-week on network television. "It's expensive and difficult and who would want to sponsor it I can't imagine, but this is how things start. You start dreaming and fulminating and something happens." Drew is an experienced glider pilot, but on this project he'll be shooting videotape from a chase plane, content to watch and record another "first" as it happens—as he planned it.

But that explanation will come later, after Drew has outlined the film's opening for Marty. Several scenes have been selected, with Drew noting their times for the narration he will write after lunch. Right now, Drew is searching for "Mt. Everest."

Marty is puzzled. "It's only labeled 'Mt. Everest'," Drew explains. "It's really the Sierras. It's supposed to be a pretty picture." But "Mt. Everest" is not where Drew's notes say it should be. Marty wonders if the time-code counter is accurate. "It better be," Drew exclaims, "or we're a day behind already!"

While Marty fast-forwards through the videotape, Drew leans back in the indirect light of the television monitors, watching gliders, pilots, and the California landscape jerk across the screens. He is sixty years old, enough heavier than in his early photographs to be noticeable, neat in pressed white shirt, gray trousers, black dress shoes and black socks. Perhaps because it is Saturday, there is no tie.

There is, however, a problem. The time code on Drew's videotapes appears to be faulty; his preview notes may be useless. Drew's second wife, Anne, has come down from the apartment on the fifth floor of the East Seventies townhouse that serves as home for the Drew family and for Drew Associates, Drew's twenty-four-year-old production company. After listening to the discussion of the time-code problem, Anne, also an editor and a producer, goes to talk to Carla, an assistant editor working in the next editing room. Marty suggests calling David, yet another editor who had worked on the tapes earlier, about the problem. Drew is getting impatient. "I'll call him! You look for Mt. Everest!"

With almost forty years in print and film journalism, Bob Drew has had to face innumerable deadlines. But mostly they have not been the shoot-and-run deadlines of hard news; they have been the longer deadlines of news magazines and television documentaries. His primary reputation is in film journalism, a film journalism judged by many to be innovative, perhaps revolutionary. Gliders are only a personal diversion—and perhaps a way to pay part of the rent.

"Mt. Everest" is beautiful. Backlighted clouds, angel-rays stretching toward the camera, the peak silhouetted in the distant background.

Then Cliff Robertson is on the screen, recalling his first conversations with Drew about the historic—if clearly out-of-the-ordinary—project. Robertson first remembers Anne Drew exclaiming, "You've got to be crazy!" And then Robertson repeats the carefully logical explanation he gave to Anne and to dozens of other curious and incredulous friends: "I've tried to stress to them that this is not a stunt. . . . It's an opportunity to do something that's never been done before. . . . It's a partnership between the wind and us." [Pause; expertly timed.] "Except there is one other partner, and He's—up there." [Perfect pacing and inflection, eyebrows arched slightly heavenward at the right moment; very professional.] Drew then exclaims, as he watches the screen, "That's wonderful."

"Something that's never been done before." Familiar ground for Robert Drew. Not just the unusual—he's already escaped from behind enemy lines in WW II, won a television Emmy, a Golden Eagle, and a Peabody and has festival awards from Cannes, Venice, and Bilboa—but "something that's never been done before": the first film system and filmmaking philosophy to show in accurate detail how real people live, struggle, and— almost—die; the first, and probably only, detailed film record of an American president and his staff in the process of crisis decision making; a planned (and partly completed) documentary series on the heads of state of the countries representing the three major international power blocs of the 1960s; and a decade-long, and partially successful, effort to revolutionize American television journalism. "Something that's never been done before." It has been a fundamental goal of Robert Drew's career.

Drew is chewing gently on the stem of his glasses, sitting hunched forward beside Marty, following the screen intently. Cliff Robertson is amiably explaining why flying an unpowered glider to the top of Mt. Everest—the one in Nepal, not Southern California—is not only possible, but reasonable. There are risks, of course, but they can be known and planned for. It will be a grand adventure, certainly one the small, select audience of this film will find worth supporting. Marty is enjoying Robertson's enthusiasm; Drew is businesslike, attentive to the skepticisms his actor-friend is now addressing. He may be hearing, an observer thinks, a comment that has become annoyingly familiar after years of proposing ideas that have never been done before. Robertson describes the initial reactions of many pilots to the plan: "There are friends of mine that just shook their heads and said, 'I hope you know what you're in for!'"

2

Beginnings

Beginnings are important, perhaps, but it is hard to know exactly how. Lives are influenced and changed by strong characters, chance meetings, even the great events of history. Such seems to have been the case in the life of Robert Drew—but, again, it is hard to know.

Robert Lincoln Drew was born 15 February 1924, in Toledo, Ohio, but he had no place he chose to call home until years later. Drew's father, Robert Woodson Drew, was a film salesman for Pathe and other film companies, who moved his family to Michigan; Denver, Colorado; Salt Lake City, Utah; and Los Angeles, California; as he sold B- and C-grade features to local theater managers in the 1920s. With the onset of the Great Depression, film sales dried up and Drew's father moved the family to his hometown of Girard, Pennsylvania, where Drew's grandfather, Frank Drew, was mayor and owner of several homes and businesses.

Frank Drew had decided on show business at age seven by running away with a circus, where he stayed for a number of years before buying a chain of burlesque houses, wax museums, and "other emporiums of entertainment." The elder Drew became a millionaire "several times—and lost it all several times."[1]

Drew's mother, Mary Way Passmore, brought a different sort of communications background to Drew's life. Her grandfather owned the newspaper in Bowling Green, Kentucky, where Mary was from. "So we had circuses on one side and newspapers on the other," Drew laughs.

By the mid-1930s, the Depression had ended, for the Drews at least. The family moved to Fort Thomas, Kentucky, when Drew's father first got another job distributing films and then became president of Seaplane Fliers, Inc. Young Robert, "Bobbie," went to school.[2]

> I ran into the guy that I think was the formative character in my youth . . . my trumpet teacher, who was much more than that. He was the leader of a band in a small town, and he insisted that everybody in that band, however squeaky the clarinet or however out of time the drum, that person was destined to be the greatest trumpet player or the greatest drummer in the world. So he taught everybody with the same wild intensity and discipline, and he'd stomp his foot on the floor and his hair would fly and he would scream and insist.
> I don't think I've ever run into anybody who thought that anything was quite that important.[3]

Mac McKenna, the music teacher, was important enough to Drew that he would recall, years later, a similar story his close associate, filmmaker Richard Leacock, told him. With three hours between international flights, Drew and Leacock decided on a quick tour of London. Leacock, an Englishman, had spent part of his youth in the city.

> It was a sentimental journey for [Leacock]. All we did was drive through the heart of London and come back in a taxi in traffic. On the way, we passed a red brick school, set in green grounds, and he said, "That's where I learned it all." Something to that effect. And I said, "What do you mean?" And he said, "There's a woodworking teacher in that school who taught me everything I know." And I said, "Well, what was it?" He said, "Well, first, it was the way he kept his tools. And then it was his idea of how to carve a leg." And he went on—he had met a guy, a disciplined guy, at a formative age. And I kind of think that happens to people.[4]

At the formative age of fifteen or sixteen, Bob asked his father to teach him to fly. "Not on your life!" was the reply. Drew's father had no objection to Bob learning to fly, only that no family member should ever try to teach another. Drew senior hired an instructor.

Seaplane Fliers operated from a barge in the Ohio River, next to the Newport Yacht Club, "a gambling establishment, run by an Italian lady who was so tough that she could and did throw grown men through plate glass windows. But during the day, it was a nice place."

Bob liked flying, and worked for Seaplane Fliers for a couple of years until the next major milestone in his life occurred. It marked the end of Seaplane Fliers, but "for me, it was absolutely heaven-sent!" The event occasioning this youthful enthusiasm was the outbreak of World War II.[5]

World War II

"Big airplanes and fighter airplanes and everything I ever dreamed of were instantly available, almost." The timing was just right, as it would be again for Robert Drew. He left high school for the Army Air Force in his last semester (Spring 1942), the first in his class to do so. He quickly passed a test showing his educational level at two years of college in order to get into officer's training as an aviation cadet: "I hadn't been to college, but I did know something about airplanes and so flying school for me was just a joy."[6]

After a year at training fields in Texas and Arkansas, Drew graduated and became an officer on his nineteenth birthday. After several months of training on the P-51 dive bomber, he began combat flying in Italy, in September 1943. He moved from an airfield near Salerno to one outside Naples that was supporting the Allied drive up the Liri River valley toward Rome. It was here that Drew had his first encounter with big-time journalism. Ernie Pyle, one of the most popular battlefield correspondents of the war, had the room next door. "And he wanders into my room one night and notices I'm addressing a letter to Lt. Robert Drew from Lt. Robert Drew. So he immortalized that exchange of letters so my mother could read about how strange it was to have two Robert Drews in the Air Force."[7] Drew's father had followed his son into the Air Force, ferrying airplanes from the United States to Europe. Robert Woodson Drew crashed and was killed in December 1944, while taking off in a snowstorm from Gander, Newfoundland.

Naples was also where Drew completed thirty successful combat missions. But Mission 31, on 31 January 1944, was notably unsuccessful, at least for Drew.

> We were divebombing the town of Fondi, where the best oranges in Italy come from. And I was the last ship . . . and we're straight down on the town and I'm seeing the bombs going off from the first ships. . . . And I don't see any German convoys there. But I do see some off . . . to one side and so—if you're straight down, to move over, you have to roll. So I'm rolling my ship and trying to get my sights on the German convoy. And I finally do and I punch the button and drop the two five-hundred pound bombs and pull out. What this means is it took me longer than the rest; you're supposed to pull out at three thousand feet and I was probably pulling out at about one thousand. So . . . what I saw was streams of flak, streams of anti-aircraft fire, coming up under my ship. So I'm pulling up and the flak is pulling up and I'm pulling up and it's pulling up and at about three thousand feet, I guess, suddenly there occurs a thunderclap and I

can't see or move or breathe. It seems like it's all over and it seems too bad.[8]

Drew managed to parachute down, landing on the roof of a house. While German soldiers searched the village for him, he escaped across the fields into the mountains. "But I find out I'm not in all that great shape. I can't see. I have to hold my eyes open with my fingers, things like that." The next day, Drew found refuge with an Italian farmer who had been expelled from the United States as a rumrunner. He spent a month hiding in the mountains during the days, eating and sleeping with the man's family at night. He celebrated his twentieth birthday avoiding German patrols.

After a month, Drew decided to get back through Allied lines and began walking his way south. "We were basically begging from Italians who were starving. It was a neat trick, but we all lost a lot of weight." Finding it impossible to just walk through the battle front because of German patrols and minefields, Drew and two Englishmen tried to swim around it. But the cold Mediterranean water forced them back, with one of Drew's companions nearly drowning from exposure and the other killed by a land mine on the beach. Drew finally made it through by hiding close to the frontlines while the Germans were pushed back by advancing French troops.

Drew had spent three and a half months behind enemy lines. He wanted to fly again, against targets he now knew first hand, but regulations at that time prevented pilots who had been shot down from flying again in the same theater of operations. So Drew was sent back to the United States, where he promptly encountered the Pentagon and discovered jet airplanes.

I went to the Pentagon after I got back from combat to find the guy—the son-of-a-bitch—who had stopped ordering A-36's. I flew a version of the P-51 called the A-36, which was a great airplane. But when I got back from being shot down, my squadron was flying P-40s, which were an old-fashioned, terrible airplane, in which the pilots ran awful risks. I wanted to find the guy who had stopped ordering P-51's . . . and question his judgment and see if he couldn't reverse it. I mean, this was not my job, as a second lieutenant in the Air Force, but I was outraged that my friends were flying this terrible equipment.

So I found this guy, and instead of getting mad—he was a colonel, and he was a very busy colonel—he invited me to lunch. And he explained the strategic theory of the invasion of Europe to me and how we needed a high altitude fighter, and how the airplane I had been flying was the perfect high altitude fighter, . . . and in order to get high altitude fighters for the invasion of the Continent and for the long-range bombing of Germany, they took the airplanes.[9]

In the course of having the Allied invasion plan of Europe explained to him over lunch, Drew also mentioned his excitement about jet airplanes. Jets were the newest, "hottest" American combat aircraft, barely beyond the experimental stages. The first jet training units were just being formed, and plenty of experienced pilots wanted to fly them. But, like Drew, they were not considered qualified to handle the new technology. The Pentagon colonel set Drew a challenge: go back to engineering school and get the education the Air Force felt was necessary to fly the jets. "I met the challenge, and he helped, I'm sure, to get me assigned to the new squadron. In fact, I know he did because when I reported to the squadron commander, he said, 'Lt. Drew, you're the first man who's been assigned to my squadron who I haven't requested, so you're going right back out.' And I said, 'Good. Let me apply to you to become a member of your squadron.' And he said, 'I'll think about it.' "[10]

After three months, Drew was "requested" back into the squadron. He was one of fifteen or twenty pilots in the First Fighter Group, the first fighter unit in the United States to be equipped with jets. Drew's next adventure was getting under way.

> All of our training was aimed at covering the islands of Japan, and we were really looking forward to that, because we had these hot airplanes that would give us an enormous advantage over the Japanese.
> The tough thing in combat is to meet an enemy who is better off than you are, or as well off as you are, and the really good thing is to meet some guy who is almost defenseless. That's what going into combat in Japan with a P-80 would have been at the time.[11]

But Drew and his fellow fliers never got the chance to fly against a "defenseless" enemy. For once, "the right time and the right place" were not in Drew's favor—or so it seemed.

> I never had a more disheartening day than the day I landed at some air base in Northern California and was walking across the apron, and I heard a radio voice talking about this enormous bomb we had dropped on Japan. And it hit me; "Oh shit, there it goes. The war will be over before I can get there."
> So at a time like that, you start thinking about what you are going to do with the rest of your life, and I guess I developed a feeling that I didn't want to fly big airplanes. . . . I guess I got the feeling that basically it was driving a bus. If you don't have a war, there doesn't seem to be a lot of purpose to that kind of flying.
> So somewhere in there I began to decide that I wanted to be a writer.[12]

3

Discovering Life

"High in the blue sky over the California desert a spectacular new air force is beginning to take shape. It is a dazzling array of P-80 Shooting Stars, the propellerless jet planes that can whisk through the air at 600 mph, make a sudden turn and spurt straight up an incredible 15,000 feet. The men who fly these planes are themselves a new breed, riding a whirlwind of power unknown to the pilots of propeller-driven airplanes."[1]

So enthused the uncredited writer of a *Life* magazine story in December 1946. Robert Drew, one of the "new breed," was flying the P-80s *Life* was spotlighting. But a "sidebar" article five pages later was to be of greater long-range importance to the young flier without a war.

THE FLIERS
Young Pilot Describes Brutal Speed Of The P-80
by Lieut. Robert Drew
Pilot of the First Fighter Group

It was Drew's first, and only, byline in *Life*. He would soon begin a fifteen-year career with the magazine, but group journalism in the 1950s rarely identified its laborers.

You are always a little excited when you ease yourself into the P-80 cockpit. It is a very "hot" plane, and it can kill you very quickly. But the nervousness vanishes when you get to work. You become a part of the plane. Your head is squeezed by a hard crash helmet around the skull and chin, by a radio set over the ears, an oxygen mask against the face, goggles over the eyes. . . . With earphone and microphone wires, oxygen hose and G-suit hose you are literally plugged into the ship.[2]

A picture inset into the half-page article shows only a young man's face, his head and torso covered by helmet, goggles (pushed up), oxygen mask (pulled down), flight suit, and flying harness. The caption: "Pilot Drew is 22, a war veteran."

> You climb. The plane zooms vertically, 2 miles in 14 seconds. Your ears pop and gas belches out of your throat. Moments later you are sitting 35,000 feet in the thin blue air, and oxygen under pressure is forcing its way down into your lungs, making it hard to exhale. . . . You look at the air-speed indicator, which has a red compressibility warning line to show when you are approaching the speed of sound when the plane can fly out of control. As the slender air-speed needle wavers closer and closer to that warning line sometimes you feel an unreasonable urge to pass the red mark, to plunge the ship into a wild, screaming dive past the speed of sound and thousands of feet down to the earth.[3]

Drew had begun his writing with prize-winning high school compositions and short stories, one of which earned the recognition of being rejected by *Reader's Digest*. But his first sustained writing was for the First Fighter Group's newspaper, *News and Views*. One of his articles on the new jet planes was seen and quoted by *Time*, and *Life* later asked him to write the personal story on jet flying that was called "Jets Are Different."[4] It was 1946, and the Drews—a year earlier he had married Rue Faris, a speech and drama major at Stanford—were living in a motel outside March Field in California. Drew was leaving the Air Force, intending to spend four years at the University of Chicago so he could become a writer. Claude Stanush, the *Life* correspondent on the jet plane story, read Drew's articles, found out what he planned to do, and asked, "Why don't you work for us?" Stanush introduced the young pilot-writer to a *Life* editor, *Life* asked Drew to come to New York to help finalize the jets story, and after a few weeks training, Drew came back to California with a job. He was a *Life* reporter, at twenty-two.

Los Angeles

As a new reporter in *Life*'s Los Angeles bureau, Drew was a cog in a large, corporate machine, producing raw copy that would be heavily rewritten into the magazine's accepted style by a writer in New York. It was an important and unplanned step in Drew's formative period—from combat fighter pilot to reporter on the most popular picture magazine in the nation—and the long-term influence of the *Life* environment was to be substantial.

Drew's limited experience had been as a writer, not as a reporter. He had no newspaper experience beyond *News and Views*, no opportunity to do the more prosaic beat and event reporting that many journalists begin their careers with. *Life*, as a national weekly, did not cover traditional beats; it knew the news stories that were important enough nationally to require coverage by experienced staff members. Less-experienced staff, and those in distant bureaus, did what was later to become known as "enterprise reporting": "I was responsible for dreaming up story ideas."

From any number and type of sources, including Time, Inc.'s enormous clipping service, Drew would find interesting and/or important stories, develop an approach to a story (sometimes to the point of writing a "shooting script"), get an editor to assign the story, and then "produce" it, "that is, taking a photographer out and aiming him in the right direction. Then he was responsible for visualizing the story."[5]

Besides suggesting a story and getting it assigned, Drew and the other reporters and correspondents also made the arrangements: "travel arrangements and every other kind of arrangement—permissions and so forth— to get the photographer in a certain place at a certain time. I almost thought of that as building a stadium, organizing a game, and getting him up to bat."[6]

And the reason? "*Life* magazine was a reporting job in which success depended on getting good pictures. So you'd find a story you wanted to report on and then you'd figure out how to get the pictures taken that would make the story work."[7]

A picture story that "worked" might be the torching of palm trees— young boys in Southern California liked to touch a match to a tinder-covered tree to see the flames race up it—or the testing of airplanes. Drew's background made him a valuable reporter when the military or California manufacturers were conducting tests: "I had a lot of aviation stories." But Drew was also willing to develop more complex topics, and the major effort of his California stay, one he refers to often, took as its modest subject the City of the Angels.

> Los Angeles was one of the first cities to get so big it broke off into pieces. And in fact Los Angeles early broke into so many pieces there were city halls all over the city. There was no downtown after a while; there was a downtown, but there was no center to the city. The academics called it "decentralization" . . . and I made an essay for *Life* magazine called, of all things, "Decentralization."
>
> So I had to try to put into pictures, or into a picture script,

something that would make an essay on decentralization, which was abstract on one hand and had to be photographic on the other. So that was the first of those kind of picture stories which had some kind of an analytical or intellectual base.[8]

Drew's efforts were at least partially successful. In a nine-page memo to *Life*'s New York office, dated October 1948, Drew suggested "an essay on a grand scale": a four-part picture story on the causes of decentralization, the effect on traffic and retail businesses, and the death of the original downtown area.[9] The resulting story, "City Against Auto," spotlighted "the world's worst traffic jam," freeway building, drive-in businesses, rush-hour traffic, and "the world's biggest motorcycle [police] force."[10] Many of Drew's picture suggestions were included. It is remarkable, considering Drew's youth and limited experience with the magazine, that of the thirteen photos in the *Life* essay, ten are suggested directly in his memo.

But the story does not include the term "decentralization."

"The Start Of Something"

"I walked out of the theater that night, stunned. And grieving, that I couldn't make films. Because I was now too old."[11]

It was 1948, and Drew was twenty-four years old. He had just seen *A Double Life*, with Ronald Coleman in an Academy Award performance as a troubled Shakespearean actor who could not separate the stage from reality. "I came out of seeing *A Double Life* and felt a little grieved that I would not be able to do that . . . , make films like that, because at age twenty-four it was already too late. I didn't have the training in dramatics and theatrics and filmmaking that was necessary. But I did start thinking about how to make films about the high voltage stuff that I was seeing as a reporter. That was the start of something."[12]

It was clearly a time, about the same time as "decentralization," in Drew's telling of it, when he was exploring new ideas. There were practical aspects to his search; if a correspondent or reporter at *Life* was to be judged on how many pages he or she got into the magazine, then perhaps novelty and/or aggressiveness in dreaming up and producing stories was a way of attracting the attention of the editors. But there was also the matter of discovering a means of maintaining the tempo of an exciting and successful life. "Now what happened in the long line is that I don't want to make fiction films. I don't want to write fiction stories . . . . What I really did was invent what I did want, which is to make real films on real people. That turned out to be the endless challenge."[13]

Although Drew actually made his first venture into filmmaking in California, assisting *Life* photographer Alan Grant make films about parades and professional wrestling, "the endless challenge" was put off for several years while Drew gained additional experience by climbing *Life*'s professional ladder.

The Detroit Workshop

One of the most difficult-to-please advertisers for *Life* was the automobile industry. Keeping it happy was a major job of the Detroit advertising office. . . . *Life*'s editorial work in Detroit and Michigan had been done on a pick-up basis by the two-man *Time* bureau in Detroit. Detroit advertisers had not been happy with editorial coverage. It was not surprising that *Life* decided to open a full-time bureau in Detroit in 1949 to keep the advertisers happy.

In the spring of 1949, Drew . . . was restless to manage his own bureau. He was told he could become chief of a new bureau in Detroit if he could generate enough stories from Michigan.[14]

Caroline Dow Dykhouse has written a detailed report of Robert Drew's experiences in the newly formed bureau. As "bureau chief in charge of myself," Drew first worked with photographers assigned out of New York. His stories had to be important enough to justify the expense and were largely limited to automobile industry activities that had national implications and nationally assigned stories that happened to be located in his coverage area.

[Drew] was in a new bureau that had no photographer and that was, essentially, virgin territory for *Life* features. He was in search of two things: career advancement and new ways to record and present the real world. He was concerned with both the superficiality of the current reporting and the barriers that the camera and equipment created to the capturing of an event. He wanted to test a theory. . . .

Drew believed that "ordinary amateurs" could find good stories by photographing the world around them and could "see" the world more clearly than professionals. So he gathered a group of what he considered "ordinary people" into a photo workshop designed to teach the theory of the essay and the art of seeing stories in everyday life.

The members of this group of potential photojournalists had so diverse racial and ethnic backgrounds that they couldn't meet in a restaurant and were unwelcome in the corporate offices of Time, Inc. The group's members were so talented, however, that some of them would dominate magazine photojournalism in Detroit for twenty years.[15]

The Detroit Workshop, as it became known, was actually a small group of photographers from widely varying professional backgrounds—advertising, newspaper, wedding and studio photography—drawn by the prospects of improving their techniques, learning how the *Life* system of shooting and selecting pictures worked, and possibly getting published in the magazine.

> Drew was not a photographer. His genius lay in his ability to generate ideas, keep a group operation moving and creative, and handle the words. He understood, however, that technical problems had to be solved. He encouraged the group to share expertise and be innovative. He and others believed that technical knowledge was a means of getting a picture, not an end in itself. This was one difference between a documentary photojournalist and a photographer. The photojournalist learned all his skills in order to convey an idea. The photographer used skills to make a picture that was an end in itself.[16]

"Drew was creating great assignment ideas. He was full of energy and we did a lot of things," recalls Howard Sochurek, a workshop member who later became a well-known *Life* magazine photographer. "But it was his enthusiasm and energy and understanding of what made a story for *Life* that finally caused me to succeed and break through and get the job."[17]

Drew's Detroit stay—approximately one-and-one-half years—was not limited to shepherding his workshop free-lancers. As the ambitious chief of a one-man bureau that he had lobbied to have created as an opportunity to display his talents, Drew was constantly submitting story ideas to New York. Since some of these ideas clearly outstripped the talents and experience of Detroit's pool of local photographers—or because New York chose otherwise—Drew had opportunities to work with some of *Life*'s best photographers: Leonard McCombe, Frances Miller, and Thomas D. McAvoy. One major essay, that Drew suggested to New York, was shot by perhaps the best-known of the *Life* photographers, Alfred Eisenstadt.

> I worked with Eisenstadt on a long story about a medical school in Michigan—the University of Michigan—and it took us I think four to six weeks, something like that. So we worked together day after day . . . and I simply absorbed some of his feeling about shooting candidly and getting the real things and getting feeling and how to handle people and so forth. . . .
>
> But I would say that Eisenstadt was not my model. There were other aspects of Eisenstadt that were the reverse of my model. He liked his name to be known, he liked to grandstand a little bit and pose pictures sometimes. So the side of Eisenstadt that was candid and that produced the great candid pictures influenced me, and the other side probably influenced me too, but in reverse.[18]

Drew succeeded in almost tripling the number of magazine pages coming out of his coverage area, with the majority of the increase coming from "enterprise" stories that originated with his bureau.[19] It was a record likely to impress any editor on the lookout for developing talent within the *Life* organization. "The way you were measured at that time in the Time, Inc. bureau was by how much of your stuff got in the magazine, and my bureau was getting more stuff in the magazine per man than any other bureau, and was considered good.

"So I then became assistant picture editor in New York [in 1950]."[20]

But at Time, Inc.'s corporate headquarters, Drew discovered another institutional feature of *Life* that had not been as prevalent, or as critical to personal success and influence, at a distant bureau. "That was the least successful effort I've ever been involved with. I worked for a year or a year and a half in a large organization in which diplomacy and organizational skill counted a lot more than reportorial ability, writing ability, or anything else. And I wasn't very good at that."[21]

So, in 1951, Drew moved back to a bureau job, as a correspondent in Chicago. No longer a manager of people, he plunged back into the routines of dreaming up and selling stories. But those were, in fact, routines for him, and he began to sense a new world of "enterprise" opportunities—television.

4

The Seeds of Revolution

"You see this picture?" It is a modest picture, covering a quarter of the page; three men are playing cards on a veranda table, with two others watching. Drew is laughing in remembrance, sorting over the pages of a *Life* essay he had produced years earlier in Chicago, tracing for a listener the involved planning, the problems of shooting and editing, and the results.

"Shall I show you the key picture?" Drew points. "That's a picture of a judge wearing a Homberg, smoking a long cigar, playing poker on the veranda of a country club, during business hours!" He is no longer laughing. "While people are *dying* because they can't get through the court jam! That son of a bitch got turned out of office because of this."

It is told as a heroic tale, the group journalist overcoming technical and institutional odds with innovation and determination to get a major essay—eight pages, thirty-three pictures—on the "Legal Log Jam in Chicago" into the magazine.[1]

> First thing I had to do was visualize this. How do you tell the story? And I wrote a suggestion that was forty pages long. Then I got called to New York to discuss it with the managing editor—who felt I hadn't researched it enough! Then I went back to Chicago, and it got assigned. And from then on, Sochurek and I became an undercover team. And we sought out these victims and we went into courtrooms. . . .
>
> I hired a private detective on my own expense account—without permission or anything. I just needed somebody to pin the judge down at the racetrack, cause that's where he usually went. . . . And

I know this guy was at the track every day. We went to the track and never found him, but—. . . .

So I heard from another source that he would be at the country club this day, and we got him! Sochurek designed a camera, a little briefcase that would contain his camera. And hide it. And he and I made our way into this country club and crept up on this judge and photographed him dealing. Opposite him is the sewer commissioner. And that picture was the pivot for the whole thing; I mean, that really pinned it down. Cause all those pictures of empty courtrooms could mean—anything. But what it did mean was that the son-of-a-gun was out goofing off.[2]

Drew clearly enjoys the retelling, enjoys the opportunity to show the complexities of the process and the initiatives it requires, not only in the field but also in the office. "I simply designed the thing, and shot it, and wrote the research story to go with it. And in New York, the managing editor laid it out and a writer wrote the captions and the text blocks. And in the process, the key picture got included, but the writer wanted to leave out of the caption the crucial information."[3]

On a page subtitled "The Obstacle" (other pages are "Apathy and Confusion," and "The Victims"), the unsuspecting judge contemplates his cards while the caption offers the following information for the benefit of *Life*'s five-million-plus readers: " 'Golf Days,' occasional country club gatherings which judges must attend to maintain their political fences, and one of the time-consuming features of judicial life. Here Judge Peter Schwaba (in hat) appears at one during court day."[4]

Drew explains the problem: "So the writer wanted to leave out 'during court day.' So I had a guy fighting me, a guy fighting the whole idea of the story, who tried to gut it. And if we didn't say that it was during a court day, then everything fell apart. So I have to have a battle. Over that one little point."[5]

This time, the decision went Drew's way. He was winning his share, clearly a competent correspondent. But a long series of frustrations was beginning to build directed against both *Life* magazine and the adversary that would eventually bring it down.

I found *Life* magazine to be a weird, weird world . . . which was so intense and ingrown that everybody there was sort of looking at everybody else there and not looking out at the world. . . . They were not looking at what television was bringing. They were not looking out at what the movies were doing. They weren't imagining that what they were doing could relate.

I may be the only guy who came out of *Life* magazine who makes candid films. That's fantastic, because I don't know of any greater training ground. I don't know of any more amazing assemblage of brain power and experience than *Life* magazine had at making candid film.[6]

A specific story crystalized Drew's attitudes toward the television of the early 1950s.

> I was working as a reporter [in Chicago], covering stories that television was covering, and I was getting real power out of the stories and still pictures, and television was getting very dull stuff . . . and I marveled at the difference. Why couldn't they do it?
>
> The example that really finally set me off was a trial in which the U.S. government broke up the DuPont Company. . . . And I was in the courtroom with Frances Miller as a photographer, . . . and into the room filed the attorneys for DuPont, and there were 100 of them, and they covered half a room, a whole wall of the room. And at an equally large table on the prosecution side there walked in one man and one girl. They were the United States attorneys. . . .
>
> And to me the drama was—it was just so obvious! Just one picture would do it. All those lawyers, and those two lawyers, and the judge.[7]

Actually, it took three pictures to do it; the judge, the government lawyers, and the "DuPont Defense": thirty-three men—directors, former and current presidents, former and current chairmen, and a substantial semicircle of lawyers—posed in a boardroomlike setting. None of the photographs used appear to have been taken in the courtroom.[8] But as pointed as Drew's courtroom observances were, the larger significance of the day, for him, lay elsewhere.

> At the end of the trial day, Miller and I and the 100 lawyers and the two Justice Department lawyers walked out the front door, and there was television. And they stopped the government lawyers and said "What happened?" And they gave them a minute's worth of what had happened and walked on.
>
> They had never had a dream of a chance of finding out what happened in that room, and why weren't they right beside me and Miller? Why weren't they shooting what happened? It would have been fantastically dramatic.
>
> A week later, the trial is postponed because the government attorney is sick or indisposed; he can't be found, he's disappeared. So I go out to his house to talk to his wife, and the door opens and I tell her who I am and that I'm trying to find her husband, as everybody is—there's a mystery about this—and she says she doesn't know anything. And as she is closing the door, a voice comes, "Don't close

the door!" And there he is. And he invites me in, and he's in a bathrobe, and he is completely manic, and I'm treated to two hours of ravings, which are alternately lucid and insane, about the evilness of the company he is fighting. And the guy has cracked under the strain, that's all. I had Francis Miller with me, and we're shooting pictures of this poor guy.[9]

Miller's three pictures in *Life* show attorney Willis Hotchkiss gesturing dramatically while reading from the opening speech he had delivered to the judge. The captions are quotations: "I say, your honor . . . what has been achieved here by this combination concentrated in this tiny handful of people is monopoly run amuck. It is arrogant, ruthless, but subtle and persuasive."[10]

> But this is all very, very dramatic and emotional, and there is no chance that television will ever see that. And so it's just a case in which I am almost revolted, and I'm saying that we've got to do something about this, we've got to make the television system work to capture what's really happening!
>
> I realized that here was a place I could make films. That is, television *needed* to look into things that tripods and the [filmmaking] systems wouldn't allow at the time.[11]

Key Picture

Drew could see the problems—and the potential—of television as a medium for journalism and, at age thirty, set out to correct it. It would be ten years before the principal elements in his proposed media solution could be developed, tested, applauded, and rejected, but the actual beginnings came in a bar in Boston without Bob Drew even being present. The chance catalyst was *Life* photographer Alan Grant, with whom Drew had first filmed parades and wrestling matches some years earlier.

> A friend of mine, Alan Grant, met a fellow named Bud Barry [the head of programming at NBC] in a bar in Boston. And as they were drinking, Grant told Barry that he and I—Grant and I, that is—could make a kind of journalistic show, a magazine of the air, that would do a lot of good for his network.
>
> So I got a phone call from Grant saying Barry would like to meet us, can you come to New York? And I did.[12]

Drew went to his meeting with NBC's Barry with clear ideas about the quality of both television journalism and the institutional climate in which television then operated.

At that time, Edward R. Murrow's *See It Now* was on the air [on CBS], but what I didn't like was that . . . it was always a set piece, . . . it didn't have any candid photography in it. You couldn't see what was going on in the world through it, and although it could be illustrated and it could be talked about, you didn't see for yourself except in a certain few cases.[13]

Television was reaching more and more people, but its documentary films were not reaching me. However interesting I might find the subject matter, I dozed off in the middle.[14]

Drew's dissatisfactions with television journalism, and the satisfactions from his experiences at *Life*, had lead him to formulate a rudimentary production plan—"a magazine show which would have the candid virtues of *Life* magazine." Drew outlined his ideas for a television magazine to Barry and got a serious reply: how much would it cost to make a pilot? Drew paused; his planning for a television revolution had not yet reached the nuts-and-bolts level. "I gulped and said 7,500 dollars. Barry said, 'Wait a minute,' and went down the hall and came back with a check for 7,500 dollars. And it was just astonishing to me that anybody could do that. So I went back and told my boss I was taking a vacation."[15]

Drew's entire professional experience had been with *Life* magazine, but institutional loyalties were not going to stand in the way of an opportunity to explore film journalism. Besides, "I didn't believe the idea would find much of a reception at Time, Inc. until it had been demonstrated." So Drew set out, with Alan Grant as cameraman, to apply his *Life* experiences to television. But a profound technological shock awaited him. "Wrestling with the big, blimped camera, the oak-hewn tripod, a table-sized 16mm tape recorder, movie lights and trunks full of cables had diverted [the crew's] attention from the finer things in filmmaking. Spontaneity didn't wait around for all this stuff to be set up, and the only real surprises that took place in front of the camera were the shock of the clap sticks and outbursts of the soundman shouting 'Cut!' "[16]

Television documentary technique in the early 1950s was anything but candid. Heavy AC-powered 35mm cameras, originally designed for theatrical filmmaking, were needed to synchronize to the speed of the AC-powered sprocketed tape recorder. The clap sticks that startled (and inhibited) Drew's subjects were necessary to establish a reference point between the separate film and tape portions of the "double-system" system. The cameras, with heavy "blimps" covering the noisy motors and film magazines to deaden the sound during recording, used fixed focal length lenses, not zoom lenses; every change in framing, from mid-shot to close-up, for example, required camera and lens adjustments and another camera/

recorder start—and clap stick. Lens focusing and camera viewfinding characteristics restricted subjects to the very simplest—or most carefully choreographed—physical movements; spontaneity was not encouraged. Film stocks were relatively insensitive and required high levels of artificial illumination every time shooting moved indoors.[17] The theatrical film industry prescribed labor union work rules for television documentary, and the crew requirements were substantial. Alfred Eisenstadt, with two thirteen-ounce still cameras, was candid and unobtrusive. Bob Drew, with a cameraman, soundman, lighting man, one or two grips, possibly a director, an assistant or two, and fourteen-hundred pounds of equipment, was not.

Drew discovered that life could not be observed with the television technology of the time: it had to be produced and directed. "And I directed it!" It took Drew and Grant five weeks to produce five stories for a forty-minute show titled *Key Picture*.

The film begins with a dramatic, low-angle shot of a super-sleek airplane being hauled out of a large body of water directly toward the camera; at just the right moment, the image is match-dissolved to a *Life*-like still photograph, from which the camera then slowly zooms back to reveal a "magazine" cover with the title "NBC Presents Key Picture." The cover then opens to a "page" with a picture and a caption, "First Look into the Heart of Hay Fever"; after a moment, that still photograph is match-dissolved into the first scene of the hay fever segment.

Drew's magazine background had provided the basic format and many lesser elements for *Key Picture*. "Hay Fever" is short and rapidly paced; "New Iron Transforms the North Woods" reports on the then-new taconite industry in Minnesota, effectively using a rather rigidly set up interview with a mining expert; "Brick Bats and Glass Houses" features a controversy over a glass-walled box that the owner finds seriously flawed; and the final segment, "Navy Gets a Plane for Tomorrow," focuses on the experimental Sea Dart, which can be rocket-launched from any ship and then land on the water for recovery. In the final scene, the Sea Dart taxis up a ramp out of the water—a repeat of the opening scene of the show—and the picture match-dissolves to the "magazine" cover, with the credit "Produced and Edited by Allan Grant and Bob Drew" superimposed on it. Drew's first attempt at film journalism was complete—except for the task of evaluation. "NBC professed to like the program and set off to try to sell a series based on it. I retreated to *Life* to try to figure out what had gone wrong."[18]

Over the next several months, Drew puzzled out the answers to "what had gone wrong." The raw material was not candid; it had to be set up and controlled to meet the demands of the filmmaking system. The editing was too static and predictable; narration—often hurried and self-conscious—tied the pieces together. *Key Picture* was very much like the *See It Now* that Drew had earlier criticized—except that it lacked the dramatic presence of Edward R. Murrow. The lessons of *Key Picture* were clear; candid film journalism would require the development of radically different equipment and methods before it could be effectively produced. Drew did not know precisely what was needed, but he knew it would be a slow, expensive process. NBC was unable to sell *Key Picture* to any clients, and the program became just another unsuccessful pilot effort. So Drew turned to another major media organization, one that he knew had the necessary resources—Time, Inc.

The Memo

I wrote a memo. . . . You see, at the time, *Time* and *Life* were the television of the time; that is, they dominated the journalistic situation in the United States, without any question. I predicted that television would dominate, and that if Time, Inc. wanted to continue its journalistic position in the world, it would take charge of that line of development. . . .

And I presented *Key Picture* to Time, Inc., with the memo and with the forecast and with the suggestion they produce a magazine show. And a meeting was convened with [Time, Inc. editor-in-chief Henry] Luce, [Time, Inc. president Roy] Larsen, and [*Life* publisher Andrew] Heiskell and the brass of Time, Inc.[19]

Robert Drew, thirty-years-old, one of the younger correspondents in *Life*'s six-person Chicago bureau, after a five-week career as a free-lance filmmaker, was asking the management of the most successful print publishing enterprise in the world to support development of a costly, untested idea in a medium that he predicted would one day put them out of business. "I presented it, I read it to them. I mean, we had a meeting and showed them the film and I said, 'Look, I'm a writer, not a speaker, so I'm going to read this thing to you.' So I read it to them and I gave them a copy."[20]

Drew's proposals are noteworthy, both for the quality—and the audacity—of his analysis and for the blueprint they provided for Drew's future theoretical and practical development. After pointing out the challenge of television, "TV will affect magazines by competing for reader time and advertising dollars," Drew outlined an offensive policy.

Life must see that good visual journalism is seen on TV.
This may look like a suicidal proposal, but look into it. TV is taking potential advertising dollars away from *Life*, but the real enemy

is not TV journalism, which takes relatively little of TV's advertising dollar. The real enemy of *Life* is entertainment TV.

In fact, *Life* has more in common with TV journalism than TV journalism has in common with entertainment TV. Time, Inc. and TV journalism stand for awareness, reality, alertness to the real problems of our time. Their effect is to equip citizens to better live their lives more intelligently, and make this democracy stronger by making it wiser. Entertainment TV, which is voraciously eating up dollars which might be going for journalism, is a threat to both. It substitutes soporific fantasies for reality reporting, and the more successful it is, the less well equipped will be our citizens and our country. *Life* and TV journalism are both living off the same fraction of the population. Their job, their mutual interest, is to increase the size of this fraction.

Time, Inc.'s offensive should be launched against entertainment TV, and it should promote journalistic TV. Time, Inc. should, in fact, lead TV journalism in developing better reporting, larger audiences, and waging a campaign for more TV journalism in terms of both time on the air and money expended.[21]

Drew predicted that the long-term struggle would not be between print and television, but between journalism and entertainment. He also suggested some specific offensive tactics: *Life* should play down entertainment television in its pages and promote examples of good "reality reporting," and should also "take leadership in TV journalism " by producing "the first high quality weekly news shows designed to attract a mass audience."

In a follow-up letter to publisher Heiskell, Drew developed his rationale for a major Time, Inc. move into television.

The weakness of TV journalism, the enormous public attention [given to television], and the great power of *Life* add up to an historic opportunity for *Life* to extend its prestige and influence into a vast and increasingly important area where it is now largely ignored. The opportunity is to show strength in a time when TV is weak—to show journalistic leadership by establishing the first, big, mass-audience TV news show. This would break through that barrier of excellence beyond which great journalistic effort will pay for itself in mass-audiences.[22]

In summary, Drew speculated that "if *Life* fails to take advantage of that opportunity, either by intention or by default, it will have marked a turning point in the growth of the influence of Time, Inc. in modern journalism."[23]

Drew's proposal seems to be near-equal parts with keen insight into the problem and impossible grandiosity in regards to a workable solution. But the reactions of Time, Inc.'s managers to the scope of the proposal seem at best businesslike, at worst a little plain. "The discussion revolved around whether Time, Inc. advertisers would be upset at having commercials in a program produced by Time, Inc. It revolved around how Time, Inc. was really paper and ink, and should they be involved in broadcasting. And if so, shouldn't they buy a network instead of just making a program."[24]

Drew laughs at the memory of a conversation three decades old. "But, you see, I was astonished that outside of the formulas, nobody was interested in what I was doing at Time, Inc. And nobody really saw the big ideas; the things we talked about were not visible to them."[25]

Time, Inc.'s management explored Drew's ideas for perhaps six months; commercials were put into *Key Picture* to see how it looked. In the end, Time, Inc. decided not to proceed. The young correspondent from Chicago had had his chance and had turned management's head in his direction for a moment. What Drew appears not to have been attentive to were the echoes his memo may have produced in the minds of his very select audience.

Background: The March of Time

Time, Inc.'s vision of Drew's proposal may have been different than he supposed. By the time the memo was read, several men in the room had been over portions of the same ground very thoroughly in the past. The corporation had developed and supported—rather reluctantly at times—a well-known ancestor of Drew's proposal, the *March of Time*.

The *March of Time* was an amalgam of newsreel and staff-photographed event footage, archive materials, re-enactments, music, graphics, and sound effects with a clipped and strident narration and a heavily dramatic structure. In production from 1935 to 1951, its popularity was considerable. By 1939, *March of Time* was booked into over half of America's nearly 19,000 theaters, was seen by thirty percent of the U.S. audience every week, and was released in British and several European editions. The series won two Academy Awards and two additional Academy nominations.[26] The voice of the announcer who was the "Voice of *Time*," most notably Westbrook Von Voorhis, was more familiar to 1930s audiences than any other in the country, with the possible exception of Franklin Roosevelt. That production experience was part of the corporate backdrop against which Drew presented his memo, but there were important administrative portions of that backdrop that were not readily apparent from the productions themselves.

March of Time was not a creation of Henry Luce, but of his closest associate, Time, Inc. president Roy Larsen. In fact, Luce chose to ignore Larsen's project, perhaps because he did not understand it or did not consider it important; there is some evidence that he resented its later popularity.[27] But in the complex and conservative bureaucracy of Time, Inc., initiative, especially combined with institutional clout, could be critically important. An example is the decision making surrounding the initial *March of Time* radio series. Luce, Larsen, and other corporation executives had gathered to hear a pilot program.

> Hardly anyone was happy with what he heard. The show was not editorially smooth like the company's magazines. Larsen said his editorial associates were "mad as hell" at him. They felt he had misused and degraded the *Time* trade mark. They thought the whole venture presumptuous of him.
>
> Fortunately, neither Luce nor his advisers really knew what to make of such a radical departure in *Time*'s affairs. Reluctantly, they approved the project. . . . In the end, said Larsen, "It was the lack of restrictions that let us proceed."[28]

"Lack of restrictions" would come to be an important factor in the career of Robert Drew; the freedom—or slackness—that sometimes prevailed in the Time, Inc. organization would allow Drew to exercise his own initiative without close administrative control. But there were other portions of the *March of Time* experience that Drew would also have to contend with, if only indirectly. Among them was the alternately colorful and troublesome personality of Louis de Rochemont, *March of Time*'s first producer.

De Rochemont was an experienced newsreel cameraman turned short subject producer whom Larsen had chosen to produce the film version of *March of Time*. He worked his subordinates too hard, pirated or sneaked footage he felt he needed, devised productions that affronted critics and outraged some segments of the audience, and attracted enough attention to his films and to Time, Inc. that the corporation felt modestly well rewarded, which was of real importance to *March of Time* and, later, to Drew.

"The *March of Time* never made any money at all. It was always an expensive series to produce compared to newsreels and other types of motion picture short subjects. . . . Because of the *March of Time*'s enormous promotional value to *Time, Life,* and *Fortune* magazines, the corporation was satisfied if it simply broke even. Whether it even managed to do that, however, seems doubtful."[29]

But after World War II, the rising costs of production outstripped the value of promotion, and television both thinned the theatrical audience and provided a no-cost alternative. So in 1951, the last editions of *March of Time* faded from the nation's screens.

Three years later, Robert Drew presented his memo, recommending a similar—at least to the management mind—excursion, into television. *March of Time* was an important part of the Time, Inc. corporate experience, a backdrop of monies spent, public identity gained, public controversy engendered, and management reputations burnished and bruised. It is significant that in eleven interviews with Drew that he never mentioned *March of Time*—nor was he asked about it.

Regardless of the influence, or lack of it, of the *March of Time* experience, Time, Inc. opted not to proceed along the lines Drew had suggested. While the decision was clearly defensible on narrow business grounds— Time, Inc. earned $376-million on revenues of $3.76-billion in 1986—the outcomes were less certain from a journalistic standpoint. *Life* was at the beginning of its downward slide, the television networks were poised for a period of explosive growth in both public influence and corporate revenues, and Time, Inc. was still debating paper and ink versus electronics.

> What I was asking for was the wherewithal to make pilot films on which to base a monster development. . . . Henry Luce was in advanced years then, and the management of the magazines, in my opinion, had become a caretaker management. The "founding" had been done. They would still originate *Sports Illustrated* and *People* and *Money* and other offshoots, but I don't think the top management had the youth and energy and vision in it to take hold of the electronic world and do something with it. They never did.[30]

Youth, Energy, and Vision

After failing in early 1954 to convince Time, Inc.'s management that *Key Picture* and the lessons flowing from it could be the basis for a revolutionary move into television journalism, Drew returned to the task of being one of *Life*'s Chicago correspondents. It gave him time to think. Thirty, married, with two small children, and a personal background of high-energy employment with two high-profile employers—the U.S. Army Air Force and *Life* magazine—Drew was reaching for yet another intellectual and creative outlet to match his goals and ambitions.

> I had time for reflection and thinking and so forth, and I really, really did miss not having been to college . . . and I thought about what it would be to spend a year. I knew I couldn't spend four years, and I wouldn't want to, but to spend a year—. . . . And then—Oh, my God, we'd made *Key Picture*, and it didn't work. *Key Picture* didn't

work the way I wanted it to work. . . . And now I was ready to go study drama, to study short story writing, and all those things that at 24 I was too old to study. I went off to spend a year at that.[31]

A Time-Life stringer in Georgia told Drew about the Nieman Fellowships at Harvard University. Loosely defined—"to promote and elevate the standards of journalism in the United States and educate persons deemed specially qualified for journalism"—and requiring only that participants complete one academic course per semester, the fellowships offered "a small group of journalists a year off during which they could partake of a moveable, intellectual feast at the nation's oldest university."[32] The results for the annual "divine dozen," and for journalism, have been mixed, of course, but one of the Nieman's greatest values may be the building of independence, distance, and perspective, away from the established routines of workaday journalism.

> Part of the Nieman year was spent trying to get over group journalism. By that, I mean that if you worked inside a tightly knit outfit like that, under that discipline, long enough, it became hard to see the world. And it becomes hard to see how they could ever be wrong. About anything. And yet, if you're going to figure something out, you have to be independent of them, mentally—or psychologically, even.
> And so I had to develop an almost corrosive view of Time, Inc., which I had never done before. But I had to develop it in order to be independent.[33]

Life valued independence, but only within limits. Managers could not see why an aspiring young correspondent in an important metropolitan bureau should want to do anything else but continue his work—and his career. Some publishers felt differently, and paid their staff members for the year's absence at Harvard.

> Time, Inc. didn't. It was a little bit disloyal to go away for a year. It was a little bit—it showed that you weren't really that serious maybe. . . . It was put to me by an immediate boss: how can you imagine that you could gain more somewhere else than you could gain right here in the next year?
> And that was part of what I was dealing with. I wasn't sure he wasn't right, you know. I was really trying to figure out some of these things for myself.[34]

Drew and his wife decided to go ahead. It would be a tough choice for any aspiring professional family—"Our life's savings to that point went into that year"—but the payoffs were to be handsome, by any of several different measures.

5

At Harvard

Walter Lippmann, William Allen White, John Grierson, Henry Adams, Robert Flaherty, Josiah Royce, George Bernard Shaw, Gustave Flaubert, Arthur Zegart, Bill McClure, Fons Ianelli, Morris Engel, and Richard Leacock: these are the names, from printed page and black-and-white TV screen, that Robert Drew remembers as the principal influences from his year at Harvard. It was an eclectic, intuitively calculated liberal arts education crammed into nine months. "I couldn't imagine ever taking more than a year. I mean, it seemed like just the maximum time one could ever take out of a career and still continue the career."[1]

In some ways a curious and idiosyncratic mixture of names and ideas, it serves—if Drew's several similar retellings of it are a significant measure— as the philosophical basis for his later adventures into journalistic revolution.

Basic Philosophies

There are three parts to Drew's philosophy: "knowledge, journalism, and storytelling." And Drew's views on the status of public knowledge and its functional relationship to the workings of a democracy begin with Henry Adams. In an analysis of varying views toward public knowledge repeated frequently in his interviews, he sees Adams and Walter Lippmann as the voices of pessimism, while a more optimistic view is presented by John Grierson—and Robert Drew.

Adams and Lippmann

In *The Education of Henry Adams*, Henry Adams goes to college maybe in the 1840s, and at that time it's expected that every young man—every well born young man—who goes to college will learn everything that there is to know, everything. Well, by the time he is writing *The Education of Henry Adams* around 1900, the world has exploded and people who speak the same language don't even speak the same language any more. The scientists can't talk to the philosophers, who can't talk to the literary people, who can't talk to the industrial people and so forth, because knowledge and control has exploded into confusion. . . .[2]

Human knowledge had burst all bonds, multiplying at such a rate that specialists could hardly know their own fields, much less other people's, and for any mind to contain [a] vision of all knowledge was clearly impossible. Darwin had destroyed man's godliness, Freud was destroying his idea of rationality and Einstein was about to destroy his certainty about the physical permanence of what he could see or feel.

As Henry Adams said it, man had lost his ability to comprehend, and therefore to control, his world. His world, in fact, was a world of dynamos, all accelerating uncontrolled, with man compelled to serve them and keep them running. It must all explode.[3]

Drew sees Walter Lippmann applying Henry Adams's pessimism to American politics a generation later.

Lippmann, . . . who was the greatest newspaper philosopher-reporter-pundit at the time, and commentator on journalism and government, carried forward [Henry Adams's] idea that mankind couldn't control itself, that democracy really couldn't work because the electorate couldn't know enough to vote on anything intelligently.[4]

The function of journalism, reporting, in a democracy, was vital, crucial, built-in, expected, and yet it was falling down because . . . the world was getting so complicated that only experts could make decisions because only they knew enough details or facts. And since you couldn't have a legislature made up of experts who knew the facts, you couldn't have a populace made up of people who knew enough, therefore democracy was in grave danger of not working.[5]

Grierson

Along with the pessimisms of Henry Adams and Walter Lippmann, the Nieman Fellowship experience also brought Drew into contact with the alternative views of John Grierson.

Grierson opposed Lippmann's pessimistic view that man could not know enough facts to maintain democracy. He opposed it with his vision of democracy functioning on a new basis of "common experience" shared through films.

And "commonly shared experience" is the way that tribes and small groups of people, and nations, until roughly this century, have proceeded to make their decisions. People understand the premises and they understand enough about the basic facts, and therefore they can come together in a town meeting or legislature and make decisions. Since this is no longer possible, in the huge, industrialized, fragmented nations, Grierson was going to sew them all back together again with films that would give everybody commonly shared experience.

So he imagined that he was going to build, or somebody was going to build, theaters in every town and hamlet across the whole of England, and these thousand, or maybe a million or more theaters, people would flock to them regularly so they could share this commonly shared experience, which would be documentary films made by himself and the people who grew out of him. That was a pretty cumbersome arrangement, but I couldn't help feeling, when television was invented and began appearing in our living rooms, that here was Grierson's million theaters gone one better in everybody's house. So we had the means for commonly shared experience.[6]

Drew's search for a journalism that provided a commonly shared experience would occupy not only the remainder of his Nieman year, but the remainder of his professional life. Before turning to the details of that search, however, it is necessary to consider the influence of Josiah Royce.

Josiah Royce

"There's a line of thinking that I don't talk about very much . . . on the philosophical side, by Josiah Royce. And he was a philosopher at Harvard at the turn of the century. And Royce wrote a book called *The Philosophy of Loyalty*. Which is not really about loyalty, but it's about how to make decisions. And how to live a life, really."[7]

Royce was professor of the history of philosophy at Harvard in 1908 when *The Philosophy of Loyalty* was published. He had attempted to establish a basis for ethical behavior in an intellectual society which had become accustomed to questioning every form of religious and ethical guidance. In opposition to the pragmatism of his teacher and colleague at Harvard, William James, Royce proposed a means "to know my duty" in life. An individual could—and must, Royce maintained—determine a socially useful cause and devote his full attention—his loyalty—to it.

Loyalty, then, fixes our attention upon some one cause, bids us look without ourselves to see what this unified cause is, shows us thus some plan of action, and then says to us, "In this cause is your life, your will, your opportunity, your fulfillment. . . ." If one could find such a cause, and hold it for his lifetime before his mind, clearly observing it, passionately loving it, and yet calmly understanding it, and steadily and practically serving it, he would have one plan of life, and this plan would be his own plan, his own will set before him, expressing all that his self-will has ever sought.[8]

Royce's propositions are wonderfully strong exhortations for single-mindedness of purpose in an individual's affairs. For Drew, it was clearly dramatic: "Royce had an inflammatory impact on me, not because he offered an answer, but because he offered an injunction: 'Plunge ahead!' "[9]

The smattering of Royce's world view contained in *The Philosophy of Loyalty* may not adequately represent the work of one of the classic American philosophers, but it clearly was a factor in fueling Drew's dedication to devising a revolution in television journalism. In the often uncertain period that lay ahead, Drew appears to have accepted Royce's advice to find a suitable cause, live for it, and be loyal to it in the face of all odds.

Sources of a New Documentary Logic

Drew had little interest in television news, which he considered primarily a headline service that had little opportunity to present the candid, "sense-making reality report" he was becoming more and more interested in. Documentaries were more clearly his concern, and as he used the Nieman opportunity to watch what television was offering, he felt considerable reason for concern.

> Most documentary films were in fact lectures. They were then, and most remain today, lectures with picture illustrations. It was as clear as the lectures I was attending every day at Harvard and thrown into relief by the novels and plays I was reading every night. In television documentaries the logic was in the words, the narration, the lecture.
>
> I tuned in to watch Murrow's *See It Now*. As the program progressed, I turned off the sound and watched the picture. The progression disintegrated. What power had been there turned to confusion. The logic left. When I turned the picture off and listened to the sound, the program tracked perfectly. Later that year Murrow's television programs were printed in book form. They read very well.[10]

Drew believed that an alternative existed, an alternative that might have made Murrow, and certainly many of his journalistic contemporaries, nervous.

Verbally based films have a limit—an automatic built-in limit—on the kind of power they can generate with an audience. Dramatically developed films have practically no limit. The only limit is how dramatic they are or how well they are told. The extreme example there is to say the nightly news show on one side—which was John Cameron Swayze talking continuously—and Hollywood movies on the other side. And as between the two it was possible for one to move you and shake you and leave you a different person almost, at the end of an experience, whereas the other one had no possibility of that at all; even reporting the start of World War Three would not do that.[11]

Early documentary films offered one set of examples and traditions, a set that Drew found lacking in relevance to the demands of a new television journalism. Drew took the principal practitioners of that earlier documentary tradition to be John Grierson and Robert Flaherty.

Grierson's documentaries were instructional in nature. That is, he, as a teacher, which he viewed himself, would come up with a thesis for information people ought to have. Then he would structure a documentary that would teach that information. And to me . . . that theory had a few holes in it, because an instructional film is not exactly exciting or inspiring or audience gathering. And Grierson's school of documentary filmmaking on reality, I thought, was propaganda. And by the way, he would almost admit that he meant propaganda, too. And propaganda doesn't work, for real people.[12]

The purposefulness of Grierson's documentaries offended Drew. Closer to his background in pictorial journalism at *Life* magazine was the sense of discovery that characterized the films of Robert Flaherty, notwithstanding the limitations in equipment, financing, and distribution of the 1920s, 30s, and 40s.

Robert Flaherty's idea was that the camera would leave the studio and its meaningless fiction to capture life as it really is. If Grierson was at heart a sociologist and a propagandist, Flaherty was at heart a naturalist, a student of nature, and his aim was to discover. [*Nanook of the North*, 1922] was a strange cross of realism and naturalism, of form from the novel, but more than that, from real life. Grierson remained cut off from real life on one hand and the great currents of story-telling on the other. Flaherty's instincts involved him deeply in life, and what he photographed demanded the employment of narrative realism in story-telling.

Now I know that Flaherty set up and posed and reposed, hired actors, did all kinds of things that defied the theory, but as a theoretician it was to me a compatible, better way of viewing the potential of film for enlightening people. And besides, my own studies had led me to believe that if we created storytellers within the motion picture medium who could match the technical advances of the medium we could be telling stories out of real life which revealed the shape of drama in real life and that that . . . drama would be the spine and strength and power of this particular reporting medium.[13]

"Drama." It would become—if it had not already, from his experiences at *Life*—a key element in Drew's "simple" approach to the revision of television journalism. It would come to him from many sources during his Nieman experience through the varied array of nineteenth and twentieth century fiction and drama Harvard presented to him.

If [Henry] Adams in 1850 thought he knew practically everything, he should have heard about a story-teller in France who that year completed a new kind of novel. [Gustave] Flaubert completed *Madame Bovary*, and let loose a kind of story-telling that has grown and expanded in the worlds of art and literature and film ever since. Its essence is a story that tells itself realistically through what a reader might see for himself if he were given access to principal characters caught up in a dramatic line of action. That viewer might also have access to the thoughts of the characters. The story consisted of a setting, a character, actions and reactions, all acutely observed as if it were actually seen in reality.[14]

Flaubert's realism was traced in Drew's readings through Proust, Conrad, Fitzgerald, Hemingway, Ibsen, and Shaw. A companion approach, naturalism, was traced from Zola through Hardy, Dreiser, Norris, Strindberg, and Gorki. But the structural differences between, and the ultimate purposes of, the realists and naturalists concerned Drew, and strongly influenced his eventual choice of a structural strategy.

Realism and naturalism were alike in that both tried to create the illusion of real life. But realism had the form of a novel, or of a play— a beginning, middle and end, a dramatic form and dramatic pacing. Naturalism on the other hand strove to present *life* experience without regard for its form. The naturalist presented experience, unshaped and unformulated. The realist presented experience, in the shape of a story or drama. The realist considered the naturalist undisciplined. The naturalist considered the realist not lifelike enough.[15]

Drew chose realism, although in one sense the observational qualities of naturalism might have been closer to the journalistic tradition he felt he represented. But it was the structural qualities of realism, "a beginning, middle and end, a dramatic form and dramatic pacing," that had the greater appeal. It was rooted in his early experiences at *Life*, where the choices of the picture editors were often governed more by dramatic than informational appeal. In many instances in his later work, if the choice had to be made between form or content, between audience appeal or literal accuracy, the scales were weighted, in varying degrees, toward form.

The force of the appeal of form—more accurately narrative form—to the young, would-be producer of innovative television documentaries was massive. Western civilization is the inheritor of well over two thousand years of experience with narrative forms that speak to audiences in satisfying, if not fully-understood, ways. Naturalistic description, though arguably more accurate, has never proved as successful or enduring. And in the twentieth century, it was narrative—after a brief initial period of simple observation—that captured the form of one of the most important influences on Drew's eventual television journalism—the movies.

> In fiction films narrative realism was picked up as *the* pattern for film story-telling. The way of looking at characters in scenes, of observing telling detail, of cutting from one view to another, of intercutting simultaneous action—all this and more was laid out by the realistic novel. The novel was made for film. Once film got the hang of rendering the realistic novel, it became the universal story-telling medium of the world. . . . This film story-telling galvanized the world, offered commonly shared diversion to millions, and began to record a weird non-historical record of our times.[16]

It became Drew's goal to apply the techniques of narrative, as developed in the novel and the fiction film, to the production of a more historically accurate "record of our times," a mixture of candid reporting and story telling structure.

> And so my theoretical view developed that we had a means of distribution [in television], we had power and drama going on in real life wherever people lived or died or worked hard or fell in love or whatever, and all we needed to do was to supply the journalist, as I thought of it, who could capture these real people, real stories, in real life, edit them in such a way that the stories would tell themselves without the aid of a lot of narration, and we would have a new form of drama on one hand, because it would be real instead of fictional, [and] a new form of journalism on another hand because it would have dramatic logic instead of verbal, schematic logic.[17]

Journalists, of those times and later, might feel uncomfortable with Drew's proposals, for they certainly contain the seeds of many of the dangers journalists have been concerned with over at least the last half-century: accuracy, the influence of form on content, the opportunity to editorialize in the guise of reporting, and so forth. They might ask—as Drew himself did—"If you have a form of communication which zeroes in on story-telling in real life through dramatic principles, how do you justify this as journalism? Why don't you just call it drama?"

The principles that were the outcome of Robert Drew's Nieman year at Harvard were: the realities and functions of public knowledge in a democracy, the flaws of mid-1950s television, and the role of drama and narrative in journalism. His theorizing, which has been maintained and embellished over thirty years, can be criticized as being overly "pat," as too simplistic to account for the practical realities of post-World War II public awareness and media power structures, or as indulging a tendency to build neatly balanced models to explain vastly complex events. Whatever the criticisms, however, these principles were to serve, with continuing refinements and retellings, as the fundamental philosophy that guided Drew's efforts for the three decades to come.

But the Harvard experience was not confined to readings and theoretical discussions about the nature of television and journalism. Much of Drew's time was spent in front of a TV set, first identifying for himself the problems of the then-current offerings, then searching for the scattered examples that could serve as clues or models to a new candid television journalism.

After dismissing the nightly newscast and the CBS/Murrow news documentary, Drew found the rudimentary beginnings of candid television journalism most frequently in the non-news documentaries that ran in television's "intellectual ghetto" on Sunday afternoons. The important programs were *Omnibus* and *The Search*, and the important names were McClure, Zegart, Ianelli, and Leacock.

Seeking Talent

Bill McClure

"From time to time, *See It Now* would have a sequence that would raise you right out of your chair, and I found out who was responsible for that. It wasn't Ed Murrow."[18] One man responsible for at least an occasional break in the lecture-like format of *See It Now* was CBS cameraman Bill McClure, "who was turning out a kind of film reporting that was psychologically penetrating."

> He made a film on diamond mining, or gold mining, in South Africa, and all he did was show how the gold miners went down, dug the gold, came back out, were examined by the physician, and went

home. . . . "Examined by the physician?" Yes. Guy looked in every orifice, pulled their mouths open as if they were animals; they expected it, the doctor did it as if he owned them. The cameraman was smart enough or sensitive enough to shoot it in such a way that you *felt* those things. So where was the magic in Bill McClure being able to do that? . . . That guy had something going that wasn't just a news photographer.[19]

The example reinforced Drew's belief that talent was a key element in designing a new form of television journalism. McClure, a cameraman, was one form of talent, but there was also the writer, the director, and the production supervisor to consider. In the case of another example of lasting importance to Drew, those three were one—Arthur Zegart.

Arthur Zegart

"I first bumped into Arthur Zegart through my TV set. I was watching a *Search* story on San Quentin prison that started off well, got better, and became great."[20]

Zegart's film was an innovation, at least to Drew, because it emphasized sound, a frequently under-utilized component of documentary filmmaking, to partially overcome the lack of flexibility of the equipment of the 1950s. Another innovation was the unusual production method that Zegart had used to make contact with his principal subjects: a lot of time and patience.

ZEGART: My basic job [was] a missionary job. I had to go into San Quentin and get the officials to give me permission to walk out in the yard alone with the prisoners. The prisoners were hostile and suspicious. Being Ed Murrow wouldn't help you walk into 4,000 prisoners and learn anything. In effect, I had to go in and say to the prisoners, "We're trying to do something different from anything you've ever seen, different from anything you've ever imagined. You'll have to put yourselves in my hands and trust me." If they would do that, I could get reality.

No outsider had ever walked out in the yard alone with the prisoners. They turned away from me and wouldn't talk. But I walked around and spotted guys I knew *could* talk. While I was casing them, they were casing me. In the second week, I got into a couple of conversations, and finally I got some prisoners to talk to me in a room. Then I set up a tape recorder.[21]

Zegart's thirteen hours of conversations had to be edited over unsynchronized pictures of the prison; Zegart was stretching the technology of television documentary to its rather modest 1950s creative limits: "No one has devised the equipment to work like this. . . . It's like trying to conduct modern warfare wearing medieval armour."

> DREW: The San Quentin film was hardly a film. It was pictures of bars, johns, light bulbs, different things you'd see in a prison, with the voices of the inmates . . . talking about their thoughts and feelings and what made them do what they did. And in a way it was that strain of documentary power that comes out of radio documentary, but it was put together with some artistry and feeling, and certainly getting it on tape must have been fantastic, was fantastic.[22]

Drew's evaluation of Zegart's film shows the importance he attached to it, and hints at the operational difficulties such methods implied.

> The result was one of the most powerful films of the *Search* series. Its high points were [eight] minutes of real reality, the inner realities of prisoners up against the prison, against society, and against themselves. . . .
>
> Television may well find other approaches to reality reporting. Zegart is practically alone in his particular point of view. To him, "reality" means the revelation of subtle psychological relationships. To many other TV reporters it means simply the true, physical surface look of a situation. But any approach to reality reporting that makes a breakthrough big enough to alter the character of TV journalism will probably have to include two of Zegart's conspicuous qualities: the vision that finds in drab reality the glowing center of significance and excitement, and some sort of moral equivalent to his overriding zeal and dedication.[23]

Fons Ianelli

"Fons Ianelli . . . was a fellow who worked with Morris Engel in the early days, and produced two pre-cinema verite films, one on an emergency ward and one on a boxer making up his mind not to box."[24]

The possibilities of candid filmmaking, free of the restrictions of heavy, theatrically-designed equipment and techniques, had begun to be explored almost a decade before Drew went to Harvard. Helen Levitt and James Agee's *In the Street* (1948) and Sidney Meyers's *The Quiet One* (1949) are considered the initial efforts. Morris Engel's *The Little Fugitive* (1953) and *Lovers and Lollipops* (1955) continued the development of the filmmaker's ability to record what critic Agee called "unrehearsed and uninvented reality," while Lionel Rogosin's *On The Bowery* (1956)—"bums on The Bowery living a terrible life . . . and destroying themselves before your very eyes"—completed the first decade of development.[25] Most were sponsored films (Meyers) or were produced for theatrical distribution (Engels, Rogosin); all except Levitt and Agee used a mixture of theatrical and documentary techniques. Their importance lies in their attempts to achieve a degree of candidness in their source material in spite of the inflexibility of the then-current equipment.

Equipment was a major stumbling block in the path of candid recording. Although Morris Engel had devised a less cumbersome, somewhat portable 35mm camera-and-sound unit, he was limited to film runs of less than one minute before having to re-load. Fons Ianelli developed one of the first 16mm hand-held synchronous sound units, using a mechanical interlock between the camera and recorder; it was too limited to allow the level of candidness Drew was looking for, but it was one of the "bits of genius" Drew was collecting from his television watching.

"[Ianelli] went into an emergency ward and shot sync sound on people coming in with, you know, broken legs and bashed heads and it was real. It was terrible—it wasn't a terrible film, it was just a terrible experience to be in an emergency ward, but this was before I made a foot of film, of real film. Ianelli did this."[26]

Emergency Ward was shot with the limitations of Ianelli's equipment; the camera stayed in place in the emergency ward and let the action come to it. The results were powerful, and innovative, but not yet fully candid. Ianelli's equipment was handheld and portable, but only within very restrictive limits. Ianelli's second film, again for *Omnibus*, was *The Young Fighter*; it was technically more flexible, but it raised another set of conceptual problems for Drew's efforts to develop a new form of candid television journalism.

> One of Ianelli's greatest lessons for me was, he made a film about a boxer deciding not to box any more, and after seeing that film I realized that one of the real traps in making reality films would be to make a film about something in which nothing ever happened, or if it did happen it all happened in somebody's mind, because it was no film, it was a failure. . . .
>
> We looked for turning points or we looked for crises that were going to have to happen, and of course we'd been used to doing that for *Life* magazine for many years. There was no point in doing a *Life* story on somebody whose life was going to be a continuum throughout the time we were there.[27]

The presence of "turning points" or "crises" in the subjects chosen by Drew for his candid journalism would become, over the years, one source of serious criticism of Drew's films. But at Harvard, in 1956, they were but one of a large number of interrelated concerns that Drew was struggling to understand and to put to effective use. Those concerns included devising effective story telling methods, overcoming the limitations of the equipment, resolving the relationship between journalistic integrity and the public's attentiveness so as to produce a journalism that "worked," and the discovery and development of filmmaking talent.

Richard Leacock

On *Omnibus*, there was a [film] called *Toby and the Tall Corn*. And . . . a lot of things happened, but here's one thing that happened that impressed me: a tent show rolls into town and the tent is put up, and as the tent is put up, you feel it go up and you feel the volume inside. . . . And people approach the tent and they fill it up. And it's endless; people filing into this one tent—it's like the midgets [coming] out of the taxicab in reverse, you know.[28]

Sitting forward on a brocade couch in his comfortable fifth-floor living room, Drew is telling the story—with enthusiasm. He is repeating what may be the most often retold story in his personal history, one of the key discoveries of his professional career.

So you have a tent, which has been visualized, a big and a large volume; you have a crowd which is built up and up and up and you have a huge crowd. Then a tent show takes place, which is funny, and people laugh and they cry and things happen. And all this happens in a cinematic way, and that is that the narration is disregardable. It's there, but it's disregardable.

So I came down to New York to find out who made it—who was responsible for this. And I talked to Bob Saudek, who was the producer of the show, and he said, "Because I assigned Russell Lynes to write the narration." So I knew Saudek didn't know anything about why it was a good show. And I went to Russell Lynes and I said, "Why was this a great show?" and he said, "Because I decided my narration would be based on the economics of the thing, cost per ticket," and so forth. And I knew Russell Lynes didn't know what the hell he'd done, either. And I got the name of the photographer, and so I went to see him and the guy was sitting in the basement of a brownstone in front of a Moviola, editing something. Leacock. And I said, "Why was it a great show?" And he said, "Because Russell Lynes wrote this great narration based on the economics of the thing." And he didn't crack a smile or anything; he went back to his Moviola. And it broke me up; I knew I'd found the guy who knew something.[29]

And the rest, as they say, is history. Drew's meeting with Leacock was, in his recountings, a pivotal event. *Toby and the Tall Corn* was hardly a fully-developed example of the candid television journalism Drew would later evolve; it was made with relatively inflexible equipment, and resembled Ianelli's *Emergency Ward* in that when the camera was shooting sync sound, it could not move to the point of the action. Leacock achieved a semblance of candidness by shooting the tent show performances several times from different camera postions—far, near, aimed away toward the audience—and then piecing the action together into a "seamless whole," much as a theatrical film editor would present a "complete" action made up of separately filmed shots placed in logical order. *Toby* only hinted at the possibilities for the future.

But Leacock was most important to Drew's future development of a new film journalism because he was an experienced innovator who was, like Drew, searching for an improved means of rendering the real world on film, and because he had strong ties to the non-journalistic "film world" that would become an important long-term influence on Drew's developments and reputation. The association between the two men lasted, professionally, into the mid-1960s (and, personally, to the present), and was so close that the resulting films became known, incorrectly, as the "Drew-Leacock films." Never a completely comfortable relationship, it was, nonetheless, of life-long importance to each of them.

Leaving Harvard

The Nieman year was pivotal for Drew. He considers it a period of serious philosophical questioning and an "examination of what I wanted to do, really." He came out of it with a mental blueprint for a new, candid form of television journalism, a television journalism with "a capacity for mobile reporting on real life in the un-public situations that make up most of what is important about the news."[30]

> TV is proud of its brief, daily smatter of facts. It is pious about the public service shows, which it puts on when the great audience isn't looking. But journalists must not be deceived. Television is a huge, voracious, expanding entertainment industry. Its informational efforts may be a sop to the government, its own pretenses, and a few individual consciences like Ed Murrow's. Until TV turns its big guns—top time, budgets, and resources—to creating informational, sense-making shows good enough to pull in mass audiences, the national mind *is* being sabotaged.[31]

The Nieman/Harvard experience had also enhanced Drew's image and reputation in New York. The life's savings that Drew and his wife had risked on the excursion into the academic world would now begin paying dividends.

[Time, Inc.] treated me differently not because I was different, but because I had done it, I guess. You know, editors would come up to have lunch with me, and suggest that I come back and do this or that, who hadn't really taken that much trouble with me before. . . .

I was kind of a hot property among the networks. . . . The news departments knew about my theories and they all read the Nieman report I wrote and the job offers came, thick and fast. . . .

And CBS and NBC were both asking me to work for them. But within their constraints: their equipment and their people and the way they did things. I knew it couldn't be done, so I wouldn't do it. And I knew that somehow I had to develop my own equipment and my own people and make my own films. And I was constantly hopeful that a network would set up a unit within itself, which I would head, and the president of NBC News at that time, Davidson Taylor, proposed it to [David] Sarnoff, Jr. [executive vice-president of NBC].[32]

A 1956 Drew memo to Davidson Taylor is typically self-confident, assertive, and in contrast to the journalistic planning of the network executives of the period.

Our real opportunity is to add our own, new dimensions to the total picture of U.S. journalism. Print, because it is abstract, has always reflected the world in a cold, bloodless light. Now we can bring alive the vital other side of the news, the feeling of what it is like to be on the scene of the story and experience its drama, color and play of personalities. . . .

I hope that *Key Picture* can be considered for what it is, a project capable of creating the first, regular night-time journalistic show, of thereby bringing into existence the journalists, the financing and the thinking to work out solutions in the various categories of public affairs and of straightening out our confused critics. . . .

With a regular, prime-time show to lead and explain the development of a true TV journalism the whole public affairs picture falls into place. The current debates of "completeness," "objectivity," and even "lateness" of TV news become manageable. The nightly news summary finds its value not as the showcase of TV journalism, but as a utilitarian compromise. The special event finds its value as a unique and valid facet of true TV journalism which must nevertheless be subject to shortening and editing to condense drama and find a proper time for presentation on the air. These values fall into perspective in an overall scheme led by a prime-time show that takes full advantage of TV's ability to range the world, see into the lives of people, edit what it sees into power reporting and pull in and inform vast audiences with this power.[33]

The closing of Drew's memo is an example of his sensitivity to the importance of network administrative and financial realities, as well as a willingness to propose challenges to the prevailing point of view.

> The breakthrough in TV journalism will come, I think, only when we have a plan of attack backed by the chiefs of our business and directed at our real problems. I know that Mr. Sarnoff has economy in mind. It is not economical to lose money and prestige when proper investment could make money and pile up a prestige of historic proportions. *Key Picture* is not only a strategic concept for an offensive but it is also a tactical battle plan that takes into account the vital logistics of talented men, technical solutions and journalistic form.[34]

Davidson Taylor—"Dear Dave" in Drew's memo—was sufficiently interested and impressed with Drew's ideas to pass them up the administrative ladder to Sarnoff with obvious enthusiasm: "The attached memorandum is from Bob Drew, the man who, so far as I know, has come closer to the solution of the problem of television news than anybody." Presumably Taylor and Sarnoff talked; then Drew was contacted: "I met with Sarnoff, Jr. and other people from NBC and it didn't happen." Drew, his concept memo, and *Key Picture* did not make a sufficiently strong impression; Davidson Taylor couldn't find the corporate backing within NBC for a separate documentary production unit—only Edward R. Murrow at CBS had the sort of semi-autonomy that Drew was looking for—and Drew returned to *Life* as a writer in New York. His mental blueprint for candid television journalism—what he would later call "the dream"—was firmly in place; the only problems that lay ahead were matters of implementation.

> "I went back to *Life* hoping to quickly assemble my teams and engineer the lightweight equipment. But I found myself running in place to try to keep up with writing and editing chores. The managers of Time, Inc.—Henry Luce, Roy Larsen—had looked at *Key Picture* and passed. Networks kept offering me jobs. I already had one of those. I was making $13,000 a year, and I needed a million dollars."[35]

6

Returning to Life

By 1956, Drew was back at work at *Life* magazine in New York, trying to develop "other things": new equipment, new talent, new forms of reporting in addition to his writing chores. He needed a million dollars, he thought, but he had failed to get such a commitment, or even much reaction, from Time, Inc.'s management, so he proceeded on a piecemeal basis. In doing so, he chose a curiously familiar vehicle for his developmental attempts: promotional films that would draw attention to upcoming issues of *Life* magazine. It was a variation on *March of Time*, with significant differences: the films would be reportorial in style, not re-enactments; they would deal only with the events of a particular *Life* cover story and not with broader issues; and they would be presented on television, not in theaters. But the fundamental corporate purpose of these first Drew films—the institutional rationale that allowed them to be made—was promotional, as the *March of Time* series had realistically been.

Drew's first concern was to begin developing his new ideas. Development required money, and access to that money required bending some of the most familiar rules of print journalism in order to get things rolling.

> I would never in a million years have walked into the publisher's office. Editorial and Publishing were completely separate.
>
> But somehow this required an investment and some action and maybe [Time, Inc. president Roy] Larsen encouraged me to do it and maybe not. So I asked [*Life* magazine publisher Andrew] Heiskell to put up the dough for the film.
>
> I said, "If I pick the right story and make it in motion pictures while *Life* makes it in still pictures, the way I imagine doing it, it will

44

be so good that it will run on the air, it will find its way on the air in prime time, and will help publicize your magazine issue. So you can have a story on the *Ed Sullivan Show* or . . ."—I am thinking of the big rated shows of the time—"or the *Steve Allen Show* or the *Today Show*, or the *Tonight Show*, and the next day your magazine is on the stands, and this will help sell the magazine."[1]

Heiskell agreed, in principle, and Drew began searching for a topic that would meet the specifications of his proposal—a *Life* cover story that would attract the attention of the producers of a major television show *and* allow Drew to develop and showcase his ideas for a new form of candid journalism.

> I'm working as a writer when I see that *Life* is going to do a story on a balloon ascension by a man in his 60s; he's going to go to the edge of the atmosphere, as it was called, about 100,000 feet, in a Navy balloon, with a telescope and the right kind of equipment, to look at Mars to see if there's water on Mars. And so I like this idea and I think it will make a great film; a candid film, even. I'll install cameras in the gondola, I'll be with the man as he suits up, I'll cover the landing of the flight, I'll "bug" it so I get the sounds and the excitement, we'll look through the telescope and see Mars, and so forth. And the biggest show on the air at that point in time is—on television—is the *Steve Allen Show*. It's a comedy show. And I get the *Steve Allen Show* to agree to run the film. And Time, Inc. to agree to finance the film.
>
> And I hire Leacock and a crew of six or seven—still a big crew— [and] go off to South Dakota to shoot the great balloon film. After thirty days—the weather hasn't been right—the balloon finally inflates. The old man is locked inside with the Navy pilot; they're in pressure suits. The balloon inflates, pops, falls back down. End of the project.[2]

The balloon's collapse was a serious setback for Drew's fledgling ideas. A large crew had waited a month on location—"expensive is what I'm saying"—and there was nothing to show for it. "The balloon fell down and I thought, gee, there goes the Drew film career."

> So I'm in South Dakota with the cameras, crew—and I pull out the old correspondent side and start calling around and I find a story. It's a football game. It's a coach whose whole career depends on winning a game, Air Force Academy against Colorado. So it's reachable, it happens the next day, I hire a plane, fly the crew down there, we shoot it and we make the first, really—the first film with much really candid stuff in it. And it's pretty good stuff. . . . A lot of the action takes place in the locker room, as a desperate coach tries to rally his

losing team. And this guy is sweating bullets and his crew are crunched and broken and it's just a horrible, wonderful situation. And I bring the stuff back to New York, edit it, show it to Heiskell. . . . The lights come up and he says, "Jesus, that's a wonderful film! How do I get back my thirty thousand dollars?"[3]

Drew laughs when retelling the story, but it may not have been so funny at the time. The football coach was not a *Life* story, let alone a cover story, and publisher Heiskell got no promotional mentions of the magazine on nationwide TV to compensate for the film's substantial expense.

American Football (1957), Drew's first attempt to use promotional filmmaking for *Life* as a cover for developing his new form of film journalism had failed to deliver what he had promised. But when he proposed another project, Heiskell again agreed: "Each of these 'yeses' bowled me over, I couldn't believe them."[4]

So *Life* is doing a story on zero gravity—weightlessness—and my film idea is fantastic. The way you simulate weightlessness on earth, if you are not in space, is to fly an aircraft through a ballistic curve, and if you do it right, you can get about 15 or 20 seconds out of it when the aircraft and everyone in it is weightless. And if you did that for a week, hour after hour after hour, you could produce on film a continuous weightlessness, which would be the first time, and it would really be remarkable. That's what I did.[5]

Drew's structural strategy for the film was to use the production of the *Life* cover as the story line; *Life* would be the story. In making that choice, Drew may have been influenced by a favorable coincidence: "Fortunately the *Life* correspondent is extremely overweight. I mean he is *heavy*."

Warren Young is his name, a lovely guy, loved him. But the fact that Warren Young was so completely earthbound, so heavy, so rotund, made it wonderful when he became weightless.

Anyway I played on that, and edited the film [*Zero Gravity*, 1958], and the film was run on the *Ed Sullivan Show*, which was probably the top rated show of the time, probably between a dog act and a juggler. The next day CBS News ran it, and it got run everywhere all over the country many times.

. . . and it made the cover of *Life*, by the way, the story: there is a picture of a guy walking on the ceiling on the cover of *Life*.[6]

From a collapsing balloon to a floating correspondent; Drew's luck appeared to have turned. Publisher Heiskell was amply repaid by the publicity given *Life*. A year after its initial collapse, the balloon carrying the space telescope finally went up. But a gondola full of scientific equipment is not a good location for sync sound filming, and a balloon at 80,000 feet makes a distant and difficult subject. *Balloon Ascension* (1958) is a choppy and fragmented attempt to tell a complex science/adventure story in which the drama—except for a potentially dangerous landing in high winds—is largely in the voice of the narrator. But the film fulfilled its "cover" purpose when it ran on NBC's *Today Show*, with Dave Garroway, while *Life* featured the balloon on its cover with a story by the pilot.[7]

Another *Life* cover story was about the "bullfight of the century," called "Stirring Drama in Spain," and *Life*'s coverage of it was the story framework for another Drew film, *Bullfight at Malaga* (1958). ABC first agreed to carry the film as a special, but cancelled the program because of protests from its affiliates about the probable audience reaction to the killing of an animal on prime time television. A shortened version ran on NBC's *Tonight Show*.

"The film was exciting and Jack Paar pulled another one of those 'I won't hold up the magazine and I'll only run ten minutes' and he ran it, and then he talked about it all night long, that is, he had two and a half hours on the air and the whole show was about this bullfight. So again *Life* magazine got its due."[8]

The most important aspect of this period was the development, the learning, that was taking place. The transition from producing magazine stories and essays to producing television documentaries—especially a new form of television documentary—was complex and difficult, both intellectually and in terms of the raw energy and initiative required. While maintaining one career, Drew was both creating the institutional climate for a new career and developing the operational skills necessary to support it. And while mindful of the institutional realities—"I didn't care what they thought—well, I did care; I hoped they liked [the films]"—Drew's creative attentions were focused on learning more about filmmaking.

> Each [of the early films] had a virtue for me of some cinematic or filmic thing I was trying to develop. The football film had candidness and character. The weightless film was trying to evoke not the size of a tent or a crowd, but the feeling of the space inside of an airplane and the feeling of becoming weightless within it. The two matadors was a drama, pure and simple, with life and death in it. One of the guys got hooked by a horn and thrown ten feet in the air and came down, got back up and killed the bull. That was really pretty dramatic.[9]

But as Drew was learning and developing his philosophy and skills, he was also becoming increasingly aware that the limitations of 1950s filmmaking equipment and techniques were preventing him from making progress toward the candid television journalism he envisioned. Drew's energy and tenacity would slowly produce a breakthrough, but it would not come about by his efforts alone. He needed, and had, the support and skill of a principal associate, Richard Leacock.

7

Other Voices—Richard Leacock

Ricky Leacock is different from Bob Drew. No townhouse in Manhattan's East 70s for the English-born filmmaker; he has warned a visitor that his Cambridge, Massachusetts, home is "not what you'd expect of an MIT professor" and he is right. The building, set at the back of an oddly-shaped narrow lot on a nondescript residential street, is old and down-at-the-heels—no thought given here to historic preservation.

The bedroom, immediately inside the door, is decorated in soft pastels, with a number of photographs, some intimate, of Leacock and friends placed about. The large kitchen-dining room is almost farmhouselike in its size, simplicity, and clutter. It is a room in which an interview can comfortably take place.

The contrast with Drew continues as Leacock invites the visitor to join him: "You've had breakfast, right? I make good Missouri pancakes. Learned how to make pancakes shooting *Toby*." Leacock is in faded blue jeans, a cotton shirt, and barefoot; he pads around the worn floors, making coffee, using the almost-antique bathroom, getting organized. He clearly has not been kept waiting by his midmorning visitor.

If Drew is directed and busy, Leacock is informal and chatty, sometimes deliberately thoughtful, and always wary of the implications of certain questions and of his answers. Both Leacock and Drew have an air of speaking for the record, for history, and they try to be careful, Drew being careful to get his points across clearly, Leacock being more often cautious. But both exhibit an intense thoughtfulness and enthusiasm for the field of documentary film, a common interest that brought them together, from vastly different directions.

The Beginning

(While stirring pancakes) "I've done a lot of filming in the Middle West; *Happy Mother's Day*, lot of stuff out there. *Toby*. . . . *Toby And The Tall Corn*. Yes, that's an important one. Drew said it was the beginning." [1]

Whether Drew meant that *Toby* was the beginning of the Drew-Leacock relationship or the beginning of a new form of candid film journalism is open to question, but it was not the beginning of Ricky Leacock's film career, or the beginning of his curiosity about the world around him and how the happenings of that curious world might be transmitted to his friends—the audience.

Leacock's first film, *Canary Bananas*, made in 1935 when he was fourteen years old, showed his English boarding school classmates the life he knew on the banana plantation his father managed in the Canary Islands. The short silent film was shown by the headmaster to the father of one of Leacock's classmates, the by-then-famous documentary director, Robert Flaherty. Flaherty told Leacock, "Someday we'll make a film together," a remark that turned out to be prophetic although it was likely only a casual comment at the time. Leacock made other short films, but his curiosity matured and his professional career in film began in World War II, where he spent four years as a combat cameraman in Asia. [2]

> I guess I am the kind of person that no matter what happens to me, I find it exciting. I'm one of these awful people who thoroughly enjoyed World War II, every moment of it. . . . I'm not saying I liked killings—I never killed anybody, never fired a shot in anger—but I was involved. And . . . thinking of people back home, in their comforts, I've always had this feeling of, "Jesus, if they could know what's happening to me now; how much more interesting than being at home!" How wild to be stuck in a third-class Indian train, that takes five days to get from Calcutta to Ceylon! [laughter] With a bunch of moaning, groaning G.I.'s, all wishing they were back in Brooklyn. And my feeling is the opposite: "I wish I could convey to my friends where I am now, because it's *unbelieveable* what's happening; what's happening to me is *incredible*." And I guess there is the deep-seated desire to share that. And, somehow, to be able to depict it.
>
> And I have the feeling that this is true of sketch artists; not ser-r-r-ious painters who sit in studios! But I don't think that Goya sat in his studios and dreamed up those sketches of the horrors of war, and the madness of bullfights. I don't know anything about art history, but I know when I see those drawings, I am electrified! I say, "Jesus! What's going on here!" And I think there's the same sense in the really perceptive still photographer; not of creating arty pictures, but

of saying "how can I convey this." And it's the same sort of thing with film, and that's an aspect of film that I'm interested in. I'm not interested in laboriously creating "facts."[3]

Meeting Flaherty

After the war, the first of two pivotal meetings in Leacock's life occurred. Out of the army in 1946, he stopped in New York to visit Flaherty. The older man, after a gap of fourteen years since directing *Man Of Aran*, had raised the money for another film.

"I visited Flaherty and he was pleased. He didn't want to discuss what I had done, wanted to see no films, didn't want to test me in any way. He asked me only, 'Are you free?' I said, 'Yes.' And he said 'O.K. We are going to Louisiana.' Just like that, bang, on the basis of a small banana film."[4]

On such an informal basis, Flaherty chose the cameraman for his final— and in visual terms, finest—film, *Louisiana Story* (1948).

Flaherty was already a legend—*Nanook of The North* (1922) and, to a lesser degree, *Man of Aran* (1934) had assured that. But he was also considered highly impractical; only *Nanook* was a true box-office success, and his deliberate, unstructured methods proved unworkable in a movie studio environment. He was equally unacceptable to noncommercial filmmakers; Grierson and the social documentarians of the 1930s and 1940s considered him a purposeless romantic, concocting personal fables instead of using the medium to uplift and educate.

But Flaherty's filmmaking strategy had longer-range effects than his critics knew. It was later called "non-preconception." To Flaherty, it meant being *curious about*, not *in control of*, the subject: "The notion that filming should flow from the filmmaker's boundless interest in his subject and that shooting should not be overly selective."[5] For Leacock, it was an incredible opportunity.

> He had the extraordinary ability to look and look and look at stuff. . . . We shot the whole drilling sequence [for *Louisiana Story*] in daylight—seemed to be the sensible way to do it—and he looked and looked and looked and it was fine, nothing wrong with it; it wasn't very interesting, wasn't very exciting, but it was fine, technically beautiful. And he suddenly said, "We've made a terrible mistake," and I thought he was crazy. He said, "We're going to reshoot it at night." I said, "We don't have any lights." He said, "Get some lights." "We don't have any money." "Well, never mind, we're going to do it anyway." And we did. And my God, was he right. It eliminated all the cruddy details that were distracting, that were carrying your eye

away from the central action. But we didn't know that. We had to find out the hard way. He was an absolutely extraordinary man.[6]

Flaherty used no script, he shot incredible amounts of rawstock (200,000 feet for the 8000 foot *Louisiana Story*, a 25:1 ratio), and it took him years to complete a film. In an era when Hollywood tolerated eccentrics so long as they were good box-office, Flaherty remained a truly unconventional— and unemployable—director. It was partially because he *thought* about film.

How do you make a tree tall? or a cliff high? His solutions were purely cinematic solutions. They weren't compositions, they weren't from paintings or stills. The obvious one is in *Moana* where the kid climbs the tree and he goes way the hell down the beach with a long telephoto lens. No cameraman in his right mind would have done that, and it's just a question of the time it takes to make the tree tall—there was no shot of that whole tree. . . . I find very, very little of this kind of thinking and feel in filmmaking. I think until filmmakers start playing with cameras themselves you're not going to get it. . . . Almost no filmmaker bothers to handle the camera himself. [Flaherty] enjoyed it. I've never known anybody who enjoyed shooting more than he did. I mean, he just would go crazy looking through that viewfinder.[7]

The viewfinder. As long as Flaherty's subjects revealed themselves through the viewfinder, through images, his films were intense, sensitive, alive. When the subject had to reveal itself through speech, the magic failed.

Already when we were working on *Louisiana Story*, I saw that when we were using small cameras, we had tremendous flexibility, we could do anything we wanted and get a wonderful sense of cinema. The moment we had to shoot dialogue, lip-sync—everything had to be locked down, the whole nature of the film changed. The whole thing seemed to stop. We had heavy disk recorders, and the camera that, instead of weighing six pounds, weighed two hundred pounds, a sort of monster. As a result of this, the whole nature of what we were doing changed. We could no longer watch things as they developed, we had to impose ourselves to such an extent upon everything that happened before us, that everything sort of died.[8]

Flaherty had, perhaps, an inkling of what might be possible, but the problem, as Leacock found, was "you couldn't do it." The medium— synchronous sound filming—smothered its subjects. Flaherty's early documentary revolution failed for want of the transistor.

Leacock's career after *Louisiana Story* was that of a moderately successful free-lance cameraman and director, making films for the de Rochemont organization, the United Nations, CBS, and number of government agencies. He worked with other prominent, if traditional, documentary directors of the period including Leo Hurwitz, Willard Van Dyke, and Irving Jacoby. But the experiences were not, at least in retrospect, particularly satisfying.

> What happened was that with this *ridiculous* equipment, we came in like a Hollywood crew. And I think that deep down, that's what many of us wanted to be. "The Movies." We were proud of those huge cameras and truckloads of equipment and microphone booms and this, that, and the other thing. . . .
> It was all so organized that we took all the life out of it. I've often said that we spent enormous amounts of effort going out into the real world and destroying the very thing we set out to record. Systematically destroying it! And somehow we didn't catch on to that.[9]

Synchronous sound recording systems had been available to filmmakers since the late 1920s, but the cost and inflexibility of the equipment made it unsuitable for any kind of genuinely candid filming. "*Toby* . . . had to be done with this—is 'arcane' the right word—this ridiculous equipment. Mitchell [camera], the tripods, . . . 35mm tape recorder. Weighed at least 150 pounds! Two men to set it up. . . . A truckload of equipment." But for all the limitations that Leacock encountered in making *Toby*, he was inching toward a workably candid system. However, it was not easy.

> We worked like crazy! It was a strange film in that these performances, tent theater, happened every night. So even though we were *incredibly* clumsy, we were able to get a bit tonight and a bit more the next night and a bit more the next night. And we did some cheating; shooting with a handheld camera, certain sequences, and laying in fake sync sound. And we worked like crazy on it. And it was my first sort of "personal" film, where I'd done my own camera work and directed it and edited it.
> And it went on the air. . . . It was prime time, national television [on *Omnibus*]. Big deal. And it went on the air, and it's a half-hour long—Zuummpptt! It was over! And there's that absolute void! . . . And I worked my pants off. For six months. And you wonder, "What the hell was that all about!" *Nothing* happened! I got a sweet note from the head of *Omnibus* saying how everybody had enjoyed it and blah-blah. It was very nice, people said it was very nice. And "Boom!" It was just like yesterday's news. Must be like making a wedding cake or something; it gets eaten, there's nothing left, except a vague "burp"

in somebody's memory! [laughter] So I was absolutely amazed when I got a call from somebody named Bob Drew.[10]

Meeting Drew

The second pivotal meeting of Leacock's career was about to take place. Drew, watching television for ideas about how to implement candid television journalism, saw *Toby* and got excited.

> He had seen the show by accident, called me up, came down to New York and this marvelous thing happened. Somebody you had never heard of in your life came in and had understood every single thing in the film. And more than understood it, had projected from it. Obviously our thinking had been very parallel.
>
> And we talked a bit about his views on television journalism, which were very strong; he thought it was a disaster. And he, coming from the *Life* tradition, which was—I think it's been a bit lost in history how remarkable the photojournalism of *Life* was. . . .
>
> And so Drew was full of this, and I didn't really understand, but I knew that in *Toby* we had desperately tried to overcome, to get back to some feeling of observation rather than organizing everything. . . . And then I didn't hear from him.[11]

Leacock continued free-lancing for *Omnibus* and others, making *How the F-100 Got Its Tail* (1955) and *Bernstein in Israel* (1958) that exacerbated his impatience with the available equipment. Others were working to solve the same problems. Morris Engel had made *Weddings and Babies* in 35mm; "He had a crazy rig—a 35mm camera, a portable tape recorder—that made it possible. I was very impressed by that." [12] Leacock, since his finished work would be seen on television, was able to use 16mm, and a new professional camera made by Auricon had improved the situation— slightly.

> And we found ourselves in Israel [filming Leonard Bernstein]. We had left the day after the opening of *West Side Story*. Bernstein was not that famous in those days, and everybody wanted to know— [because of] these *rave* reviews—"What is it like? What does it sound like?" There's no recording.
>
> And one night at the hotel, Felicia, Lenny's wife, and Lenny, with a little piano and this group of friends—including Teddy Kollek, the mayor of Jerusalem, I think was there—between the two of them played and sang the whole *West Side Story*! Singing all the parts. It was hilarious! And where was the camera? Locked up in a garage someplace! No place! We were always—we missed everything! But we managed to make a half-assed film.[13]

The actual devising of a handheld camera and separately synchronized recorder would take several years, but Drew and Leacock continued their occasional efforts toward that goal—and got to know each other better.

> Somehow Drew was able to get some equipment built, by a guy out in Hollywood, . . . Loren Ryder, sweet old guy . . . he put together an unbelieveable contraption; a sound recorder with all these boxes attached to them, cables connecting them, and an Auricon camera.
>
> And it arrived in a box, and Drew called me with this *insane* idea, of going to Malaga [Spain] to film a bullfight. No permission, no arrangements, no nothing! And we didn't even—this thing had just arrived from Hollywood, in these cardboard boxes. Didn't even open them; we just prayed! . . .
>
> I remember we took off for Paris, and then there were no flights left from Paris to Madrid, cause everyone was going to this bullfight; it was one of the biggest bullfights in history, whatever that means. And I remember we were stuck in Paris, and then the *Life* aspect of Drew emerged. I mean, I would have quietly packed my bags and gone home or gone got drunk or something. Not Drew. He came in smiling and said, "I've chartered a twin-engine Beechcraft, with pilot, co-pilot, and beautiful attendant, and we're flying to Madrid." [laughter] It's incredible![14]

Leacock's laughter credits Drew at his finest, the producer who can produce—in spite of the odds.

> I remember we got to Madrid on a Saturday night, the bullfight was on Sunday. . . . We unpacked the equipment in the hotel. And it didn't work. Period. It didn't work! At all. No, nothing happened! [laughter] So I got the hotel electrician, with some screwdrivers and a voltmeter and things, and we managed to get it working. Some connections wrong in the cables; nothing serious. And we flew down to Malaga, with the bullfighters, and [Ernest] Hemingway was along; it was pretty wild. In a DC-3. And there were officials chasing us around, because we had no permission to be there or to shoot; I mean, it was absolutely mad. And I think—I was loaded down with this crazy camera, the cables connecting me to Drew, to different boxes all over the place. And I think at the end, as the first bull died, somewhere around there, the camera stopped! [laughter] It was madness!
>
> So we borrowed a spring-driven camera, shot it anyway. We did get some [sound] footage. . . . It's fragments. I think it's probably the best bullfight film ever done, in a funny way. But there are those amazing moments when [matador Luis Miquel] Dominguin is tossed in the air . . . and that strange scene of Dominguin undressing after

losing the fight. I mean, it's fragments! Miniscule fragments. But somehow we generated a lot of excitement around us.[15]

After more than twenty years of film apprenticeship, experience, and exasperation, Leacock could finally count some bits of progress: the camera was off the tripod and in the cameraman's hands, and "miniscule fragments" of real human activity had been captured, with accompanying sound. He could begin to glimpse the future that might be possible. But progress would not come from enthusiasm and excitement about what might be possible; it would come only with argument, cunning, salesmanship—and luck. It would come, finally, with the intervention of a producer.

8

Getting Equipped

"You can't begin to do dramatic, real-life stuff if you wipe out the drama in the process of recording it. So you have to learn to shoot candidly. And since we were able to shoot candidly—that is, without disturbing too much the reality that was going on—in still pictures, we had to develop that in motion pictures. And that, I did. We did."[1]

An important part of Robert Drew's contribution to the development of cinema verite in America was to shepherd the development of a new—and radical—generation of filmmaking equipment. Drew is not a cameraman or a technician, although he frequently recorded sound as part of a filmmaking team on his early productions. Drew's contributions to solving the problems of equipment limitations lay chiefly in motivating and managing—and financing—the new developments. That equipment may eventually have cost Time, Inc. a half-million dollars and only Drew had the level of vision and initiative, and the right institutional positioning, to make it happen. In rudimentary ways, films on a football coach, a weightless correspondent, a balloon astronomer, and two bullfighters showed the way. But this was not his vision of candid film journalism. He needed more opportunities, more money, and more time to continue his developments. And he was still working for *Life*.

"We're cooking along and what I'm really doing is building up a library of films that I can stick together to show how a magazine show would work. So I finally do that; stick them together and show this to [publisher Andrew] Heiskell. Who shows it to [Roy Larsen] . . . the chairman of the company. And I get summoned to [Larsen's] office, and he says, 'Would you please leave *Life*.' "[2]

"Please leave *Life!*" Even when retelling the incident, there is a note of surprise and apprehension in the way Drew inflects the phrase. He had spent his entire professional journalism career with the magazine, developed his skills, studied his field, proposed a forward-looking plan for redirecting his company, so why was he being asked to leave? "Because, Bob, the Broadcasting Division has a capital budget for equipment." Larsen was proposing an institutional solution to Drew's problems, a way to give Drew a chance.

"I needed money and the Broadcast Division had capital expenditure budgets for equipment. So whereas for *Life* magazine, it looked like a lot of money to put out a hundred thousand bucks for this or that, for the Broadcast Division, they were used to spending a hundred thousand bucks for this or that."[3]

Time-Life Broadcasting consisted of five television stations in less-than-major-markets—Minneapolis, Indianapolis, Denver, San Diego, and Grand Rapids. Drew and Wes Pullen, head of Time-Life Broadcasting, struck a deal: in return for his production expertise, Drew would have the money he needed to develop his filmmaking system. Drew had reservations about the workability of the arrangement from the Time-Life Broadcasting side, but he was not about to state them so long as the money was available.[4]

But money alone would not mean development. Drew was not a technician; Leacock understood the technical principles, but had little detailed technical experience. Fortunately, a person with experience both as an engineer and as a filmmaker was at hand—Donn Alan Pennebaker.

9

Other Voices—Donn Alan Pennebaker

At various levels, Donn Alan Pennebaker is a hard man to reach. Several attempts to contact him by phone are unsuccessful; he is getting ready to leave for a European shoot, or just getting back, or some other bit of business is pressing in. When finally contacted, he is reluctant to be interviewed. "I don't want to get into a hassle . . . there were real differences with Drew, so I quit . . . the operation had become bathed in vagueness," but finally agrees to take a call later in the week. The caller has the feeling it may be very brief.

On the callback, Pennebaker cannot be more helpful or thoughtful. The interview lasts two-and-a-half hours, the first hour a nonstopped response to "Tell me how it started." He is frank, intensely interested in telling the story and making the nuances clear to the listener. Alternately excited, skeptical, and regretful in his recollections of the film history he has been a part of, Pennebaker is both a strong supporter and sharp critic of his former boss, Robert Drew. It is a remarkable and fascinating call.

The Equipment Prospects

I'd known Ricky [Leacock]—and Ricky had come to Russia [to film Leonard Bernstein in 1959] with a sync sound rig, and it made quite an impression on me. Although it was very ugly; I could see that the mechanics of it, the electronics of it, were totally not worked out. But . . . it became clear to me that what was really fantastic about a sync sound rig was that you got things that you didn't expect to get. And so when we came back to the States, I was really kind of interested in technically taking that and trying to see if I could work [it] out—

59

and make it really portable, cause it was just not portable; it took about three of us to haul it around.[1]

With the money from Time-Life Broadcasting in place, the next steps in Drew's plan could be be developed. Pennebaker willingly provided some of the technical support.

> The equipment prospects, the equipment problems, were *so* enormous, that it was kind of interesting and took most of my energy. And that and setting up the studio to be able to accommodate a dozen or so editors, with equipment that didn't exist—that is, just the problem of, a typical problem was that up until then, most editors used hot splicers, as they worked. The idea of tape splicing, for tape and film, using this same piece of equipment, simply didn't exist, to my knowledge. And we built little things with pins in them; little pieces of wood that you could hold in your hand, and actually make splices. . . . And we were working with [magnetic] tracks, of course. And [magnetic] tracks were relatively new. I mean, probably within four years, three years, prior to that, most of the tracks in the New York documentary were actually optical. . . .
>
> And I know it was a frustration for Drew, but no matter how much money he had available, the problem was that there just weren't many people that you could go to who could give you solutions, who would know them; it took time to work them out. And between Otto Propelka, who ran MagnaTech, and Mitch Bogdanovitch, [a camera repairman/designer] who operated in some sort of limbo uptown, we were getting our equipment painfully slowly, but sort of sorted out.[2]

Although much of his background was technical, Pennebaker's chief interest was in filmmaking. He understood equipment, its limitations and the possibilities it held, and his goals were to unlock those possibilities in service of a filmmaking concept equally as revolutionary as Drew's, but somewhat differently directed.

> Drew had swung around from putting together a kind of magazine format, with little short bits, to something with what we were talking about; what Ricky and I both [thought] was the concept of a major film. Of doing films which were one hour, minimum, in length. Possibly longer. Because it just didn't seem worth setting up and going into situations unless that's what you were going to come out with.
>
> And Drew began to swing around toward this. Maybe it was easier to sell to the magazine, I don't know. But the old idea of the short little bits began to disappear.[3]

The basic elements of revolution were in place; Drew as producer, Leacock as principal filmmaker, and Pennebaker providing logistical support, at least initially. But the combination was loosely knit, with Drew the only Time-Life Broadcasting staff person in the beginning, Leacock and Pennebaker on free-lance arrangements, and all three bringing different skills, temperaments, and long-range goals to the endeavor. The common elements were hope and vision: the hope of breaking through the barriers to sync sound filmmaking, and the vision of a new approach to documentary film that had truly not been possible, technically or conceptually, before.

> We both had a lotta faith in Drew! I think you have to understand that Ricky and I were both very won over to Drew, not just because he was coming in at the right time, and was something we needed, because you can't go on with silent cameras. . . .
>
> But in the beginning, we were both impressed with Drew's ability, his willingness to go ahead and kind of push out into this void, and try to carry the magazine with him. And he seemed to understand the equipment problems, and understood that it had to be dealt with; that you just couldn't push people around with the old equipment. Which is what most producers would have done. They don't really believe that equipment makes that much difference. So, they would just say "Well, listen, just get somebody to help you carry it if it's heavy!" without comprehending what that would do to our [shooting] situation. But Drew was really totally aware of all the—you know, he made himself aware of all the problems, and how we did it, and how you got—how you were able to get some sort of entre to a person and how crucial that entre was. And all this time, of course, we were working out, in long discussions, what it was that made good stories good and the bad ones bad.[4]

10

The Primary Experience

The stage was set for a breakthrough. Drew now had some experience: the candid shooting with *Life* photographers, the inflexibility lessons of *Key Picture*, and the production and institutional experiences of the *Life* promotional films. He had talented co-workers; Leacock was director and cameraman, and Pennebaker was helping to make everything work. And, Drew had Time-Life Broadcasting's money. All that was lacking was an appropriate story, a story with importance, drama, and the opportunity for candid reporting. Drew's choice was characteristically grand—he would film the election of the next president of the United States.

"Probably in January of 1960, I found my story: this attractive young senator [John F. Kennedy] running for president. And . . . he was approaching a primary contest with Hubert Humphrey in Wisconsin. And Humphrey was an interesting character too. And my idea was that the camera would live with each of these men throughout the period of the primary and tell their story."[1]

But even in 1960, even before the spate of assassinations of mid-decade, a television producer-reporter could not simply decide, on his own, to make an intimate documentary of the political process. Permissions were necessary; the participants had to be briefed and agree to at least the presence of the camera team during the campaigning. Access to the subject, at least at some acceptable level, was soon recognized as a key element in Drew's developing methodology.

> I go out and visit Kennedy in Detroit, fly back to Washington on his plane, talk to him the next morning in Georgetown, and tell him basically what we've got—a new form of filmmaking, which is a new

form of reporting, which is a new form of history. That it would require the camera—a team, myself and Leacock—to be with him from morning till night, every day, for a number of days. That he can't worry about when the camera is on or off or what we're shooting. This way, we'll get a record which can be edited as a story to tell itself. He says, "What's in it for me?" I say, "I don't know, maybe nothing, but if you happen to win and you look good, it might be useful to you. At the very least, it will be part of the—it will be good history."[2]

And he gave me a long look in the eye and said, "If I don't call you by tomorrow, we're on." And he didn't call me and we were on.

And then I visit Humphrey and got the same kind of agreement from him. So *Primary* was set up.[3]

But between setup and completion there would be both anguish and elation for all concerned. Drew was operating under a commitment to Time-Life Broadcasting, which he did not strongly agree with, to show the corporation's stations how to produce more sophisticated films. In 1960, local television stations were shooting mostly silent film of automobile accidents, football games, community meetings, and drugstore holdups; sound film was limited almost entirely to interviews, speeches, and occasional public hearings. The equipment available to the news departments of the Time-Life stations was crude, suitable only for the most rudimentary form of filmmaking.[4]

The stations don't have the equipment, either the cameras or the editing equipment, to make sophisticated films. That means films with multiple sound tracks. And there are not mixing studios in the Time, Inc. cities, a lot of them. So I get Loren Ryder on the West Coast . . . to design a portable sound studio and editing and mixing system that we can pack up in suitcases and take from city to city and use in hotel rooms. I have Mitch Bogdanovitch in New York putting together an Auricon that's been silenced and cut down and made lighter so we can shoot candidly so the characters don't hear the clacking and clanging and are not aware that we're shooting. A wire [with the sync signal] goes from this to a Perfectone recorder, which I carry, with a directional microphone.[5]

With these tools, Drew; Leacock; Al Maysles, a young New York cameraman recommended by Leacock and Pennebaker; Terence Macartney-Filgate, a Canadian cameraman familiar with some portable filming experiments done by the National Film Board of Canada; and Bill Knoll, a free-lance cameraman, arrived in Minneapolis. Time-Life Broadcasting's station, WTCN-TV, would be their base of operations for covering the presidential primary campaign in neighboring Wisconsin. With Drew and Leacock working as one team, Maysles and a local newspaper reporter hired to handle the recorder as a second team, and Macartney-Filgate and Knoll generally with silent cameras, the filming began.

> Leacock and I would travel the day with Kennedy. And Kennedy would sweep into a town, and get his picture taken, go to the high school and make a speech or stand on a street corner and try to shake hands with all the factory workers, appear on a radio show and talk about religion, which is a big issue at the moment. And Humphrey would be doing the same thing. Mainly, though, Humphrey would concentrate on farmers and Kennedy would concentrate on workers. And at night, we would reassemble and see what the other crew had shot . . . and find out what had been done and where we stood and think through what the assignments would be for the next day and assign them. And it basically went like that, day after day. And night after night.[6]

The shooting was under way. From Racine to Madison, Beloit to Sparta, eight years of thinking, planning, trials and errors, and scrapping together both equipment and talent was being tested in the little farming towns and crowded union halls of Wisconsin.

Drew's notes for the shooting reveal a broad attentiveness to detail, and a desire for control, that clearly equated with his earlier *Life* experience of "building a stadium, organizing a game, and getting [the photographer] up to bat." A week before the election, he still had to "persuade Humphrey [to] be close election night," to "check with Pierre Salinger [to] get [Kennedy's] schedule," and to spend the "evening at typewriter—compose script [and] ops plan." Time was scheduled to have photographers "out casing" locations. A generalized shooting plan for "moving into a town" was drawn up:

> —Ricky on candidate - sound, wide at start - close on face.
> —Maisels [Al Maysles] over shoulder - close in on faces.
> —[Bill] Knoll special effects - extreme close-ups of reactions, excitement, candidate.
> —Filgate - special effects, articulating - spelling Ricky, Maisels, Knoll - sound, quotes.
> —Drew - mikes for Perfectone, Auricon.[7]

A similar "outdoor meeting" plan envisioned:

> —Leacock arrives with candidate, stays on him, extreme close-ups - I'm wild with Perfectone - it goes on and on.

—Knoll with Auricon gets jokes, passion, all references to importance of campaign.
—Maisels bores in on people reaching with Aire [Arriflex camera], pretty girls - sex.[8]

It is of some interest that all of the notes which have survived that identify a particular candidate deal with appearances by John Kennedy.

Drew's planning was clearly justified. The 1960 election would have a profound effect on America's future, and Wisconsin would mark its real beginning: political writer Theodore White stated, "If [Kennedy and Humphrey] could not at the primaries prove their strength in the hearts of Americans, the Party bosses would cut their hearts out in the backrooms of Los Angeles."[9] But for Drew and his crew members, the "primary" question in the beginning was, "what are we getting?"

"The Very First Time"

We were getting real stuff, on the move, for the first time, maybe in history, in sync sound. People were not noticing us, things were happening in front of the camera, we were recording and getting it. And the very first time it worked, Kennedy bounded out of the car, walked into a photographer's studio, had his picture taken. The guy was outrageous, the photographer; posing Kennedy's fingers, bending them around and making dumb jokes and shooting his cuffs and so forth. Kennedy is sitting there being a good sport. So [Ricky and I] shot them getting out of the car, going through the door, into the studio, everything that took place, Kennedy walks back out, gets in the car, drives off—it's *all on film and tape, continuously!* When we got back in the car, Leacock and I looked at each other, and this was it! This was our dream—the first time ever!!

And we were thrilled to death. Our sense was that we were *getting* the story.[10]

For five crowded shooting days, the struggle to begin a revolution continued: in a car with Hubert Humphrey, who seemed completely unaware of the amateur-like "gun" camera and minirecorder Leacock was using, and at a rally where Jacqueline Kennedy was observed—and filmed—nervously twisting her white gloves behind her back as she spoke to the working-class crowd out front. Humphrey was trying hard to be lively and upbeat in a slow-moving radio interview while Kennedy was effortlessly greeting supporters leaving a rally. The election was the beginning of a major change in the face of American politics. Drew's coverage of it marked the beginning of a major change in the way human events at all levels were recorded and reported.

> In hotel rooms and a television studio the night that the primary was decided . . . there were no sync sound cameras at all covering anything that we were covering. There was a lot of press around and a lot of radio people, people with tape recorders, but people had honestly never seen anything like our rigs, and I have a feeling they really didn't know what it was and what was happening. . . .
>
> . . . I met *Life* editors in the hallways who laughed at what appeared to be heavy equipment we were carrying. And who had no idea what we were getting and what would result.[11]

But breakthroughs do not "happen"; they are planned and pushed, hard enough to make the break occur. Equipment, talent, vision, and leadership were the real forces behind the making of *Primary*.

> In Leacock, and Pennebaker and Filgate, . . . I tried to develop a feeling that this was their story, and what they got on film was *their* responsibility and interest, and that it was continuous and that you started at dawn and wound up at midnight, and you were most interested in a character. And if the technical side had to go, then it went, but you were with that character, and if the lights went off, you know, whatever happened, you maintained yourself in position with the character. . . . So I did everything I did with the *Life* photographer; I got him up to bat.[12]

As producer, it was Drew's responsibility to see that the camera was where things happened, to see to it that material was collected, and that the record was established—in sum, to *produce*. But the excitement, the sense of breakthrough, was not Drew's alone. For his principal associate, "It was incredible!"

> LEACOCK: It was insane. After five days of shooting on *Primary*, none of us could even stand up. There was a hotel room; it looked like a pile of dirty laundry. It was all of us asleep, all over the godamned floor. It was a killer.
>
> But we loved it. I said, at night, we'd all be like a bunch of thieves; telling each other what we had stolen that day. Bunch of pickpockets! And some of it was true, some of it patent nonsense. [laughter] And Drew was right part of it.
>
> There's a wonderful sense of craziness; this is not—you've got to go back to the time. If you were serious documentary people, you're worrying [about] your godamned tripods, you were worrying about being steady, having enough light, all this stuff. We just said, "To hell with that."
>
> And we had this weird set of rules. They were spoken. Never ask anybody anything. Don't *ever* ask anybody to repeat anything you

missed. Don't ask them questions. Don't—this was the rule of the game. And this was contrary to what everybody was doing. There was, you know, *See It Now* or whatever it's called; questions, questions, yak, yak, yak, yak, one cigarette after another. . . . And we weren't searching for absolute truth; that's all bullshit. We were trying to get at what . . . Drew talks about, or talked about when he saw *Toby*, the sense of being there.[13]

Twenty-five years later, the pioneers of cinema verite recall their reactions to "the sense of being there," and doing something for "the first time ever" with remarkable vividness. The experiences of that week in Wisconsin, and of the weeks to follow as the film was laboriously completed in Minneapolis, were important—and satisfying—moments in their lives. But the vividness is also partly the result of having repeated the story hundreds of times; *Primary* was, in fact, a breakthrough. It would introduce the realistic possibility of a new form of television journalism—and of documentary filmmaking; it would also make its makers well-known in their field. The film from that late-winter shoot would irrevocably change the face of documentary, in America and abroad.

But first the film had to be completed. Drew had sent Pennebaker to Minneapolis to help Loren Ryder set up the sound and editing equipment.

And when I got there, I went up to the door of the hotel room and opened it and it was a ballroom! And it was full! And the cables were running all over the place, color-coded every color of the rainbow. And I walk in and Penny looked up and said, "Don't worry, I've wired the busses!" Meaning he'd wired the fuses. Oh, shit! We're going to burn down the hotel!

So, then started a very rough period, because the camera and recorder Leacock and I had so very carefully kept together with a wire to carry the sync signal, turned out the wire had been broken the whole time; we didn't have any sync signal.[14]

The broken wire was a catastrophe. The time and energy spent shooting, the hours of film and tape, the institutional risks taken in proposing this project, the money—all would be wasted. Ten hours of unsynchronizable film and sound, while they could be edited along conventional lines, would hardly be the breakthrough Drew was seeking. "But Ryder had built an amazing device into this machine of his; you could turn a crank and vary the speed of the transfer of the sound. So I would say [it took] three weeks, day and night, of turning the crank to transfer the sound from 1/4" to 16mm for editing. We got it roughly in sync."[15]

With the sound transferred from 1/4-inch tape to 16mm magnetic film and synchronized with the picture rolls, editing could begin. And at this point, Drew introduced yet another innovation: the cameraman would be the editor. "Every man was supposed to be able to do everything." The filmmakers—Leacock, Pennebaker, Macartney-Filgate, and Maysles— were placed at editing benches, each editing a sequence for the finished film. "The idea was that we were all kind of equal," Drew recalls, "but as things developed, somebody had to coordinate and criticize, and we all criticized each other's work, but I developed into the supervising editor, of course."[16] In practice, Maysles proved not to be a satisfactory editor and returned to New York; Macartney-Filgate was let go because of personality difficulties; and Leacock and Pennebaker did most of the editing.

> PENNEBAKER: When we did *Primary*, sitting in that room . . . Filgate the Nonbeliever saying, "You're all full of shit—what you're doing. You could do this just as well in . . . Canada in a mixing studio." And the rest of us—Al [Maysles] wheeling this film back and forth . . . just watching it. And Ricky and I editing all night long, night after night. It was like a religious experience—and for Drew, too. And all of us perceiving, suddenly, the possibilities of something we had dreamt up before anybody'd done it.
>
> We'd done it in a crude way. Mechanically, it was very imperfect. But it was there. And we'd done it in a way that was very simple— simpler than anybody'd imagined. Just because we'd been on the right horse. And that was a fantastic thing. I mean, we came away from that thing just really changed. I mean, there was no possibility of doing anything else, ever, for Ricky and I.[17]
>
> DREW: In the end, Kennedy wins a squeaker, and what we have is two parallel stories which we can intercut, so the editing works. And the characters play off against each other stylistically, so that works. We show the film to the networks—and they don't understand it. . . . you know, they wonder where the narration is.[18]

The Results—Today

Primary is a hard film to get excited about today. It is crude and primitive; the sound quality, the camera work, the editing patterns, and the overall structure are all extremely marginal by today's standards. The innovations have become cliches; a viewer must continually remind himself that this film has to be seen in its time. Were it not for its historical value— political, social, and filmic—it could easily be overlooked.

But *Primary* is important, and watchable, for two reasons. First, it *is* historic; there are glimpses of what the future held, and there is a sense of what an improvement over the past it then was. And second, there are some moments of real intensity and insight into the characters and the task they were about that are of interest and importance today: Kennedy's speech to a Milwaukee rally, much of it in tight closeup and perfect synchronization, showing the personal intensity, sincerity, and courage of the polished young Easterner facing a Mid-Western, workingclass urban ethnic audience; Humphrey as television director, directing the actual director, as well as his wife and a political associate, on how to handle the opening for a local telethon; an excruciating—and now well-known—one-minute-twenty-second wide-angle follow shot, by Al Maysles, of Kennedy entering a jammed rally hall and making his way through a crush of bodies and outstretched hands to a stage where the seemingly endless crowd spreads to the edges of the frame.

These moments of record, of observation, moments of humor and intensity and insight into the personality of the candidates, are enough to validate Drew's dream, or at least the promise that it held. Unencumbered, for the most part, by the "cinema-antics" that came to plague some early cinema verite followers of Drew—the snap-zooms and pans, finding focus in the middle of important action, use of the tight zoom lens to spotlight "important" details as a means of visual commentary—*Primary*, at its best, is very, very good.

And at its worst, it is horrid. Or at least it is confusing, meaningless, and a mish-mash of inadequacies and trials and errors: closeups of Humphrey's feet walking this way and that during on-the-street campaigning, a cliche in its own time; Kennedy receiving election returns in his hotel room with the sound quality and synchronization so poor, and the content of the conversation fragments so complex, that even an attentive and informed audience cannot follow the significance of the action.

And at the level of analytical generalization, of synthesizing an explanation of what it all means, *Primary* was clearly inadequate. Theodore White, in his book *The Making of the President: 1960*—itself a revolution in reporting—had been able to make such a synthesis, but White was not concerned with trying to develop a complex new technology at the same time. Drew had not intended to provide a political analysis, or even a verbal narration that would provide a roadmap to the viewer, but an audience—especially a 1960 audience—could reasonably have expected more help in understanding both the specific details of the events presented and the broad significance of those individual events for the political process. A scrap of handwritten narration from Drew's editing notes apparently was intended to address the problem: "You may have sensed that the camera has indeed brought you something new. This has been an experiment—to see how closely you could be made to participate in the event and to see how, after it is all said and done, this new experience affected you. I hope you will let us know."[19]

This preliminary narration was not included in the final script. In spite of the best efforts of Drew and his associates, *Primary* is not self-explanatory; the details of "dramatic logic" had not yet been worked out.

But the inadequacies for the present day viewer are not the point. It is in the context of its own time that *Primary* is most important, not as a historic example of filmmaking practice, but as an example of a historic filmmaking influence. It was "a breakthrough," and in reality "it broke the mold." These are over heated, but accurate, terms and phrases. For those for whom *Primary* and its companion films struck a chord of recognition, the excitement was genuine and far-reaching. No matter what Drew's commercial or critical success, this first example of candid television journalism had provided a model of what the future might, and would, be. There have been many modifications and imitations of Drew's dream, many that Drew would not claim any kinship with. But the seminal nature of these early films can be clearly traced through the work of later cinema verite filmmakers who have used, at least as a point of departure, the fundamental observational stance toward documenting human activity taken first by Robert Drew.

The Results—1960

"You've got some nice footage there, Bob."[20]

That was the reaction of an NBC News vice-president to *Primary*. Eight years of planning, reflecting, experimenting, gathering talent and equipment, and then: "You've got some nice footage." And the network executive was a friend! Elmer Lower had been a *Life* correspondent in Los Angeles in the late 1940s with Drew, had become a *Life* bureau chief, and then joined NBC. Lower had many of the same journalistic roots as Drew; perhaps he was more comfortable with the "lecture logic" Drew found so limiting in documentary than with the "picture logic" Drew was struggling to establish.

> His implication was that, somehow, we didn't pull it together. And he clearly missed the narration, you know, a lot of narration.
> [*Primary*] broke the mold and if you didn't see it, if you didn't see it for what it was, it looked like hash. And I've seen how that can happen with the kind of film we made. If you don't understand that you're looking for yourself, [then] you're really depending on somebody to tell you what you're seeing; [if] you're really in that

verbal mode and one of these films hits you, if you're not looking for
character and you're not following the action, it can look that way.[21]

Primary was never broadcast by a network. It ran, in a 26-minute version,
on Time-Life stations in Minneapolis, Indianapolis, and elsewhere; the
RKO-General chain and other independent stations ran the program in
Los Angeles, New York, and other major cities at odd times and with little
critical or public notice.[22] One major factor in this lack of notice was the
fact that *Primary* appeared several months after the Wisconsin primary
was over, after Kennedy had crushed Humphrey out of the presidential
campaign in the West Virginia primary, after the Massachusetts senator
had captured the Democratic nomination and shifted the nation's attention
to his general election battle with Richard Nixon, after Hubert Humphrey
versus Jack Kennedy in the snowy Mid-West had long since ceased to be
news. Other documentaries of the Wisconsin primary had come on the air,
in more timely fashion, and been forgotten. Only *Primary* survives, and
then largely because of the enthusiasm of its makers and its importance to
film history. There were no reviews of these initial broadcasts. The program
passed before the 1960 television audience without making the slightest
visible ripple. But at least one audience, beyond the makers and their
friends, found *Primary*.

> It gets shown in Europe, and what comes back is a furor. I mean, in
> Europe, some people either got it, or got something out of it, but
> people are going crazy. They begin visiting—people are flying across
> the Atlantic to see us, to find out what kind of camera we're using,
> how we did it, and so forth. And within the next eight months, or
> year, fiction films begin coming out of France using our techniques,
> as if it's good to have shaky cameras. We're trying our damnedest to
> make the shaky camera smoother and over there they're making them
> shaky to look like us! So *Breathless* (1961) appears, *Tom Jones* (1963),
> and a whole succession of films that are using our "look" to—I don't
> know, to gain authenticity, I guess. Or expressiveness, or whatever.[23]

But what Drew and the others could sense even then, from the scattered
positive reactions—and the predictable negative ones—was that the at-
traction, the distinctiveness, of *Primary* was more than the camera simply
moving off the tripod and following the character; they sensed that, in
Primary, in the hands of a skilled observer, the camera was finally free
enough of its former inflexibilities to begin, at long last, to "see."

> You'll never see it again. I mean, it'll never be seen again the way
> it was then. And that stuff is automatic now. . . . On the other hand,
> it isn't automatic. I see an awful lot of stuff in which today the camera

gets out of the car, goes in, shoots what happens, comes back out,
but—you haven't seen into the man. You haven't seen the wit, humor,
irony, character. It's somehow we're awful good at shooting physical
things today, but some of those things were psychological things
that we were shooting, even if we shot them physically. And that
psychological shooting is something we had from the first film on. . . .
So Kennedy's charm and wit and so forth was great, but the
psychological approach that saw into Kennedy was also seeing into
the other character. And in the end, the Humphrey people really
thought we did Kennedy in, you know. And the Kennedy people
really thought we did Humphrey in.[24]

Drew may have been pleased by the reactions of his subjects, but that
was small reward given some of the stresses inherent in the process.

The main pressure is to deliver your dream. . . . I mean, in *Primary*
I'd been working for five years to make the breakout film, right. And
so then . . . here it was, and I was under the pressure to make that
film. That was my greatest pressure. That was the only pressure that
would have given me a cerebral hemorrhage or a heart attack. . . .
. . . *Primary* was tough, and *Eddie* [1961] was tough and a lot of
the early—in fact, the first five or eight films were—each one was so
chancy and risky and tough it was frightening.[25]

Drew, in creating a rudimentary breakthrough with *Primary*, had fulfilled part of his commitment to Time-Life Broadcasting, to produce "my
kind of film," but the remainder of the commitment was hardly a success.
Local television stations were not accustomed to the effort necessary for
documentary filmmaking.

We worked around the clock. We did what we had to do to make a
film and there was no way those people could have invested that kind
of time and energy in making a film, in editing a film.
Not only could they not invest the time we were willing to invest
to make the film but honestly, it was quite an illustration of what kind
of talent you need to make a film. People who work day to day in a
TV station keeping the system going just don't have the kind of
minds, or at least didn't then, that it takes to painstakingly edit
sequences for weeks at a time and make a film.[26]

Primary had failed to provide a useful example of documentary filmmaking that the Time-Life stations could use in the production of their own
films, had failed to ignite the interest of audiences unaccustomed to "picture
logic" presentations, and had failed to receive a network play. But for all
its limitations, *Primary* had apparently caught the attention of Time-Life

Broadcasting's management, or perhaps it had only set the system's ponderous corporate wheels in motion. In any case, "they asked me to make another film."

The Wisconsin primary had been April 5th; with the synchronization problems and the delays caused by the unwieldy cameraman-as-editor concept, editing had taken more than six weeks. The next assignment was for May 30th, Memorial Day, at a racetrack in Indianapolis.

11

Discovering Eddie

We had done something for Minneapolis. The next station we were going to do something for was Indianapolis, and the Indianapolis 500 was going to be run and it was the big event of the year in Indianapolis, and Wes Pullen asked me if I would look into doing a story on Indianapolis. And I felt that we had just made really an historic leap in making this important film on American politics, and the idea of going to shoot an automobile race didn't appeal to me at all, and I tried to get out of it and talk him out of it, and finally I agreed to go out and look at it.[1]

Auto racing was clearly not Drew's principal interest. He would shoot a quick, short film to satisfy the president of Time-Life Broadcasting and then get back to serious business. But Bob Drew was about to discover something important about the revolution he was shepherding, something about the importance of "characters in action" that would have a powerful influence on his filmmaking future.

I was at the Indianapolis Speedway during the time trials one day in the lunchroom when a man came busting through the door and put a dime in a telephone and made a phone call, and began describing how you turn a corner in a race car, and before he was through my hair was standing on end practically—not on how you turn a corner, but at this character, this guy, how he felt about racing and so forth.

So I found out who he was, and he was Eddie Sachs and he had the pole position, . . . meaning that he had gone faster than anyone else in the time trials, and that he would start the race off in front. It gave him some chance of winning the race.

So I talked to Sachs, and when I went back to New York I was now enthusiastic about making a film about this race driver, really. But it was still going to be a 20 minute film. I had upped it from 15 minutes to 20 minutes. It was going to be a 20 minute film.[2]

Was *Primary* really "this important film on American politics"? Or was it a personal portrait of two men engaged in a decisive contest? Was candid television journalism's future to lie with more animated treatments of the vast topics of our times, or would its focus be on the intricate workings of personality and interpersonal politics among individuals engaged in some personal quest or struggle? The questions remained (and remain) unresolved, with examples supporting each view available in Drew's work, and in the work of others who have come after him. But the importance of Eddie Sachs's phone call is clear: without Eddie, and *On the Pole*, Drew's revolution might have had a distinctly different flavor.

> But when I got to thinking about how to shoot a race and a race driver, and planning it, I needed a lot of cameras and a lot of crews. In fact I needed more people than I needed for *Primary*. . . . You had to get cars entering the turn, making it through the turn, missing the wall, going down the straightaway, . . . panning shots, . . . static shots, somebody to be with Eddie Sachs and somebody shooting the action in the infield, . . . So . . . without even thinking about it we shot a one hour special. I mean we shot what we thought we had to shoot to get this 20 minute film, and it was a one hour special.[3]

The Results—Today

In the beginning, there are the balloons, thousands of them against the sky, signalling festival and celebration. Then there are the people, mostly young, lounging, playing, in "summer Sunday" fashion. There is a singer: "Back home again in Indiana . . ." in that ponderous voice reserved for ceremonial occasions. And there is a narrator, a steadily-tense, never-seen "voice of God" guiding us carefully into the adventure the producer has devised for us.

If *Primary* is a hard film to get excited about today, if it is crude and primitive, then *On the Pole* is nearly its opposite. There are lapses, but in the few weeks between the April 5th Wisconsin primary and the Memorial Day running of the Indianapolis 500, Drew and his associates had progressed from barely acceptable to nearly fully developed in terms of cinema verite filmmaking. *On the Pole* is informative and often engrossing; it is also an important example of the promise of candid television journalism.

There are two ways in which this promise is displayed: in the depth and abundance of intimate detail the camera teams were able to record, and in the sophistication of the structure—the story-telling—of the film. Both are remarkable historically; both are pleasing, and in some respects fascinating, today. *On the Pole*, only the second of the Drew documentaries to be made, with the marginally adequate equipment still being developed, is an almost-completely-modern cinema verite film.

Structurally, *On the Pole* is rather simple. It is the story of the Indianapolis 500 told through the experiences of one of the principal drivers. There is a sophisticated parallel development of the stories of the race and the driver, the public event and the private person. The skill in crossing back and forth between the two events, in balancing the energies, and gaps, in each, is one measure of *On the Pole*'s sophistication, a mark of the progress that had been made in only a few short weeks.

But it is at the level of intimate detail that the film's remarkable qualities are most apparent. The amount, variety, and intimacy of the detail displayed in *On the Pole* had never been achieved before in a documentary film. Misjudged initially by Drew as an inappropriate follow-up to an "important film on American politics," *On the Pole* is a "small" film made large by the accumulation of human detail it presents, told with a fresh innovativeness that will never be seen in quite the same way again.

But there is yet another feature of *On the Pole*, beyond the recording of detail and the structure of storytelling, that was to become fundamentally important to Drew and his approach to documentary filmmaking: casting, or as Drew might term it, storyfinding. Although it was not fully recognized at first, casting/storyfinding gradually came to be understood as a basic ingredient in successful cinema verite. Understanding which stories "worked" became a preoccupation with Drew and his associates.

Structure and Detail

On the Pole opens with a teaser, the sounds, pictures, and narration introducing the audience first to an event of some sort; then to a "hair-raising American ritual"; then hinting at the real subject—"the private struggle of one of its heroes." And then the slow widening of the information pool: identifying the event as the Indianapolis 500; revealing the real subject of the film as "the man on the pole" as the title appears over a pack of cars moving to the start of the race; awakening the audience to the life-and-death aspects of high-speed auto racing with a wrenching scene of a car spinning out of control across and back across the track as other cars maneuver to avoid it; obliquely introducing the specific subject of the film with the track announcer's description of the crash, "Eddie Sachs looses control . . . Eddie Sachs [has] lost control!" and then a new voice, obviously a principal character, partially voice-over the end of the crash scene, partially voice-over a medium close-up of a man's hands on a steering wheel, gesturing emphatically as he says, "As I took the thousand-foot slide last year. . . ."

Welcome to Indianapolis. Meet Eddie Sachs.

The teaser/titles/introduction brings the audience quickly through mood, setting, history, and danger directly into dramatic, intimate contact with the principal subject, Eddie Sachs. The narrator—there is noticeably more narration in *On the Pole* than in *Primary*, less reliance on the audience's ability to apprehend oblique details in a fast-moving flow of images and sound—reviews the situation and sets up the promise of the hour ahead: "Two days before the race, Eddie is already wound up for the most exciting moment of his life."

Then, a carefully edited and artfully disguised background on the Indianapolis 500, auto racing, and—most importantly—Eddie Sachs, follows. Eddie, at a prerace ceremony, accepts a trophy for winning the pole position; his acceptance and his plug for his car's sponsor is awkward and uncertainly delivered. A detail: Eddie is the only one of the thirty-three drivers seated in the stands who is wearing a coat and tie. Then Eddie, shown driving a passenger car, explains with vividness and enthusiasm how a race driver slides his car at the wall to make a high-speed turn and how wind currents cause a dangerous "floating" effect on his car as he accelerates down the straightaways. Eddie's awkwardness in public ceremonies, contrasted with his almost manic intensity when explaining the racing techniques he knows and practices so well, are a preview, a build-up, for moments of even greater awkwardness and intensity later on.

There are unfortunate moments in the film, when the significance of synchronous sound is forcefully demonstrated. As youngsters frolic in a motel swimming pool, Eddie's wife says voice-over that Eddie isn't getting enough rest; then, in sync, that the pressure is wearing him down and making him nervous. Then, after the narrator mentions Eddie's several crashes—"Dark memories that return even on a summer day"—there is thirty-seconds of Mrs. Sachs, again voice-over, in concerned-but-matter-of-fact tones, describing Eddie's most recent accident. She recalls how badly he was injured, how he had lost part of his face and ear, and how plastic surgeons had repaired the damage—"They even put little tiny holes in his eyelids so eyelashes would grow. I think that's a wonderful thing!" Meanwhile, the picture shows happy children splashing in the pool. Did the camera fail? Was the sync cable broken? Was the cameraman reloading, or just not interested in the wife's story? The awareness of the loss of facial expression at a tense and important moment is an example of how quickly— nine minutes into the second American cinema verite film—an audience (or at least a critic) becomes accustomed to the innovation of portable synchronous sound.

"And here we go, right out onto *my* fabulous Indianapolis Motor Speedway!" Eddie is in the front seat of a station wagon, and the camera is in back—Eddie turns full around on "*my*"—and the film's exploration of Eddie continues: "thrills, excitement, 'gran-dor' (mispronounced), prestige." Eddie drives the oval track at a very modest speed, giving the audience the driver's view, as well as continuing their view of the driver. And, finally, "the clincher," to parallel the strategy of a *Life* picture essay script: "I guess my whole heart is right here—." The scene is a medium shot of Eddie, the camera is in the front seat looking into his earnest face, his expression is serious, intense, but also awkward, his heart clearly on his sleeve. It is also a shot made while driving on the highway, not on the track, placed here for dramatic effect, and it is unlikely any first-viewing audience ever noticed, or cared. "—My whole heart, just everything I've ever dreamed of, everything I've ever wanted, is right here inside of these two concrete walls." Eddie becomes clearer with every moment as the story unwinds.

Now the pace and direction change. There are scenes in "Gasoline Alley," the shop area; information on cars; and an introduction of the chief mechanic and the owner. There is a brief sequence from the prerace driver's meeting with track safety officials; Eddie is characteristically late, and the only one dressed in suit and tie. Then the chief mechanic explains the repairs being made to a blown engine by gently chiding Eddie that he "took out of the pits too fast [on a test run] and didn't even up the temperatures in the engine." Eddie listens blankly, then smiles sheepishly and says, "Well, that's a good thing to know; I'm glad to know that," then bumps into another mechanic and says, "I'll get out of your way." The sequence *reveals*: Eddie is an intense, boisterous driver not that familiar or at ease with the machine he drives or the T-shirted mechanics in his garage. But it also previews a later, and more serious, racing problem, one that will affect the outcome of the race itself. As detail, the sequence is interesting and a valuable addition to Eddie's portrait; structurally, it reveals a complexity of story line often not present in films made years or even decades later.

Detail continues to build. Day-before-the-gates-open crowds are watching through chain-link fences. There is parallel cross-cutting between mechanics breaking in the rebuilt engine and Eddie eating breakfast with rival driver Jim Rathman. The pit crew tries to change four tires in eighteen seconds—and takes forty. Eddie gives them advice on how to do it faster, and gets testy replies.

And then the tension-builder, the beginning of a demonstration of the "psychological shooting" Drew prized, as the camera is simply present and observant, able to "see into the man." After patiently placating some pushy, picture-taking fans—"they're just wonderful . . . they drive you nuts . . . wonderful, wonderful people"—Eddie launches into a remarkable trackside confidence, delivered almost directly to the camera, apparently without any prompting.

> I'm getting tremendously tensed up. . . . I'm getting excited inside. My system's getting nervous; I'm going to the men's room every hour, I can't control my system. . . . It's just once a year—one big chance! And it's gonna happen; it's just a matter of finishing my work now and some rest and coming out here and putting my helmet and my goggles on and going—fast!! . . . And I've never been this nervous before. And I want to do *so* well. I've never thought I'd win the race until now.[4]

Partly in medium closeup, partly in cut-away close-up's of Eddie's slowly wringing hands, it is the heart of Eddie Sachs. "And I want to do *so* well." The inflexibility Drew fought to overcome, the mobility he sought, the observational talent he found in Ricky Leacock, all begin to coalesce in this sequence.

Then, almost abruptly, the pace is changed, the tension allowed to subside. At a pre-race dinner, natty in a sleek dark suit, the other drivers more plainly dressed, Eddie speculates whether he would—or could—quit driving if he wins, wondering, "if I didn't win the race next year, I'm a has-been. Actually a has-been!" There is a frantic sequence of the Speedway gates opening very early on race day, a gatekeeper's mocking "Gentlemen, start your engines!" and then a frenzied rush of cars to the best parking locations.

Race cars are wheeled out, majorettes strut by, lines of late-arriving cars creep through the gates, the track announcer fills time with introductions and perfunctory interviews, programs and souvenirs are for sale, and fans sleep away the long morning before the start. Eddie sits on the pit wall, making small talk, taping his goggles down to narrow slits: "I'm only looking in one direction . . . I'm not interested in sightseeing!" It is a small moment, demonstrating the importance of film as a recording medium, the importance of facial expression and voice inflection to a fuller understanding of the event, large or small, taking place before the camera. The competitive side of the cheery driver begins to emerge, the "gran-dor" begins to recede.

There is the starting-line commotion: brief clips of Eddie seated in his car and smiling broadly, his wife standing outside the pits area talking to those—all males—inside, mechanics making final unexplained adjustments, Eddie shaking hands, more smiles.

And then, beginning calmly enough, the film's climactic moment, only 31 minutes into a 52-minute production, is proof of the potential Drew had believed in, the possibility and promise of cinema verite equipment and techniques. The camera, at eye level, looks slightly down on Eddie in the cockpit of his car as the chief mechanic leans in to talk intermittently, Eddie somewhat distracted, his mind elsewhere. Then Sachs slowly, precisely, crosses himself and prays, for fifteen seconds, with intense concentration in the midst of the purposeful confusion around him. The sound track, clearly placed for dramatic effect, is the celebrity singer: "Back home again in In-di-a-na—" Eddie looks up, his moment of prayer over, smiling shyly at a crew member, then shaking the man's offered hand. As the crew rustles about, Eddie wipes apparent tears from his eyes, slowly shaking his head in some moment of private wonderment, perhaps, at his place at the center of all this activity, the man "on the pole." After a moment, he raises both hands to his eyes and deeply bows his head.

"—The new-mown hay is on its wagon, from the hills I used to roam—." A cutaway shows Eddie's wife looking on, serious and alone along the fence, licking her lips in apparent tension and concern. Then Eddie again, wiping his eyes, smiling shyly, to no one in particular, then searching for a handkerchief while the chief mechanic leans in very close to the obviously emotional driver for a few private words, a slap on the shoulder and a few more words, Eddie slowly regaining his normal composure, looking more confident and businesslike, the hard edge of the competitor starting to return.

The camera remains in medium-shot to medium close-up throughout; no super-intimate close-ups, only two brief cut-aways, no cinema-antics. The four scenes last one-minute-and-twenty-seconds, a considerable time, even in documentary; they are marvelous moments, remarkably simple and intense, among the best in cinema verite then or now.

"—My In-di-a-na home." Thousands of balloons are released, officials clear the starting line, "Gentlemen, start your engines!" comes over the public-address system, and the cars are pushed off for the parade lap. Eddie is seen in medium close-up, waving to the crowd as he drives out of the limited range of the telephoto lens. But the emotional peak has passed with the drying of Eddie's tears; the race is almost an anti-climax, and takes up only nineteen minutes of the total film time.

At the start, Eddie's "on the pole" advantage lasts only a few yards as he looses first place on the first turn, forced back by a more aggressive driver. He roars back, takes the lead, makes a pit stop, loses the lead, is reported "falling back" and comes into the pits with a steering problem that costs him over two minutes. The pit area at crisis time is hard territory for a camera crew; things happen fast, good sound is impossible, only a general sense of confusion can be recorded and communicated. Back on the track, in ninth position, Eddie tries to gain ground. "Eddie's driving furiously!" explains the narrator, as Sachs moves up to fifth place. There is a series of extremely long telephoto shots of Eddie's car flashing between trackside obstructions, the flashing adding visual reference points for the sense of speed that is otherwise difficult to convey. Then, "Something's wrong!" and Eddie pulls back into the pits once more. "A broken piston— the same one that blew on the practice lap—and the end of the race for Eddie" is the narrator's explanation; there is the intimation that the mechanic's warning against driving too hard too soon after a pit stop, the warning Eddie considered "a good thing to know," was forgotten in the furious attempt to regain first place. Eddie's drive to succeed, it seems, may have caused him to lose.

Friend/competitor Jim Rathman wins; the camera follows Eddie as he unnecessarily plays traffic cop for Rathman's quick dash down the pit lane to the winner's circle. The winner's ceremony is collapsed into cliches of wife's kiss, trophy handed, winner's victory fist upraised. The camera returns to Eddie, wandering through the pit crowd, getting an occasional word or two, clearly not the winner. Watching the smiling but obviously strained face of Eddie as a loser, it is possible, perhaps, to recall his earlier remark: "And I want to do *so* well!"

At the victory dinner, Eddie wears an elegant white suit; Jim Rathman is plainly dressed as he accepts the winner's check of $110,000. The next morning at breakfast, Eddie kids Rathman about having won the race by cheating, cutting across the infield while the judges weren't looking; both men laugh, Rathman easily, Eddie less so.

And then a final moment, probably contrived, and completely de-lightful. Eddie and his wife are driving down the highway, the camera in the back seat. Eddie: "Well, kid, we won't get a chance to retire . . . we have to race for another year." And his wife replies, "What would we have done all summer . . . ?" The camera stays on Eddie's wife, and after an almost professionally dramatic pause, she says, "Next year, Eddie." The picture cuts to a medium close-up of Eddie's hands on the wheel, driving along. Racing car sounds are brought into the background, and then "Back home again in In-di-a-na—" as the credits appear. After dreams of glory and moments of defeat, *On the Pole* ends with a soft, dramatic "kicker."

On the Pole is first-rate cinema verite, important historically, and impressive today. It is a transition film, utilizing many of the conventional montage editing conventions of the time—the furious rush of cars as the gates open, the bits-and-pieces evoking of holiday mood—along with the patient presentation of longish segments of sync sound that personalize and, slowly, dramatize the film. The structure is sure, the accumulation of detail purposeful, and the ability of the cameraman to recognize and record intimate and important moments genuinely impressive.

But the film is certainly not traditional "journalism": there is no consideration of the economics of racing, for the drivers or for the city of Indianapolis; there is only passing attention paid to spectacle-versus-safety issues; and Eddie's off-season career as a hair dresser is conveniently overlooked.

The film can also be charged with trading shamelessly on Eddie Sachs's kooky personality by showing Eddie's awkwardness, bombast, and teary moments as occasions for audience unease rather than as a sharing of the experience. But it is the image on the screen, its intensity and authenticity, that effectively disputes such charges. *On the Pole* is not a sentimental film about an American hero, or a clever ridicule of emotional intensity; it is rather a limited and direct record of a sometimes awkward and sentimental man, trying as hard as possible to succeed in a high-profile and dangerous profession. It is a never-before-seen form of television journalism—cinema verite.

The Results—1960

"The film had a strong effect on everybody who saw it. CBS ran it. And then—that was the first review I remember—a reviewer said something like, 'This is what television ought to be doing.' And I chalked that up as being our first perceptive reviewer, because basically what the film did was let you see what it was like to be in Indianapolis during the race through a character."[5]

The tangible payoffs, for Drew and for Time-Life Broadcasting, of *On the Pole* were greater than for *Primary*; CBS bought the program as a sports special, which probably repaid the production costs, and the reviewers—partly as a result of the network's promotion efforts—had taken at least passing notice.[6]

But these were still halting steps. The old documentary mold had been pierced, but hardly broken; the attempt to create a new mold, a new form for candid television journalism, was still tentative and uncertain.

> We threw away the props that support documentary—the lecture
> logic, the script, the script writer, the director. We said that we would

do better by capturing real stories in real life, and that this could only be done by a new kind of story-telling photographer.

. . . Frankly, it was a big leap and we were not sure. But the first time out [*Primary*] we were surprised. We had a number of extraordinarily lucky happenstances. And we came back with more power, and truth, than the old documentary system would have allowed. However, due to all the luck we had to acknowledge, we were no more confident than before that our ideas were a solid substitute for the conventional props.

The second time out [*On the Pole*] we again had unbelieveable luck in the unpredictable wonders that took place in front of us while our cameras were turning. One could not hope to be that lucky again.[7]

It would, of course, turn out to be only partly luck. Chance often plays a part in human affairs, but ability, motivation, and opportunity are also important factors. Drew's desire for a more satisfactory form of reporting, his maneuvering to develop the improved equipment he knew would be necessary, his institutional background and position at Time, Inc. could not all be characterized as merely luck. As he had done years earlier in making arrangements for *Life* photographers, Drew was engaged in "building a stadium, organizing a game, and getting [the filmmaker] up to bat."[8]

In the over-all development of cinema verite in America, *On the Pole* was important as an early example of what might be possible. In a more immediate way, it caused an important reaction in two men. One was a *Life* reporter, Gregory Shuker, and the other was an ABC vice-president, Tom Moore. And their decisions as a result of seeing *On the Pole* were to have important effects on Drew's career, and dream.

12

Other Voices—Gregory Shuker

Greg Shuker is, like Donn Pennebaker, a busy man, an independent film and video producer interested in documentary, industrial, and feature projects; pre-arrangements are necessary to make sure there is time to talk. And, like Pennebaker, he is voluble in an interview, providing the detail and nuance necessary to fill in the spaces in what might otherwise be a bare, informational record. Unlike Pennebaker, he was not there at the beginning. He became one of the most productive and long-lasting of Drew's associates, but his was a different beginning.

The Beginning

Shuker, like Drew, got his early professional journalism experience on *Life* magazine; and again like Drew, he got his job through fortuitous circumstances—luck.

In 1954, Shuker was editor of Northwestern University's student newspaper when he was chosen to visit Russia on one of the first good-will exchanges following Stalin's death. While there, he shot some 35mm color slides, and when *Life*'s Paris bureau queried the returning students about pictures, Shuker volunteered his. The results: in a photo essay on Americans in Russia titled "Russia's Wintry Look," six of nine pictures, including three of four full-page blow-ups, were credited to Gregory Shuker.[1] Friendly contacts at the magazine led to a correspondent's job after his military service was completed in 1959.

So Shuker and Drew worked for the same magazine, in the same building, but Drew was on "the other floor," a "back-of-the-book" editor, handling pre-planned features while Shuker worked on last-minute foreign and domestic news. But though they had not met personally, Shuker and Drew shared an important element in common, the experience of being a *Life* correspondent.

> The correspondent and the photographer were the *Life* journalists, and our competitor at the time . . . was *Look* magazine, and the reason I mention that is that *Look* used to give credit lines on stories and they'd say "photographed by —" and then they'd say "produced by —." And that was quite accurate because the producer . . . of a picture story was very much like the producer of a verite documentary because that was the person who usually concocted the story and dealt with the logistics of it and often researched it in advance of the photographer and figured out, not how to shoot the pictures, cause that's the photographer's job, but *where* to shoot the pictures, often, and what the sequence of events might be.[2]

Another important element Shuker and Drew shared was the friendship of *Life* photographer Howard Sochurek, whose skills and contacts Drew had helped develop in Detroit. The friendship resulted in a phone call that proved pivotal to Shuker, and to Drew.

> In the summer of 1960, . . . I was sitting at my desk one afternoon, at Newsfront, which was what the domestic news place was called, and my phone rang. It was Howard, calling me from a room on the 34th floor of the Time-Life Building.
> . . . He said he was upstairs and he was looking at something that might be interesting to me, if I had a few minutes to look at it. . . . I said, sure, and I went upstairs, and found this little room in the middle of the corridor, with no windows, and went in—and this is very vivid in my mind—I went in, closed the door of the room, the room was dark, and I was aware of a lot of people standing around this *tiny* little screen, of what I now know was called a Moviola, but I didn't know what a Moviola was, and there was this little screen flickering with this rattling machine and a . . . 16mm magnetic sound track running with this thing. And I kind of peered over a few heads.[3]

The heads Shuker was peering over were those of Drew, Pennebaker, Al Maysles and others, and the little flickering screen was displaying a rough-cut version of *On the Pole*.

> There was this little black-and-white picture of this man, who I later found out was named Eddie Sachs, wandering around a racetrack in Indianapolis, having lost—having had his car crap out on him and he had lost the race, and he was wandering around the track trying to

catch the attention of people who were all streaming in the other direction, heading toward the winner's circle. And on the sound track you could hear the announcer saying congratulations and so forth to the winner. And you could hear this guy, Eddie Sachs, saying something like, "Well, next year." "Wait till next year." And, "If you can lead the race, you can win the race," he said.

And the camera was *right with him*. And, I mean, he was kind of turning around, 360-degrees, and he was waving, and he was trying to get people's attention—nobody was paying any attention to him! And there was this *incredible* sense of *being there*. I'd never seen anything like that. I mean, you know, the sound was there, and there was another sound track, which was his voice recorded at a different place—I didn't know what "voice-over" meant, I didn't know what "Moviola" meant, I didn't know what "hand-held" meant. . . . And I didn't know any of that, except I just saw and heard this little black-and-white image. . . .

And the lights came up and there was Howard Sochurek, and he grinned and said, "Do you know Bob?" and I said I'd seen him and I shook his hand. . . . And Bob looked at me and said, "Well, what did you think of it?"[4]

Shuker laughs. It is clearly a familiar retelling, done with relish and an appreciation for the importance of a small moment that has had long-lasting effects. "I mean, this really happened!!"

"And Howard was standing there, grinning, and I said—and this really happened, too, because we've talked about this—I said, 'I don't know what that was that I was looking at, but whatever that was, I want to do that!' That was the beginning. Right there."[5]

Shuker soon got his chance. Over the next three years, he worked on a number of Drew films and produced two of the most important ones—*The Chair* (1962) and *Crisis: Behind a Presidential Commitment* (1963). The thirty-fourth floor screening of the rough cut of *On the Pole* may have been only a minor step in the production of that film, but for Gregory Shuker, it was a turning point. "I hounded [Drew] after that. I wanted to work on that kind of stuff."

13

The ABC Connection, 1

Greg Shuker's reaction to the rough-cut of *On the Pole* was only the first of many individual reactions that were to influence Drew's career and plans in significant ways. Another and more immediately important reaction came about shortly after the film was finished.

"I had been talking to Tom Moore, who was vice president in charge of programming for ABC, for perhaps a year and showing him my films. I showed him the balloon film and . . . the first football film and . . . *Primary*. And I showed him *On the Pole*. He had a strong reaction, and he said, 'Let me borrow that film.' And he did borrow it for a weekend, and at the end of that weekend he called me in."[1]

Tom Moore was a neighbor of Drew in Darien, Connecticut, and had seen much of Drew's work; in fact, he had scheduled *Bullfight In Malaga* as an ABC special a year earlier before it was dropped because of protests of animal cruelty. Moore also knew that Leonard Goldensen, president of American Broadcasting Company-Paramount Theaters, wanted a high-visibility documentary made for ABC. CBS had just done a two-part special on Africa and Goldensen wanted ABC to counter. Moore wanted to know if Drew would be interested in doing "an hour, say, on Latin America." Drew tried to turn him down.

> I told Moore that I would not, that I disagreed with doing an hour on a continent, that what I would do is find a story within a continent which in the telling would reveal something about the continent, but that's the way I thought television ought to work, and that really they might have the wrong man.
>
> And Moore said, "No, I'd like you to do this one, and will you at

least research it, look into it for a week and tell me what you think then. . . ."

So after a week of investigation I found out that there was a story, a story of Latin America, which was an obvious big overall important summary of that part of the world, and that there were certainly events coming up which would illuminate that story and put it into action in terms of people.[2]

Drew's Latin America story is a generally familiar one today, but it was not well known to television audiences in 1960. It was the story of the poverty and extreme wealth that existed side by side in much of Latin America, of societies and governments that ranged from paternalistic to exploitative, and of the emergence of Fidel Castro as a popular hero—and the United States as a popular villain—in much of the area.

Drew also learned that a climactic moment was at hand: a political confrontation between the United States and Cuba at an upcoming meeting of the Organization of American States (OAS) in San Jose, Costa Rica.

The key fact was that if and when the United States was able to engineer the expulsion of Cuba from [the OAS], there were a lot of people throughout Latin America who would protest, and the protest would take spectacular form—in some places violence, in some places parades, in some places God knows what. And certainly in Cuba Castro would be led to make a huge protest, and Castro at that time was—as he still is—a great showman. So I expected some combination of a political event in Costa Rica with turmoil and protest in other countries, and a monster demonstration of some kind in Cuba.[3]

Drew quickly rough-scripted and budgeted his idea and Goldensen approved. Then Drew scrambled to get on top of the story: "It depended on just picking up and flying out of town almost immediately." Al Maysles and soundman William Worthy were sent to Cuba, while Drew and Leacock left for the OAS meeting in San Jose. The meeting was as confrontational as Drew anticipated, and his insistence on flexible equipment and talented personnel proved crucial to the coverage, as Donn Pennebaker recalls.

Ricky went down to San Jose to do *Yanki No!* on the conflicts. . . . [U.S. Secretary of State Christian] Herter blows up and righteously declares how evil the Cubans had been to have these [Russian] missiles, and that all of South America must join in condemning these missiles. And a lot of South American countries did not want to rise up and condemn Cuba. They weren't sure they didn't want missiles, themselves. But it was a real tough one, because the Americans were putting on a lot of pressure. So in the end, they took a vote, and Herter won. The conference there in San Jose decided to vote to condemn Cuba.

Now, there's ten different newsreel cameras down there, all set up, recording all this, some better, some worse. And Ricky's just another camera, right? At this point, [Raoul] Roa, who's the foreign minister from Cuba, jumps up and says, "This is outrageous. I know that half the people present in this room realize that this is an absolute farce, and that what they're doing represents—they're going against their real feelings. And I'm not going to be present anymore to be insulted in this way. I'm leaving."

And with that, the whole Cuban mission, the whole Cuban group, rises up and walks out, singing the Cuban national anthem. Well, Ricky just walked out with them. He wasn't plugged into any wall. He didn't have any tripod. They walked up the street to the hotel, singing all the way. They go up to the hotel room. And that's how you meet Roa.[4]

Mobility and flexibility were important features of Drew's approach to journalistic revolution, but not the most important. As Drew's technical developments became more widely known and spread to other areas of the news and documentary industry, discerning audiences might have noticed that the new tools did not always bring new or more revealing forms of filmmaking. The creative impulse was still required. The filmmaker, although freed from the limitations of the static and immobile camera and recorder, was faced with a previously unanticipated series of challenges: how to fit into a filmmaking situation he no longer had to—or wanted to—control; how to effectively observe and record the significance of an important human moment; how to overcome his faulty preconceptions of how the world really worked. Although Drew and his associates had begun to consider these questions, most filmmakers had not even asked them. Drew, Leacock, and Pennebaker were, in the truest sense, pioneers; there were almost no guidelines to follow, beyond those Drew had absorbed at *Life* and was now adapting to the vastly more complex media of film and television. Even now, in their third attempt at breaking out of the old filmmaking limitations, the process of learning how to do "something that had never been done before" seemed always to be taking place.

Yanki No!

It begins with crowds. Crowds celebrating, perhaps, or chanting; it is hard to tell which, the sound is muffled badly. A narrator—and then the title, flashing on and off on the screen—explains: "*Yanki No!*" The narrator says, "This is a film editorial, a warning to you that a dangerous gulf is opening between you and millions of your neighbors. You are about to see into Latin America from the viewpoint of the people who shout, 'Yanki no!' "

"From the viewpoint of the people." Drew chose to structure his material around the various people he, Leacock, and Al Maysles had filmed. It represented a departure from the format of interviews with experts and heavily narrated silent location footage that characterized conventional network documentaries of the period. For Drew, it was an opportunity to advertise the difference. The narrator says, "Now meet some 'Yanki no!' people: Arcaya, Junior, a Venezuelan student; Aba, Cuban revolutionary; Gabriel, and his wife Maria, of Caracas; Jesus and his wife, of Cuba; Arcaya, Senior, Venezuelan diplomat; Roa, Cuban foreign minister; newlyweds in Havana; Ivan, a Russian in the Caribbean; Fidel, in Cuba."

The recitation, intended to call attention to the personal nature of the program, is also an index; the program follows the introduction almost exactly.

Yanki No! is uneven, technically and structurally. The camerawork is shaky at times, the lens choices ineffective, some footage is very dark; the sound is often muffled or plagued by high levels of background noise. But there are flashes of intensity and innovation that provide promise, and there is little that is technically "pat" or conventional.

Structurally, the pattern is mixed. The OAS meeting, which might have been the focus of a more conventional documentary, becomes a point of departure for a more personal examination of the problems that are of concern to the people of the area: Foreign Minister Arcaya leaving the Presidential Palace the next day and explaining informally to Drew that he has been fired by the prime minister for supporting Cuba too strongly; the "ranchero" of Gabriel and Maria Manzanilla, Gabriel trying to anchor the dirt floor of the ragged shelter against a downpour that threatens to wash it away, then talking at length with a friend about being unemployed for over five months, the narrator translating, "I'll try again . . . I have nothing . . . I'm cleaned out." There is also more conventional coverage, but it is the personal moments that stand out.

Over half of *Yanki No!* is material shot in Cuba by Al Maysles: Jesus Marrero moving his family from his fisherman's shack into a government-built house, the narrator saying, "This is a big day in Jesus's life; *he* doesn't want anything to happen to the Revolution"; Ivan, a sailor from a Russian cargo ship on a "mission of friendship"; and Fidel.

It is Al Maysles's coverage of Fidel Castro's massive demonstration to denounce the U. S.-backed condemnation of Cuba that many critics noticed. Seldom had (or have) U. S. audiences been brought so intimately into contact with Castro's oratory. Beginning in afternoon daylight and continuing until after dark, with only sparse translations and many cutaways of individual listeners and vast crowds, and ending with a long extreme close-up of Castro's conclusion—"We are really free and sovereign . . . and we have learned to say 'No!'"—the speech, the enthusiastic chanting of the crowds, and the dancing and flag-waving, are the dramaturgical climax of the film, setting up Drew's closing recital of the potential dangers growing in the slums of Latin America.

And then an unusual note, a closing editorial.

> NARRATOR: Against the easy promise of Communism, and the impatience of the angry masses, the stark truth is that the forces for democratic development are starting late and against perilous odds. The cry, "Yanki, no!" is a cry for help, a cry of warning, a cry for you, Yankee, to care about your neighbors. You, Yankee, must be prepared to follow through, with understanding, effort, and dollars; to act quickly and strongly in their behalf—your own behalf—and on behalf of freedom in the world.

It is a rare statement in a Drew film, a departure from description into prescription, perhaps included to enhance the statesmanlike role ABC's president wanted to assume in the broadcasting industry. Drew insists otherwise: "It was the only time I ever did it, and it was because this film had a mission, which was to sort of wake the American people up to the situation." Or perhaps Drew's closing was only part of an overall effort to make a splash.[5]

The Results

"It made a splash with the critics and the public. ABC's news vice president quit because his management had made the film with an independent. The sponsor, Bell and Howell, asked for more."[6]

All three elements of Drew's statement are true, and important. *Yanki No!*, by virtue of being programmed as part of the Bell and Howell-sponsored *Close Up!* series on ABC, received broad—and favorable—attention from reviewers.

> JACK GOULD, *New York Times*: An arresting and fascinating study of Communist infiltration in Latin America, a presentation greatly expanding the techniques of visual reportage. . . .
> The use of portable cameras was especially brilliant in trips through the slums of Cuba and Venezuela and in attendance at the huge rallies

of Premier Castro. A viewer had an uncanny feeling not only of personal presence but also of emotional involvement.[7]

LAWRENCE LAURENT, *Washington Post*: [Bell and Howell president Charles H.] Percy and ABC may as well brace themselves for the protests that will surely follow tonight's telecast of "Yanki No!" It does not offer a pretty or a comforting report on the Latin America's view of the United States.[8]

Time Magazine: The hour-long show had a rough-and-ready quality about it. Frequently the sound was so bad that words were indistinguishable. Some of the camera work was shaky, some of the cutting rough. As an editorial, the program was impassioned rather than closely reasoned. But the report hit like a fist and left some haunting images in the viewer's mind: the despair of an out-of-work electrician's helper in a dirt-floored hut in Caracas; the satisfaction of a fisherman whose family has a fine new cottage in a Cuban cooperative.[9]

Part of the splash, for some reviewers, was the companion controversy surrounding the resignation of John Daly, vice president for news, special events, and public affairs for ABC. A month before the program aired, the *New York Times* reported that Daly had resigned, citing "fundamental policy differences," after learning of Leonard Goldensen's commitment to buy *Yanki No!* and three other Drew-produced films from Time, Inc. Daly claimed Goldensen "had violated the 'traditional policy' that all news and public affairs programs be prepared entirely by the network and not by outsiders." But the *Times* also reported the resignation as part of "a longstanding internal struggle at ABC over control of news and public affairs programs."[10] The *Washington Post* reported that "ABC executives complained that Daly's main programming 'principle' was a steadfast dedication to radio techniques, with incidental pictures for television."[11] In an ensuing reorganization, public affairs production was moved to the programming department; the vice president for programming was Drew's friend Tom Moore.

Moore's actions not only precipitated Daly's departure, but also briefly made himself, Drew, and Time, Inc. a center of attention and speculation in the broadcasting community. *Variety* pointed out that Moore, with the support of ABC president Ollie Treyz, had assumed control of news, public affairs and sports programming in addition to the entertainment programs he had previously been in charge of. This was contrasted to the separation of news and public affairs from other types of programming at CBS and NBC.[12] Other trade publication headlines such as "Time Marches On— Right Into ABC's Bell [and] Howell Pubaffairs Production" and "ABC and Bob Drew (Time, Inc.) Expand Program Vistas as Newest Success Story in Pubaffairs Area," and reports that "Time, Inc. is expected to play a much bigger role in ABC-TV public affairs than anyone . . . thought" may have triggered concerns among network news managers.[13] The prospects of Time, Inc. directing its considerable resources into the distinctly proprietary area of network news and public affairs production was certain to have an unsettling effect, especially since the entry route was through one of the networks' own news division. The insiders, quite naturally, adopted a defensive position that was to create long-term negative difficulties for Drew, his parent organization, and for cinema verite.

But, for the moment, Drew's approach was fresh. By simply not trying to better CBS and NBC in the interview-and-analysis format, by bypassing the more traditional, and familiar, format for a more realistic and novel one, Drew had captured the interest of both critics, and network sponsors.

> I made *Yanki No!* . . . [and ABC] offered it to Bell and Howell—who gladly sponsored it. Then I was called in to a meeting . . . at which I threw out ideas for documentary programming. The ABC people liked the ideas, and the president of ABC jumped up and ran around the table and said, "I see a new day dawning," and he showed some signs of excitement which being a good salesman might have been his style, I don't know, but he professed to see a new day dawning and sent me out to Chicago to make a presentation to the Bell and Howell people. Now remember I was working for Time, Inc., so Time, Inc. shortly thereafter concluded a deal with ABC to produce a lot of the Bell and Howell programs.[14]

The Time, Inc. deal with ABC was an institutional breakthrough, an initial fulfillment of the plans Drew had offered his superiors half a decade earlier. With the ABC contract, Drew and Time, Inc. had access to the audiences, and the program publicizing and reviewing structure, that the Time, Inc. stations lacked. It was a development not likely to be lost on some of Time, Inc.'s senior management.

And in another institutional breakthrough, Drew was about to become an independent organization; a journalistic entrepreneur, with a production schedule, a measure of management control, and a staff.

> There [hadn't been] any staff; I was simply doing films as they came along. As the subject came along, I'd do a film and hire people to do it. . . . We made *Primary* on that basis. Then we made . . . *On the Pole.* . . . Then *Yanki No!*; all of this on free-lance.
>
> But then in '61, late '60 and early '61, ABC decided to buy a series of shows from Time, Inc., that is, my stuff from Time, Inc. Time, Inc. asked me to produce it within the company, and I think I was reluctant to do that. They suggested we set up Drew Associates.[15]

Drew insisted on a measure of independence from his parent organization because of his familiarity with, and suspicion of, Time, Inc.'s management methods. He succeeded in gaining that independence because he had developed the talent and the equipment to produce attention-getting documentaries with candid intimacy and a real-life quality, and because nobody else could do it. Drew was the producer of the only show of its kind in town; he was in a strong position to insist on independence.

> I wasn't willing to do it as an employee. . . . I didn't want them to be able to tell me how to do it, because I knew how to do it, and if we didn't do it my way it wasn't going to work. . . . [And] they very quickly regarded that as the way it ought to be. They agreed to that. I mean, what we were doing—[laughter]—it's hard to imagine what it was like, but what we were doing nobody else could do. . . . At that point, it was pretty hard to say, "We'll hire a guy from CBS to do it," cause CBS just couldn't do it.[16]

14

Drew Associates, 1

In general terms, Drew knew the kind of films he wanted to make, knew the kind of journalistic revolution he wanted to bring about, and knew the kind of creative control that would be necessary. Following the formation of his production company and his resignation from *Life*, he set about creating an organization that would be able to meet those requirements.

> We formed a company and made the . . . associates stockholders, paid a salary. And the salary was roughly the going rates for that kind of work at that time.
> So my system was set up with me as the managing editor, hiring and firing and managing the editorial side and editing. And editing means, in the magazine world, finding the ideas and developing and scripting them . . . and assigning the people to do the particular jobs within that, and then editing the material into finished form.[1]

Drew's intent was clear enough in his own mind: "I set the aim of making everyone—cameraman, correspondents, editors in some cases—into 'filmmakers', people who could go beyond their specialties to conceive and produce whole films."[2] But "filmmaker" became a misunderstood, even controversial, term; it did not convey the meaning Drew had intended. "Filmmaker" implied that that individual was in full creative control of the final film product. It was a misconception that Drew has long struggled to set right.

> Though I produced each of the early films, came up with the ideas, assigned crews, field-produced and schemed and managed the editing, photographers and filmmakers also joined in these functions as well,

recording pictures or sound by day, helping edit by night and doing strategy planning the next morning.

So I used the title "filmmaker" for people who thus joined in the making of the film. It did not mean, as the term filmmaker implies today [1982], that they were *the* filmmaker or that they had made a whole film.[3]

Drew, based on his group journalism experiences, utilized the talent and ideas of his associates as needed throughout the production of a film. Rather than a single "filmmaker" creating a finished film, the entire staff could participate.

All the key people would screen the [uncut] film, and a lot of the non-key people would screen it, too, and we would try not to discuss it very much, because we would try not to impinge our ideas on each other. . . . And then would come the day when we all got together in the same room, closed the door, and whoever had been named film-maker on the film would begin reading his scheme.[4]

In the case of Shuker, he would have screened material and made notes and he would read from his notes. . . . He would start at the opening shot and he would go through the film. And at that point, Leacock or [James] Lipscomb or someone who was on the story would, at various points, remonstrate and complain and ask for changes, and arguments would ensue, and a view would emerge of what the best structure and details would be. . . .

A scheme would then be assigned. And the guy who was to manage the editing would disappear for eight or ten weeks and then there would be a screening. And after that screening, people would be throwing typewriters through windows, quiting their jobs, going off to the islands, so forth. Or, more typically, drowning themselves in martinis at the Algonquin Hotel.

And, then, if the film was coming along like, say, *Football*, the filmmaker would proceed to make a fine cut. If it weren't coming along, like most other films, I would sit down and start editing. And that's generally the way Drew Associates operated.[5]

Drew's organizational model was set in place, with Drew as managing editor and a staff of correspondents and photographers ready to do the assigned work of production. However, both the organizational and personal relationships were quite complicated in practice. To take one example: with the formation of Drew Associates, Time, Inc., in what may have been proper corporate fashion, insisted on something more than a loose verbal agreement among the parties. The contract between Drew Associates and Time, Inc., which gave Time, Inc. exclusive rights to Drew Associates productions for a period of time, was "very complex," according to Drew. For Drew's associates, the situation was different, but equally complex.

> PENNEBAKER: I'm sure they were very nervous. They dwelt in a world where people just stole everything they could get ahold of. So [Time, Inc. was] constantly concerned that they would be putting up a lot of money for equipment and technology and even a kind of purposeful conceptualizing that would be snatched away from them. And they'd have nothing. And I'm sure that probably happened to them there, in their normal dealing with editors and photographers and what-not. So they signed people to various—like contracts, you know, that worked for them.[6]

Pennebaker implies that the contracts may have represented more than simply protection for Time, Inc. The motivations of Drew and the reactions of his associates with regards to these formal contracts appear to have been quite different.

> PENNEBAKER: [Drew] was afraid it might get snatched away from him. He was very guarded about it, in some ways. And the idea [was] that it would suddenly be—you know, that I could go to *Life* magazine and say, "Well, this is Pennebaker Films, you know; why don't you deal with me?" [laughter] And, of course, none of us were interested in doing that because none of us wanted to deal with *Life* magazine at *all*! And we really liked dealing with Drew. So, from our point of view, there was no reason to worry about it.
>
> But I think Drew, and maybe the magazine, were concerned. . . .
>
> Al [Maysles] wouldn't sign the contract. He sat on it for months and months. Finally decided he couldn't do it. That Drew was really not acting in his [Maysles's] best interest, and that in the end, he'd get wiped out. So he didn't. Ricky and I sort of thought about it for a half an hour and said, "If this is gonna fuck us up, it's gonna fuck us up, and we'll walk away, that's all. But we just have to trust that what's happened so far, and what's possible, is *so* interesting and so important that a little contractual device can't stand between us." So we both simply signed it.[7]

The situation Pennebaker reports, of the nervousness of Drew and Time, Inc. and of his own skepticism, may not be fully accurate; time and events have a way of coloring an individual's memory. But it does show that there were clearly different motivations present on the part of Drew, Time, Inc., and the various associates, motivations that would have important long-range effects on Drew's dream of a candid television journalism that would present a series of commonly shared experiences to the American television audience.

15

The ABC Connection, 2

Bell and Howell . . . sponsored a whole series of documentaries on ABC called *Close Up!*, which were generally not very exciting documentaries. And documentaries of the old school. Bell and Howell saw my films and got excited, and renewed for another year on the basis that I would be the producer, or at least a major source of their documentaries. . . .

The egos involved [at ABC and Time, Inc.] were diametrically opposed, however, so it was an interesting balance as long as it lasted. Which was about one season.[1]

The ABC connection proved to be fraught with problems. It did, however, allow the production of the first four films of Drew Associates, films that were produced in something more than the developmental, freelance atmosphere that had prevailed earlier. Less critically satisfying than *Primary*, *On the Pole*, and *Yanki No!*, they were to be a training ground for one of Drew's more interesting achievements—a network documentary production unit located outside a network.

The Pilot Project

Scott Crossfield says, "Well, I'm gonna get out of here; I'm a pilot, not an actor," and the narrator replies, "He's too busy to explain anything more."[2]

Less than three minutes into *X-Pilot*, the fundamental defect of the film is clearly stated, as the principal subject turns and walks away from the camera and, effectively, from the film. Although the narrator continues,

98

"You'll discover a great deal about Scott Crossfield just by being with him," critic Stephen Mamber is closer to the truth: "Crossfield's reticence is an unconquerable obstacle."[3] Although the camera faithfully follows Crossfield through a test-stand firing of the X-15 experimental airplane's rocket engine, through preflight meetings and "Scott Crossfield's last rocket flight," it is kept outside the important human moments. The narration tries to add information, explaining some of Crossfield's personal reactions that can't be shown effectively, but Crossfield is no Eddie Sachs, heart and emotions on his sleeve, with a clear and easily comprehensible test to be passed or failed.

There are several possible explanations for the characteristics and weaknesses of *X-Pilot*. A plausible one is that Drew may have simply misjudged the ability of his adopted medium to render important but nondramatic events in ways that sustained audience interest. *Life* magazine could have moderate success with one dramatic image, some additional informational images, and good copy. Drew needed to sustain a story-line over 26-minutes, with either a moderately dramatic personality on which to base his "picture-logic" or a return to the narration-with-illustration "word logic" he was trying to escape from.

Another explanation of the weaknesses of *X-Pilot* may be that Drew had not yet fully realized the importance of casting in his development of candid television journalism. With Scott Crossfield and the test firing of the X-15, Drew may have found the right moment, but his principal subject displayed only workman-like reactions.

A final explanation is that at the time *X-Pilot* was being produced Drew was in the process of organizing his newly independent production company, a process that was not yet fully worked out in terms of adequate staffing and field production control. And the time devoted to organizing and managing meant that Drew was spending less time in the field than he had previously done; he was forced to take "some pretty good sized gambles" in sending new and almost always inexperienced filmmakers out on major, high-cost, high-visibility projects. Drew's theories, and his field experience and long-developing story sense, could not be immediately communicated to the newcomers.

And he was attempting to innovate under intense professional scrutiny from the documentary producers and managers at the three commercial networks, ABC included, who, if they could not innovate, could reliably turn out a conventional product that met conventional standards better than *X-Pilot*. The contract with ABC, however, provided some time to get Drew Associates better organized, some time to better learn, and to teach others the complex realities of candid documentary filmmaking.

Watching Integration

While *X-Pilot* was still shooting, in the fall of 1960, another story began breaking in New Orleans, and Drew sent Leacock, Shuker, and others to cover the integration of white schools by "Negro" children. It was a news story, but Drew's investment in equipment development allowed Leacock to cover it in a manner much different from the nightly newscasts.[4]

> LEACOCK: Most of the time, nobody paid a helluva lot of attention to us. Remember, we were not a common sight at that point. People with portable rigs didn't exist. The newsreels and the TV people were all still on tripods, pretty much. Except for little [spring-driven silent] hand cameras. And so we were fairly unique at that point. It was later in the civil rights movement that people started identifying media as the bad boys. In Mississippi and things. A lot later.[5]

Leacock's New Orleans shooting took him to the Frantz School, where crowds of white parents gathered to jeer a few black parents; to interviews with segregationist leaders and officials of the National Association for the Advancement of Colored People; and finally to Mrs. James Gabriel, a white mother seen taking her six-year-old daughter to the integrated school through a crowd of angry white parents, then leading her daughter back out and swinging her purse at someone in the crowd as the narrator intones: "Violence! And Mrs. Gabriel fights back." Then to Mrs. Gabriel's home, her two daughters inside with her, a son in the angry crowd outside, her husband at work, as the narrator describes the situation: "The crowd is growing louder outside . . . Now the crowd is hammering on the doors and windows . . . Mrs. Gabriel looks for the police."

Unfortunately, the narrator must—and does, extensively—describe the situation. *The Children Were Watching* is fragmented and oddly incomplete, as if too much were happening, too fast, and at too great an emotional distance, to be fully satisfying, or even comprehensible, without plenty of narration. The angry white parents in the street, whose facial expressions and emotional phrases were to become so familiar over the next several years, are too often rendered indistinctly by the poor quality sound recording techniques of the period. The film's most important sequence, in the Gabriel home with the crowd hammering on the doors, is a testament to the potential of Drew and Leacock's vision of making the camera a direct observer of significant human events. The camera watches as the family endures the rock-throwing, window-pounding crowd with obvious apprehension. The sequence suffers, however, from diffuse sound, distant photography, muddy image quality, and jerky editing, with the narrator explaining almost the entire chain of events, and their significance. Drew

THE ABC CONNECTION, 2

Associates, at this early point in its development, could not fully meet the opportunities of that moment. But it is to their credit, perhaps, that they tried even what they knew they might not achieve.

"Nothing would have come out of there if people had stuck to light levels and sound levels that were considered acceptable. It was an example of the kind of risks that I urged people to take, and of the kind of risks I was willing to try to make films from. So, how satisfied was I: I was *appalled* at all the problems and the lack of technical quality, and I was thrilled by the fact that I'd never in my life seen anything like it."[6]

Structurally, Drew's emphasis on the theme of "the children were watching" is a strong, unannounced editorial statement not fully supported by the film material. There are several scenes of angry white parents in which children in the scene are in fact watching the adults, but in most scenes involving children they are simply watching; what, the audience does not know. And the narration unmistakably proposes and supports the theme. The narrator says, " 'The Children Were Watching'—one week in New Orleans early this school year. They were watching their parents struggle in fearful conflict over integration of schools. By their parents' example, the children were learning lessons—deep lessons, taught and learned unconsciously, but as powerful and direct as milk from mother to child."[7]

It is a recurring problem in documentary films: how to present the most important and significant material in a way that will capture the attention and interest of an audience both diffuse and distant (in terms of emotional engagement with the material) without distorting the reality of the original situation. Drew feels that the film material supports the title fully, in part because "I had more of [children watching]. . . . I didn't want to make the whole film that," although he recognizes that "it is overemphasized." All reporters, in all media, make choices and selections in fashioning their stories: *The Children Were Watching* was Drew's choice.

And the film should not be too heavily criticized for what it is not; in the context of the limited news coverage given the school integration process in the South at that time, it was an important effort to go beyond the headline reports to the fundamental differences in viewpoint that were so graphically on display.

The Reactions

"I thought that as soon as those people saw themselves with a third eye, as soon as they saw how they were behaving, they would all reform and stop and be ashamed of themselves and be converted to a proper view of the world. So I was surprised when the New Orleans stations didn't carry the broadcast, and I was surprised that other people of the then southern persuasion were not instantly converted by seeing the film."[8]

The television audience constituted one important set of reactions for Drew to consider but, beyond the resentments of local New Orleans residents, there is no evidence they were noticeably impressed. But another important audience was being invited to take notice. *The Children Were Watching* occasioned a two-and-one-half page feature article on Drew and his films in *Broadcasting* magazine, the principal trade journal of the broadcasting industry. The writer credited Drew with "a new form of television picture journalism," and observed that the zoom lens "in the hands of Drew's cameraman is the ultimate photographic weapon."

> In Mr. Drew's approach, the camera is the most important ingredient. His crew uses it somewhat in the way a doctor uses a surgical probe. Relying heavily on facial close-ups, the camera, in a typical Drew documentary searches for expressions that show how people on the scene are reacting to an event.
>
> The basic theory behind his technique, according to Mr. Drew, is that "everywhere news is taking place, people are under stress." He and his team try to capture the dramatic structure of the story by using as few adornments as possible.
>
> "I want to do shows that employ dramatic logic—where the story tells itself through pictures, not through word logic, lecture logic, written logic or interviews," Mr. Drew says.[9]

The *Broadcasting* article was a chance for Drew to advertise his methods and himself, a normal move by a producer attempting innovation in a competitive and success-conscious industry. But the intensity of Drew's photographic material and the unvarnished manner in which he presented it led a variety of more conventional producers and critics to object to the manner of presentation, if not to the material itself. They constituted an important audience whose reactions Drew would later have to take into account, at one level or another.

William Bluem

The Children Were Watching, along with a later Drew production, *Crisis: Behind a Presidential Commitment* (1963), drew the particular ire of critic A. William Bluem. A professor at the Newhouse Communication Center at Syracuse University, Bluem was founding editor of *Television Quarterly*, the journal of The National Academy of Television Arts and Sciences, awarders of the Emmy. Bluem's establishment view was well reflected in a chapter titled "News Documentary: The Crisis Within," in which he examined "those issues related to technique which Robert Drew posed for all of TV journalism."[10]

Bluem claimed that "These new types of experimental film-makers—the exponents of *verite* . . . [assume] at the outset that the camera is the only real reporter and must not be subservient to script, to preconceived thematic statement, to plotted narrative, to someone's idea of a story—to anything, in fact, but the chronological unfolding of events."[11]

Bluem termed Drew's method *verite*, "a TV adaptation of *cinéma-vérité*," and provided this assessment.

> It offers excitement—an overlay of blurred and breathless movement which can, of course, grip the emotions. By proposing to let us experience life (as well as merely see and hear about it), it stakes out a claim for continuing development in documentary television.
>
> But *verite* has shown us also that it can nullify an essentially intellectual message—or impede, in annoying fashion, our appreciation and understanding of it. Because it can interfere with rationality (it is *designed* to do so), the question fundamentally is whether *verite* is legitimate in News Documentary.[12]

Bluem's objections to the candid television journalism Drew was seeking to develop and establish were fundamental ones. They were deeply rooted in a respected journalistic ethic that had been established, at considerable professional cost, over many years, by Edward R. Murrow and Fred Friendly at CBS, Reuven Frank at NBC, and many other dedicated news professionals. Bluem's reactions to *The Children Were Watching*, while more articulate and pointed than most, were similar to those of many of the leaders of network journalism.

> Following upon his instincts to react spontaneously to a fluctuating situation, Leacock resolved to remain as unobtrusive as possible and record the story to the finish. His handheld camera gave us a sequence of unsteady pictures, as the loose pan, the zoom in and out (and the momentary adjustment of focus), and every other kind of externally imposed movement was introduced. Projected thus into the milling crowds outside the school, we began to experience the restless energy of the crowd in close-ups of elbows, backs of heads, and twisted faces.[13]

Bluem then gives a lengthy description of *The Children Were Watching*:

> Now we hear the word "nigger" spoken in contempt, and the frame drops to show a small child, listening. There is a momentary pause on a man's unshaven face as he speaks of "gittin' a shotgun"—and above and behind all of this the ugly shouts and screams of the racist

women fill our ears. We move back to the semi-peaceful Negro home, where nerves are taut, and overhear the parents talk of their plans for their daughter's future. The camera pans to the family dog and to the father petting him.

Abruptly, with the briefest narrational transition, we are inside a car, riding along the trouble-ridden streets and listening to the words of the driver [the P.T.A. president], a white segregationist leader. In a distorted blur his words crackle: ". . . half of them are uninterested in bettering themselves."[14]

Bluem's description is hardly a neutral one; there are the "screaming racist women" and the segregationist leader, presented "in a distorted blur," whose "words crackle." A more detached critic might have chosen less colorful, and more accurate, descriptions of the film.

Then Bluem offers his evaluation: he raises legitimate journalistic questions and concerns, questions and concerns that deserve thoughtful, not rhetorical, treatment.

Is this a valid recourse for the journalistic documentary in a society groping to find answers to grave questions? Could it, by any honest measure of journalism, be called a report, or even a record, of an event? These questions must be answered, for what we see in "The Children Were Watching" is a drama affected not only by the mere choice of a climactic moment in a crucial social situation (which may, after all, be what journalism is all about), but largely by cinematic techniques.

Leacock went to New Orleans seeking to witness the same ugly miscarriage of justice which all thinking men knew was occurring there. But, while others were trying to explain the meaning of these events in order to invoke the sobriety of reason, he was disposed to show only hate and fear at its most tumultuous level, leaving us no room, no avenue, for thoughtful action.

What *CBS Reports* had done in its "Mississippi and the 15th Amendment" was not far distant, in some ways, from what the Drew unit recorded. We saw the hate there, too; we experienced the same sense of disgust with the machinations of the racists; and we felt the same sympathy with those being denied their basic liberties. But we saw it all in the framework of journalism to which drama was merely an additive. In "The Children Were Watching" we witnessed not only the drama, but were made participants in it. Emotional involvement in this Drew production was no longer a method by which to lead people to intellectual involvement, but an end in itself. When used in this way, *verite* is a negation of that virtue which underlies the documentary idea.[15]

"He's idiotic." Richard Leacock is not the most unbiased observer in the matter, but in responding to Bluem's description and evaluation from his background as a filmmaker, and based on his presence at the scene, Leacock clearly has a differently informed view than Dr. Bluem.

> LEACOCK: The whole thing in that film is the woman [Mrs. Gabriel] who chose to be different. What he's saying is idiotic. The strength of that film is that the white woman who chose to send her children has the guts and the faith to do so. And what he is saying is moronic. He was [not] there, . . . and I think the picture he painted of the crowd outside is inflammatory. The film itself is not. It is quite moderate. And the balance of the film is between the two views. The view of the guy who is the inflamer [the white P.T.A. president] is very straightforward—I just think that's idiotic. . . .
> . . . It gets down to basics. If you want to go look at what's going on, or do you want to create preconceived notions of what's going on. I'd think documenting a lady who has some guts is a lot more interesting than what all those guys pieced together out of their limited experience and imaginations [referring to another ABC *Close Up!* documentary on race relations, *Walk In My Shoes*, produced by Nicholas Webster in 1962, that Bluem cited for "skill and maturity"].[16]

"[Do] you want to look at what's going on, or do you want to create preconceived notions of what's going on." This basic premise, stated simply by Leacock, is the fundamental difference of opinion that exists between cinema verite filmmakers and more traditional producers and reporters. These filmmakers appreciate the intensity and complexity of the moment; they are concerned first with what has, in fact, happened. The traditional producers more fully appreciate the background leading up to, and the broad range of effects following from, the event. To chose between the two points of view would be to lose the advantages of one, but the making of a satisfactory marriage between them has been difficult in practice. Bluem's criticism displays little in the way of deep understanding of the potential role of candid television journalism, but he successfully previewed a theoretical and practical controversy that continues to the present day.

> DREW: He's talking about rational explaining, "reason", "sobriety"; those things which are of value in print journalism and are of value in *CBS Reports* journalism and beyond which somebody has to go if they want to make film live. And—in fact, he says he resents having been made a participant in a drama; now that's a compliment, because that's what we were trying to do, make him a participant. And his feeling that you can't participate in a drama and think about it is

haywire! The way people get stimulated to think is by having [an] experience and then thinking about it.[17]

The questioning of the validity and appropriateness of Drew's developing methods was only beginning. Both the new journalistic capabilities and the controversy over them would produce far-reaching changes in how television journalism, and documentary filmmaking generally, was done. The changes would not be those that Drew had initially sought; "picture logic," at least by Drew's definition, has never replaced, or even seriously challenged, "word logic." But Drew's more immediate challenge was to establish an organization that could support the next steps in his long-range plans, and at the same time provide ABC with successful programs.

New Frontiers

The narrator says, "Now you will begin to move with the President, seeing and hearing for yourself in a new kind of report; not a filmed version of summary and opinion you can find in print, but rather a personal adventure with the President as he confronts the great problems of the U.S. and the world."[18]

In the third, and most ambitious, of the *Close Up!* programs, Drew returned to familiar ground for both his subject—John Fitzgerald Kennedy, the winner in *Primary*—and his method. *Life* magazine had often attempted to personalize those in positions of power with dramatic, insider photographs and copy, and *Adventures on the New Frontier* attempted to adapt that approach to a documentary film. The results, in the short-term, seem astonishingly poor: "It got bombed by the critics." But in the long term, it helped lay the groundwork for one of the most important of the Drew films, *Crisis: Behind a Presidential Commitment*, and also provided the contacts that became *Kenya*, the fourth Drew film in the *Close Up!* series.

John Kennedy, as candidate and as president, displayed a finely tuned, and generally friendly, political understanding of the power and importance of the news and opinion media in national affairs. His understanding of television's importance was particularly strong, and favorable. He had earlier consented to the making of what was to become one of the most revealing documents of political campaigning at the presidential level, *Primary*; he would become the first president in history to allow his news conferences to be filmed and telecast live, without any presidential controls; and he also displayed an interest in the documentary.

An invitation from Pierre Salinger, the president-elect's press secretary, brought Drew to the Kennedy vacation retreat in West Palm Beach, Florida, in November of 1960. On two successive evenings, he showed Kennedy copies of *Primary* and *Yanki No!*, the latter in the company of Senator J. William Fulbright, soon to become chairman of the Foreign Relations Committee.

After the screenings, both Jack and Jacqueline Kennedy "expressed delight with *Primary*," and Drew made his pitch for a new project.

> [Kennedy] considered himself to be something of a historian, . . . and I made the point to him that when he entered the White House he would find the record of past Presidents, and there would be pictures of men shaking hands in front of automobiles and making speeches, and still pictures, and motion pictures, and there would be official papers, but that he wouldn't see the expression on the man's face, and he wouldn't actually see for himself how a President felt about anything in the past. . . .
>
> And Kennedy picked up on that and said, "Yes. Think of what it would be like if I could see what Franklin Roosevelt did in the 24 hours before World War Two was declared, before America's declaration of war was declared."
>
> And I proposed that I have two teams, one team would move into the White House with him and show what happened when he walked in and sat down at the desk or whatever. And one team would go with his wife. . . . So he called Jacqueline over and put it to her the way I put it to him. One team would move in with her and one team would move in with him. And she had been very complimentary and very sweet up to this point and she said, "No team is going to move in with me!" And he realized that we had made a mistake and sort of tried to ease over that by saying, "That's all right. We can do the office part."[19]

So Drew had obtained Kennedy's permission to film. The next step was to see if the presidency could tolerate the camera. Drew and Pennebaker spent a portion of two days in the Oval Office. Staff members took their lead from the president as conversations were filmed: "He had to be reminded that we were there after a while. . . . This was a deal between me and Kennedy, and I was proving to him that we could do it."[20]

Later, other crews—Leacock; Pennebaker; Al Maysles with his brother, David, taking sound; Shuker; and others—shot stories that would relate to what had been discussed in the president's office. In the meantime, Drew was busy with the network and the sponsor.

> Bell and Howell was complaining about a show which ABC was making for them, and I remember feeling that we had some unfair advantage at that time over the network people because the network producer [John Secondari] was asked to unveil his best idea for a

documentary, and his idea was to do a film on water pollution. Then he showed some endless pictures of septic tanks and sewage treatment plants and so forth.

Then I was asked what I had to offer. The inauguration of a new administration, the first look at a President at work in his office, and so we had a lot of momentum, let's say, and we were able to do practically all the films we wanted to do there, at least for that season.[21]

But if Drew had the advantage of access to the Kennedy personality, "the office part" was, as he had anticipated, often dull and fragmentary for the casual viewer. He introduced a series of brief illustrative excursions to selected problem areas: Pigeon Creek, West Virginia, with unemployed miner Tom Muncy, to illustrate unemployment problems; Addis Ababa, Ethiopia, with former Michigan governor G. Mennen Williams as Kennedy's roving ambassador, to illustrate African economic problems. They helped the pacing of the final film, perhaps, but the sequences seem too clipped and tentative to be either satisfying, or fully comprehensible.

However, Drew's reasons for making *Adventures on the New Frontier*, and presumably for making it as he did, are not always apparent in a screening of the program itself.

> The purpose of this filming would be to see if [Kennedy] could tolerate the camera, if the work of the Presidency could really proceed with the camera there. He had been oblivious of it in the shooting of *Primary* but he wasn't so sure that he could be so oblivious of it conducting business in the Oval Office. So [*Adventures on the New Frontier*] would be in advance of a real film, a real story that we would do at some other time.
>
> I pointed out that . . . if we could find a story out somewhere that was happening about which the President was making decisions . . . and if this decision, whatever it was, pressed the President to the wall, that is, if it were tough for him and he had to decide something that was not easy, then we would have a real story and a real film.
>
> He saw all that in the time it took to talk about it and agreed with it and it was a matter of then working it out. The crisis film that we finally made [*Crisis: Behind a Presidential Commitment*, 1963] we shot, I think, two years after that. It took two years to find a crisis. In the meantime, we had shot the early stuff in the Oval Office. It turned out that we became part of the woodwork there as we did most every place else. Business went on so naturally that at one point in a Joint Chiefs of Staff meeting, I think it was Admiral Arleigh Burke had to remind the President that he was being filmed at that moment, and it was about time for us to leave the Joint Chiefs of Staff room where they were talking about maneuvers off Cuba.[22]

Drew found that Kennedy was able to tolerate the camera in a number of instances, and the day-to-day business of the White House went on in apparently uninhibited fashion before a new candid television journalism. But there were important, and not always revealed, reservations on Kennedy's part; the "maneuvers" about to be discussed when Drew was asked to leave the Joint Chiefs of Staff meeting turned out to be the unsuccessful invasion of Cuba at the Bay of Pigs.

Kenya

Kenya is, in one sense, a happy accident, an example of what Drew Associates' now-developed equipment base and still-flexible internal structure could occasionally accomplish. *Kenya* was not a result of careful planning and thoughtful consideration by a managing editor, but rather owed its initiation and much of its limited power to the filmmaking intuitions of Richard Leacock.

LEACOCK: We were following [former Michigan governor G. Mennen] "Soapy" Williams, Kennedy's African expert or some bullshit, something like that, through Africa [for materials eventually incorporated into *Adventures on the New Frontier*]. And we were getting absolutely no place. This was a non-film; all we were getting was State Department handouts. Nothing. Getting off planes, getting onto planes, shaking hands with prime ministers, *boooorring*! And we weren't about to interview; why would we want to interview "Soapy" Williams! And we finally got to Kenya, and found ourselves just before the first election for the black-dominated parliament. It was *electrifying*! And I didn't talk to Drew, I didn't do anything, I just made a decision; we are staying here, goodbye "Soapy" Williams, there's no film there, we've got one right here. Sitting under our faces.

Did I get fired? No! You could do this. And I knew Bob, he'd back me to the hilt. It was a period of a kind of freedom that I'd never experienced before, or since.[23]

But for all Leacock's effort and enthusiasm, *Kenya* is only partly successful. Scheduled to be presented on two successive weeks, "Part One: Land of the White Ghost" is principally a result of Leacock's shooting with white settlers in the White Highlands section of the country, while "Part Two: Land of the Black Ghost" focuses on the upcoming elections and the absence of black leader Jomo Kenyatta, who was being held in prison for alleged Mau-Mau atrocities, from the process. Leacock's portrait of farmer Jim Hughes is revealing of the attitudes of the land-owning white minority toward the black native population; however, the material on Hughes is scattered almost haphazardly throughout Part One, interrupted repeatedly by interviews, scenes from election rallies and independence celebrations, and sequences contrasting "the good [white] life" and native poverty.

Part Two is even less coherent, more concerned with the obscure Kenyan politics involved, and far less personal. Jomo Kenyatta, the personality who is used as the contrast to farmer Jim Hughes, could not be photographed in prison, and so an eerie superimposition of Kenyatta's face from an old still photograph is used repeatedly over other material to show his hidden, or perhaps only unknown, influence on the upcoming election.

Kenya remains an imperfect and pedestrian film. Other than *Yanki No!*, the five Drew Associates-Time, Inc. films for ABC's *Close Up!* were not especially notable with audiences, reviewers, or broadcast industry professionals. The films were, in Drew's view, "doing things that had never been done before and which were astonishing." But while the films were quite different from other *Close Up!*s with which they were presented, candid television journalism had not captured the attention or interest of any of the significant audience groups, and the most important outcome of these productions may have been the learning experience they provided for Robert Drew and his associates.

16

Drew Associates, 2

The ABC contract with Time, Inc. gave Drew Associates some audience and reviewer visibility, some organizational standing within Time, Inc., and some time to organize, plan, and produce. The years of formulating concepts such as "commonly shared experience," of memos to management and last-minute charter flights to find, or follow, a story: all these challenges were prologue. Drew would now have to take his chances. And the most immediate problems were organization and stories.

Drew generated many of the early ideas at Drew Associates; only Greg Shuker, whose experiences at *Life* may have given him a reportorial outlook similar to Drew's, was able to consistently turn up story ideas that Drew found acceptable. But the evolution of the method that made cinema verite a workable reality involved the reconciliation of a number of different points of view.

PENNEBAKER: When they came back from [shooting *Yanki No!*], we sat down and started to talk about stories, and [Drew] started bringing in people—reporters from the magazine. And I could see that he was going to pay them a lot of money. And they had no idea [what we were doing]. And I thought, suddenly, that the possibility of deciding what films I wanted to make was not going to be mine any longer. Somebody else was going to make it. And that began to bother me a little bit. . . .

Ricky had the same problem. In other words, we all kept saying, "Well, we want to do a film about such and such," or we knew of something or this was going to happen. Then we all had to sit down and think, well, was it going to be commercially saleable? In other words, what made a good story? We weren't sure. We began to try to evolve ways of deciding, and I could see that the reporters at the magazine did know something about stories. I mean, they had learned something, or they knew something before then, that I'd never thought about. And I wasn't sure what made a good story, and I guess I was—I thought I just would sort of look at somebody and if they glowed in the dark, I knew that they were going to be a good story. I mean, I just assumed that.[1]

Drew always maintained the role of managing editor, with final control of story selection and film editing. But, increasingly, his staff did the implementing; the informal, non-traditional organizational structure of Drew Associates, especially in the early months, not only allowed principal staff members to formulate their own approaches to stories but almost required it.

But the possibilities opened up by candid television journalism in the hands of talented filmmakers like Pennebaker and Leacock, were a source of continuing tension within Drew Associates. One reason may have been that the experience of filming—the experience of looking through the viewfinder, of making the choice of framing close up or framing wide, of making decisions on when to roll the camera to record selected actions and ignore others, of sensing and following the complex interactions of individuals and "the story" in a way that could later be condensed in editing—was somewhat different from the role of the correspondent or field producer, who had gotten the photographer "up to bat" and continued to control the course of shooting in various ways, but who participated in the actual event being filmed in a different way. In taking sound, the correspondent's recorder often ran continuously, so there was less decision-making as to when to record. The microphone was almost always aimed broadly at the principal sound source, so there was no choice to be made between the principal speaker and the reactions of others. And the correspondent could not closely control whether, or when, the photographer would zoom out or in or pan or focus on a significant visual detail. The result was, for photographers such as Leacock and Pennebaker, a closer identification with the actual filmic event, a different understanding of the intimate details of a particular interaction.[2]

The correspondent, and the executive producer, had a necessarily broader view, more of a sense of the context of the particular filmic event in a larger story, more of a concern with the "weight" of an event and its probable clarity and meaning to the eventual audience(s) in relation to the hundreds or even thousands of other events available from shooting. The tension between these two viewpoints, the intimate detail recorders and the broader storytellers, was a subject of frequent consideration among Drew and his associates. And questions of form and structure, drama versus stricter reporting types of journalism, were becoming more apparent.

> PENNEBAKER: It became clear to me that what we were making was feature films. And whether we wanted to or not, or even had an outlet for them or not, that's what everything was moving toward, that whole concept. Because that's what we'd been raised on; we all understood what that was. The documentary as such . . . required a different kind of approach than any of us knew how to do. It required . . . that peculiar objectivity that the magazine kept; you know, "*Life* Goes To A Debutante Party," where *Life* was seen as the cunning and fantastically capable cameraman [who] comes sneaking in the windows while these little children cavort unseen, you know, without noticing [him]. And above it all, came this commentary, to tell you how that fitted in with the national weal at that moment.
>
> What we were able to do was to go out and slip into situations and film them, but none of us really felt up to commenting on them. Especially in that kind of documentary tradition. And neither did Drew, really. But it became clear that that was going to be the requirement. If we were going into television with the stuff, that was going to be the requirement of the material. And Drew began to get, I think, split up. He began to see that he was going to have to deliver to Time-Life, and ABC, programs that fitted in with what they had in mind, but that Ricky and I were speeding very fast in another direction.[3]

ABC was a television network, not a feature film distribution company, and the demands of that medium, at least as they were defined by those with the power to make production and programming decisions, had to be met.

> PENNEBAKER: In a way, I think he was more perceptive than we were about the medium. People do miss things on television, because they don't pay attention. Whereas, in feature films, they watch them quite closely. And Ricky and I were making films in which we assumed that everybody was watching closely. But Drew was saying, "No, they're gonna miss stuff, so you're gonna have to have a narration to explain to them what they miss, and tell them to look at things that are about to happen so they won't miss them." We found this very redundant, and kind of awkward, and it was the beginning of the problem we had, which was that . . . you almost didn't have to make the film![4]

The variation in viewpoints, which often came down to the correspondents supporting one view and the photographers another, was, in part, a function of Drew's distance from actual field production. When the initial methodology of cinema verite had been worked out, Drew had been directly involved at every level of production; taking sound in the field, supervising the editing directly, providing a model of his ideas in action for his associates.[5]

> PENNEBAKER: He was an extraordinary producer in the field. He would never settle for anything but the best . . . there were very few people as good as Bob. I mean he just wouldn't stop! He'd charter airplanes to get places. I mean, this, of course, was what you learned at *Life*. You know, the jugular vein-type [approach]; you know, never let go, never settle for less if you think there is more there. And money is nothing to stop and worry about. I'm sure he did worry about those things [but] I never got such a sense of the worry.[5]
>
> LEACOCK: And each of the films of that Drew period were wild adventures. I didn't give a good goddamn about automobile racing. We fell in love with Eddie Sachs. This crazy idiot! We had no idea we were going to make a film about him. We just came to do a few days shooting. And so these were—the events themselves were adventures. . . .
>
> And there was a problem between Drew and most of the people working with him about the amount of narration. But he was under tremendous pressure; he came from the journalistic tradition, of "what is it, where is it, who is it?" et cetera. And there were conflicts. But we didn't have the tremendous pressure that Drew had, to succeed in the marketplace. We just wanted to have our fun.[6]

But the role of managing editor, which Drew increasingly began to assume with the initiation of the ABC contract, did not realistically allow time for in-the-field participation in most individual productions. In many cases, on-the-scene initiative and control had to be delegated; important decisions in many Drew films were made by correspondents and photographers.

> See, I had a deal with the devil. The deal with my people was I wanted them to become managing editors, in effect. The other end of my deal was, I would deliver great programs. So, what generally happened was, I would give somebody twelve weeks to edit a program and look at it, and it wouldn't be right, wouldn't be good enough or something. So then I would edit it. And that was very hard for morale in the organization, and later I realized that I'd made a big mistake. That, you know, great pitchers don't have to be great home run

hitters. There are first basemen, second basemen, and so forth. And so, now I realized there are great photographers, there are great editors, and there are producers and so forth.[7]

It was very destructive to the idea of building filmmakers. And it was [an] impolitic, and unpopular, way to do it. . . . But the fact is that everybody's future and reputation were riding on it, every film.[8]

As the operational distance between Drew and the story increased, editing became more and more the means by which he would influence and shape his films. Much of the later controversy surrounding both the crediting and evaluation of the Drew films centers on the editing, and the real editor was Robert Drew.

> SHUKER: Bob, I would say, is a great editor. He was not the easiest guy in the world at the time, either. I always had to remember then, Bob's background early, as a very young man, was as a fighter pilot. And a fighter pilot's different from a bomber pilot, or transport pilot. A fighter pilot flies alone. And makes the decisions to do whatever he does. And so Bob was sometimes difficult on the people who worked for him. His patience didn't last too long sometimes. . . .
>
> But he's a great editor. [And] his great strength is . . . not just in the cutting room, but also at the typewriter. And he's very good at seeing—just as the managing editor of *Life* was—seeing the whole story. You know, all this material is sitting there and, "What's the story? What's the logic of the story here? What's the beginning, middle, and end?"[9]

But Drew also faced the more mundane problems of effectively organizing a production company. His plans were expanding; the concept of a series of "commonly shared experiences" for a nationwide audience had begun to take an even firmer hold on him. But those plans would have to be implemented. As the boundaries of the dream of a candid television journalism widened, and the practicality of direct personal control and supervision diminished, Robert Drew became ever more the *managing* editor, ever more dependent on the personal visions of individuals who might, or might not, share his sense of what was possible and necessary.

> LEACOCK: Bob had the same problem Flaherty always had, of the need to make something that "works." That's always a conflict. . . . There's always the danger that we had to grapple with of taking material and shaping it so that it conforms with a preconceived notion of what happened. That people are sad at a funeral, instead of discovering that they're having a ball. That's not an accurate way of doing it.
>
> See, sometimes we found ourselves, I think, simplifying the dra-

matic line. Because you've got to get it into an hour, you've got an audience, you're trying to hold their attention. I think that always—I felt, at least; I won't speak for others—that in simplifying and condensing you sometimes mutilate the sense of what happened.[10]

SHUKER: I think of the image from that book, *The Hustler*; one can be a great pool player—but you can't shoot championship pool unless you're in the poolhall that has the championship game held in it. The table has to be there to play on. Bob provided the pool table. For people that were already very talented. It's like a coach. A good coach. And the players had their own brilliant abilities, but without the coach and a team, you didn't have any place to play.[11]

PENNEBAKER: In the beginning, you see, part of his problem was: he wanted to have control of those films and he really was afraid. He wouldn't let Ricky or I make our films. And he was afraid that we would make little artistic treats that just wouldn't be saleable on the market that he was talking in. He was talking to the Department of Sales, trying to sell this as a series. . . .

Finally, he figured out that he could keep control on these films by having a kind of minimal input all the way, looking periodically at stuff, maybe looking at a rough cut. But in the end, if he could get his hands on a film one or two weeks before the mix, and get somebody who could write narration—get a narrator—he could by-and-large control the way the film looked, and at least [the] content, in a way that was satisfactory to him. . . . And it just seemed that we didn't have time to worry about what happened to the films.

And that began to bother me, and I knew it bothered Ricky, who always felt very troubled by the fact that everybody was in such a hurry to get the damned things done that nobody was really looking—and the films, instead of getting better, were getting worse. It was clear they were getting worse.[12]

17

Breaking the Connection

"Time, Inc. and ABC were giants who competed. They both owned television stations. ABC 'stole' a Time, Inc. station. A Time, Inc. executive insulted ABC's president. Time, Inc. lost its access to ABC air time."[1]

Twenty years later, Drew would dismiss the end of the ABC contract in a single, brief paragraph. But the substance of that ending was somewhat more complex. Candid television journalism—cinema verite—was clearly not designed for news work. *Yanki No!* may have revealed, in new and more intense ways, the human complexities that were a part of even global politics and *The Children Were Watching* may have previewed the contrasting attitudes underlying the coming civil rights struggle, but they were not "news"; they did not seek out, report, and explain the day's events in commonly understood and accepted ways.

The films of Drew and his associates were not even documentaries in the conventional sense. They avoided the prescriptive designs of the social documentary films of the 1930s and 1940s, and they avoided the descriptive, "word logic" structure of the network television documentaries of the 1950s. The Drew films sought to explore a new capability, the capability to see and record, at first hand, the activities of human beings at important moments in their lives and to see those moments with greater intensity and perception than had previously been possible, and without preconceptions. It was a capability that, in its deepest sense, the audience, and the profession that both guided and served that audience, had not realized was possible, had not asked for, and did not fully recognize or understand. Cinema verite, in the hands of Drew, the journalist, had not yet made a conceptual breakthrough similar to the technical breakthrough of *Primary* and *On the Pole*. *Yanki No!* had made a splash with reviewers, "prestige" audiences, and some professionals, but Drew and his associates were not able to sustain the same level of interest, or novelty, in succeeding programs.

And there were practical considerations such as justifying the cost of independently produced documentaries to network executives and the question of the propriety of a television news division allowing an outside producer to present programs in its name over which the network had not exercised full editorial control.

> DREW: Every network I've ever worked for, produced films for, has had the editorial control, final editorial control. They've never used it, but they've always had it. So, in actual practice, there are easy ways around it. But it's a convenient thing to raise up if you want to keep somebody out. I think it's two things; I think it's ego and overhead.[2]
> PENNEBAKER: [ABC was] not, I don't think, unhappy about sustaining [the programs]. I mean in terms of the amount of money, it was peanuts, sustaining a documentary show, but they didn't like sustaining Time-Life doing it. They wanted to do it.[3]
> DREW: I think [ABC vice-president for programming, Tom] Moore felt he'd been insulted somehow, and I don't know. Personalities begin to figure. Organizational sensitivities and personalities begin to figure, and it was beyond my scope to affect.[4]

So, for complex and perhaps not fully revealed reasons, the ABC contract ended. Drew's productions for the network had not been splashy breakthroughs that attracted critical acclaim; institutional realities, in Drew's organization and in those he served, caused his plans for exploiting the ABC arrangement to falter. In the process of becoming quasi-independent, developing a competent production organization, and adapting his "dream" to the practical realities posed by network audiences and bureaucracies, Drew had perhaps underemphasized a critical area.

> I was a salesman within Time, Inc. . . . until I had gotten out the first few films. And those films were winning a lot of recognition and were useful on the air and people seemed to like them, and I thought, "Good. I've done it. It's over. I'll never have to sell again." I thought the films would sell themselves. I felt the idea would sell itself. And Roy Larsen, who was chairman of Time, Inc. at the time, warned me, "Bob, you've got to really sell this now." This was after *Yanki No!*, which had achieved—it had the greatest impact of any documentary maybe ever on television. And here was Roy Larsen telling me that I had to marshall opinion leaders and find ways to gather in the

opinion leaders of the country and get them behind this. And I couldn't help feeling that Larsen had missed the point—that this thing was already making its own [way]. I'd set a ship a-sailing. It would make its way. But I think Larsen was right. Nothing sells itself.[5]

18

The Living Camera

"Against my feverish advice, Time, Inc. placed a multimillion dollar order with Drew Associates for a dozen new programs. I could see disaster for Time, Inc.'s pocketbook and my whole editorial idea if I produced a revolution on film that could not find its way to the public via regular scheduling on a network.

"Time, Inc. ordered the programs. I produced them."[1]

Drew and Time, Inc. found themselves in an uncomfortable position. Time, Inc. wanted to continue the experiment they had invested in with Drew Associates, but had lost access to network airtime; Drew also wanted to continue the experimentation, but wanted to reach a large, national audience in order to validate his methods.

> I think I wanted Drew Associates to become independent, and we would make our own deal with the networks. . . . I wasn't manipulating those guys, but under the circumstances I thought it was going to be very rough going for Time, Inc. . . . See, Time, Inc. had to commit the twelve hours to hold Drew Associates; if they committed to it without an outlet, they were going to run the possibility of failing and that was going to run the possibility of screwing up my revolution.[2]

Bob Drew's memories of the year and a half following the termination of the ABC contract are not entirely satisfying ones, but that period was both the most anguished and the most innovative in Drew's attempt to develop a workable form of cinema verite. The basic elements—equipment, staff, and experience—were in place; the challenge would be to turn theory into workable practice, "a journalism that worked." Time, Inc.'s program order, reported by Drew to be worth two million dollars, provided both opportunity and obligation, and the initial opportunity was to choose an editorial direction for the new programs—and for cinema verite.

"It was up to me to decide which way to go, [and] I decided to go the route of the personal story a la Eddie Sachs at Indianapolis, rather than the news story a la *Yanki No!*. And that was a matter of my decision, but it was also a matter, I thought, of trying to sum up where our filmmaking and intellectual and emotional currents were leading us, the things that proceeded out of ourselves."[3]

It was a decisive choice: people, and drama, instead of news. Although a choice of news would have involved Drew and his associates in examinations of people under stress, it would also have involved them in the controversy between emotional involvement and intellectual involvement. And while the format of news was a familiar one, known and accepted by professionals and audiences alike, a shift away from news would allow greater concentration of creative energy on cinema verite's strongest points. Drew's films—*Primary*, portions of *Yanki No!*, *The Children Were Watching*, and *Kenya*, Part One, and especially *On the Pole*—had succeeded best when they were most personal. Influenced by story-finding discussions with Leacock, Pennebaker, Shuker, and others, and by his earlier experiences studying drama, the short story, and the novel at Harvard, Drew chose to direct his two-million-dollar opportunity toward stories about people.

The shift in emphasis would produce grinding stresses within his own organization, in his relations with Time, Inc., and in his long-range image before industry professionals, critics, and audiences. But it also produced a series of films remarkable for their then-audacious subject selection and production approach, a series that was to later become known, partly for merchandising purposes, as "The Living Camera."

Eddie, Again

The narrator says, "[A. J.] Foyt wins. Eddie is second, by seven seconds." Eddie Sachs replies, "Oh, yeah, I'll never give up. Hell, I keep doing better every year. I didn't finish last year!"[4]

Neither, apparently, did Drew. With the decision made to concentrate on personal stories, Drew sent his teams back to the Indianapolis 500.[5] This time, they would have color film, better access to Mrs. Sachs's reactions as one of the more personally involved spectators, and Eddie again "on the pole."

But *Eddie* (1961) lacks the tension and personal involvement generated by *On the Pole*, in spite of the fact that the 1961 race is more traditionally dramatic than the one a year earlier: after the lead has repeatedly changed hands, Eddie is forced to make an unwanted pit stop with only three laps to go when a tire begins to fail. "Just about the last lap, or half way around, I would have blown it and hit the wall and spun out and had nothing." Eddie's choice, to take second place rather than chance losing everything, is both dramatic and a fine irony, given the anything-to-win Eddie Sachs of 1960.

A more important difference may have been in the subject himself. Eddie Sachs had had the experience, which few others had had at that point, of seeing himself in the intensity of a cinema verite film. Some of his most personal and, in an odd sense, private moments had been recorded, and then displayed on television. The experience must have occasioned at least some reservations on Sachs's part toward his behavior, and that may have made him more cautious and reserved in his second encounter with the camera. Cinema verite may not often be able to return to a subject who has once seen himself as photographers, correspondents, editors, and producers have seen him.

Drew's decision to shoot again at Indianapolis was probably a logical one at the time, but even Drew has been clear about the film: "*Eddie* was a remake of the previous *On the Pole*. *David* was the first film of the new push."

David, by the Sea

"[I] even played with 'Bird' [jazz saxophonist Charlie Parker] a couple times . . . , a great moment of my life. I was so nervous."[6]

David Allen was a musician, a trumpeter whose professional high point seems to have been playing "second horn" to the well-known Parker at a Chicago jazz club. But David and "Bird" shared another interest beyond music—drugs. Addiction killed Parker, in 1955; for David Allen, in *David*, in 1961, the outcome was still in doubt.

The narrator says, "This is the story of what actually happened to David, one week, by the sea—."[7]

David is clearly a transition film, and the strains within Drew Associates—drama versus journalism, documentary versus theatrical approaches—were beginning to be fully explored. Drew's story of "what actually happened" at the Synanon drug rehabilitation community in Santa Monica, California, originated with a story suggestion from *Life* magazine and Shuker and Pennebaker got the assignment. They were laboring to discover and to make practical a filmmaking form that would exploit the resources that Drew had put in place. Despite the assurance of Time, Inc.'s two million dollars—or perhaps because of it—the next year and a half would be a period of groping, of discovery, of trial-and-error, for all concerned.

> PENNEBAKER: I was really making a story about one person, and I didn't give a damn about the TV or anything else. When we came back, it became clear that that was what I'd filmed. Shuker had filmed some other material, and it kinda got to be a struggle to see which film would prevail. And in the end, Drew kind of got won over and we went with the dramatic film; we kind of made a feature film. We didn't—it wasn't quite—it was hoked up a little bit. And I guess that bothered Ricky and I some. But—it was better than not having it hoked up! [Laughter] And we went along with it.[8]
>
> DREW: [A] film that reflected a lot of Pennebaker's taste was *David*, the Synanon film, which again had some of these characteristics of just being there rather than being propelled through a story. In a way *David* was our film in which a guy decided not to do something. Ha![9]

The conflict between "just being there" and "being propelled through a story" would remain, essentially unresolved, until the end of the initial formulation of Drew Associates. Sometimes "just being there" slides into a confusing diffuseness, while there is also the occasional sense of "being propelled" too aggressively through the story. And larger questions of how the filmmakers could successfully fit into and accurately film very personal human actions, and then produce an interesting, or even exciting, film from unplanned, uncontrolled, often disparate footage, remained. And one of the subchallenges, more to Drew than to the others, was the question of how to educate the audience to the strengths of his new journalistic form.

> NARRATOR: This has been a story of a struggle, by the sea. Some lost. David won—that week. He stayed. What you have seen actually happened. It is a true story.[10]
>
> DREW: At the time . . . films weren't done this way, and audiences didn't know—or at least we were pretty sure that the audiences didn't know from time to time—that this wasn't acted or that it was real, so we made a point of trying to say that . . .
>
> The point is you just didn't see people really laugh or cry or weep or make love or get angry and so forth on television, unless it was fiction, at the time. You just didn't see that, and here we were showing those things. When Jane Fonda [in *Jane*, a later film] gets up and kisses her boyfriend who has given her a present, nobody had ever seen Jane Fonda kiss anybody that hadn't been directed or written. . . . And I am not sure we did a very good job of it either of

letting people know how, let's say, how extraordinary this was at the time, and it's hard looking back to imagine how extraordinary it was at the time.[11]

Petey and Johnny

"*Petey and Johnny* could not have failed so thoroughly had it not been . . . such a daring attempt in the first place."[12]

Critic Stephen Mamber is doing more than damning with faint praise; *Petey and Johnny* is hardly a fully satisfying cinema verite documentary, but it is a recognizably difficult, complex, and challenging undertaking. To have failed, as indeed *Petey and Johnny* does as a successfully integrated film, does not mean that talent, time, and money were not applied; in fact, one of the problems of the film may have been that too much of each element *was* applied.

> DREW: Most films we had to put a lot of work into to make work. But this one went on for so long, and it had so many twists and turns among the characters, and it was so dangerous that we could say more effort went into this film than most.[13]
>
> LEACOCK: It was interesting. We started out assigning—I sort of produced that one—and at first we sent Jim Lipscomb and . . . Bill Ray . . . out to hang out with the gang. So the gangs are smart, they caught on, these guys have lots of money, they were buying them ammunition, taking them on picnics, paying for this, paying for that—nothing was ever going to happen! Why should it? Who needs to rumble when you've got *Life*'s money! So then we had to pull back. I said we shouldn't concentrate on the gang, we should concentrate on Petey. And then we had to sort of react to things.[14]

The producers of *Petey and Johnny* set forth on an extremely difficult task in trying to make a personal documentary on street gangs in Spanish Harlem, something that was probably better suited to the more flexible, episodic format demands of a *Life* magazine story. They attempted, without perhaps fully understanding the potential difficulties, to move into and understand—and film, without disrupting—another culture. This was not a one-or two-day shoot in a Venezuelan slum, but a months-long observation in a city in which both cultures lived; yet the distance between filmmaker and subject seems as great in one location as in the other.[15]

As the shooting progressed over the summer of 1961, Petey Thomas, a street worker for a religiously oriented youth agency, takes gang members to the beach to keep them "cool," supervises a fist-fight between two rival gang leaders, shows the scars of a shooting incident during his own days growing up as a gang member, and recalls his part in a gang shootout in which he was wounded and then sentenced to fifteen years in Sing-Sing.

Intercut with Petey are scenes of Juan Morales, also known as Johnny Christian, the president of a teenage fighting gang, as he takes his pregnant girlfriend, Maria, to a street festival; is arrested for carrying a gun, "a major crime under the Sullivan Act"; has his charges reduced to a misdemeanor and shyly marries Maria in a traditional church ceremony; and is released on probation, "a chance to break with the gang."

And interspersed among the events with Petey and Johnny are minor events and marginal characters that seem to have no direct relation to the principals.

> LEACOCK: What it became was this weird patchwork. . . . The baby was born. They got married. He went to jail. But there were—for me—some absolutely superb sequences. Confrontation of the gang kids. Those wonderful scenes of kids playing in the streets. The fire hydrants. There are just these wonderful scenes. Buying the wedding tiara. Johnny and his baby. I mean, there's incredible stuff in there.
>
> But to make it work, we had to play all sorts of tricks [in editing]. As one means of making it work. That's why we always used to get mad at Drew; but [we] would have ended up with a completely unacceptable television film.[16]
>
> DREW: The editing of this film could have gone many directions, and it did, and in the end I came in and edited the damn thing, you know, really edited it. And there were filmmakers who shot tremendous, wonderful sequences of street scenes who wanted to see those street scenes in the film, and there were people who felt that it should have concentrated on one character rather than another, or that we should have concentrated on the Spanish side rather than the non-Spanish side, and on and on. So, since everybody worked on it and it was close to home, there was less of a cohesive view of what the film was by the time we got into editing. Anyway at some point I did sit down and really edit the film.[17]

The editing of *Petey and Johnny* occasioned more than the usual level of controversy, both within the Drew organization and outside. Patricia Jaffee, a professional film editor hired by Drew, was sufficiently exercised that she wrote an article in which she first outlined her approach to editing cinema verite films.

> JAFFEE: When you view many hours of material in a screening room (fifty hours as I did when working on *Petey and Johnny*), you sit through miles of banal ordinary conversation and action, some technically worthless footage, and a few absolutely electrifying moments.

What begins to emerge out of this experience is *a kind of pattern—a rhythm of life*, so to speak. People are doing something or talking in the ordinary, disjointed, inarticulate way. Then something begins to happen between them. Tensions build, and bam! . . . a moment bursts upon the screen so true, so real that it is greater than any theatrical re-creation could ever be. It is these moments that make direct cinema so powerful a medium. The big question then is how to sort them out and to *reserve this initial excitement* for the viewer. It is my firm conviction that the answer lies in *allowing the viewer to experience what the filmmaker felt in the screening room.*[18]

Like the photographers who see the film principally through the lens while trying to sense and record the complexities of an interaction, Jaffee's attention, as an editor, was focused on a different set of professional interests than was Drew, as the producer.

JAFFEE: Many of the Drew films were flawed by pushing the material into a mold where none existed. This tendency to create a story or constant excitement, to keep the film moving from one headline to another, is a result of Drew's inclination and experience. Basically a journalist, he feels it necessary to keep the audience at a high pitch of interest and excitement. . . .

The best Drew films are those shot in self-contained situations having a natural beginning, middle and end, like [*Mooney vs. Fowle*] and *On the Pole*. Drew's films ran into trouble when there was no inherent structure. In the case of *Petey and Johnny*, . . . there were volumes of material with no real core idea. . . . Drew decided that Petey's relationship to Johnny should be the film's central idea, a concept that the material did not support. In an attempt to structure this difficult film, all the exciting moments were pulled from the footage and strung together with a force that did violence to the final film. . . . The sequences themselves were never allowed to play themselves out but instead were cut to the bone, so that only the "moment" remained. The film has no air, no connective tissue. There is only Petey's narration to bridge the sequences and to embellish and keep alive the scant story of Johnny. The final result is a confusing, incoherent film, sometimes exciting but mostly banal. In spite of the film's frantic pace, its lack of exploratory footage—the refusal to *let what was there come alive by itself*—makes the film confusing and sometimes even dull.[19]

In viewing the film, it is possible to find a basis for agreement with Jaffee; *Petey and Johnny* is crowded, hasty in its treatment of very complex events and relationships, and often overwhelmed by Petey's preachy narration. But without a more complete knowledge of the original material, it is difficult to determine whether the weaknesses in the final film are a result of the apparently massive ambiguity of the original situation in Spanish Harlem or of Drew's editing.

Controversy among various contributors seems to be a staple of almost any collaborative creative effort, but the controversy within Drew Associates between varying ideals and practical reality served to stretch and broaden the creative environment. Daring attempts always run the risk of failure, but without them little, creative growth could take place and few unanticipated discoveries could be made.

> PENNEBAKER: And *Petey and Johnny* was interesting because it became clear that the first characters [we filmed]—who seemed terrific, had great names, looked terrific—were, in fact, not interesting. So you had to find somebody who was, and that meant you had to sit in and go through a lot of stuff and take a lot of time. And when you did find them, what was interesting about them wasn't just . . . a win-or-lose situation, but the fact that of all these kids, the twenty or so that [the producers] were involved with, every one of them was in jail for murder within three years. Every one of them. . . . What is that? Is every one of them a bad person? In other words, [in] the process of filming there we might find out something nobody knew. I mean, that was really heady stuff, and Ricky wanted to sit on that story for three years. Well, we couldn't do that, or Drew couldn't do that. . . .
>
> But in a way, what we were saying was: Here's this process of filmmaking, and even as we start out on it and develop it to where we can follow stories, we're going to find stories that we couldn't imagine existed, and things that we can do with it that are going to really be extraordinary. Rather than just make a copy of the last film with a different set of characters.
>
> And I don't think Drew . . . was uninterested in doing it that way, but he had the problem of—he had to sell it, finally. And he had to sell a certain number. And he couldn't tie up all this stuff just because it was interesting, for two or three years.[20]

Mooney and Fowle

"Lipscomb's *Football* was good from start to finish. All I did was cut it down a little."[21]

Mooney vs. Fowle, which is frequently referred to as *Football* by Drew and his associates, was the happiest example of Drew's concept of a filmmaker. James Lipscomb, a former *Life* correspondent whom Drew recruited, produced the film without Drew's close supervision.

> I was in Europe at the time with the Aga Kahn or something, and Lipscomb called out the whole outfit; he had Leacock, Pennebaker,

and every other cameraman and correspondent we had, working on this film, shot an immense amount of film, came back and organized a complex editing system with at least a half dozen editors I would say. . . .

It was the best realized film that I as the managing editor received. I had to do less to it to sign off on it than I did to any other film.[22]

Mooney vs. Fowle pits coaches Otis Mooney (Miami High) and Haywood Fowle (Edison High) in "the game of the year for Florida's two greatest high school teams." The rivalry between the two schools will decide the city and state championships, bring forty-thousand spectators to the Orange Bowl for the game, and is "an event so momentous for its coaches that it becomes one of the great moments of their lives."[23] It is an exceptional subject: a tight, manageable drama, two open and assertive individuals, and an event of some importance. And it is stunningly executed. The photography is loose and relaxed early on, then tighter and more involved as game time arrives and the tension increases, and the editing is controlled and flowing, extracting every imaginable bit of information, contrast, excitement, and drama from the original materials.

And it is a crowd pleaser. There is the hard work, and constant "motivation," of the practices; the pageantry and silliness of band, cheerleaders, and crowd; there is locker-room psychology and sideline Prussianism. There is play-by-play, a pattern of development in the flow of the game, players in pain, coaches angry and shouting, tense and anguished looks on the faces of the cheerleaders, and the uncontrollable flexing of cheek muscles by one coach as the critical moments of the game grind on. And finally, in the winner's locker room, there is the coach: "We beat their ass!!"

Oh, yes: Mooney won. Miami High scored an upset victory, and Lipscomb had a film.

Mooney vs. Fowle had, in many respects, all the values that Drew sought: intense personalities, dramatic structure, and ample access for the camera. It is a strong example of what cinema verite could accomplish in certain subject matter areas, an example of "The Living Camera" concept at its best.

LEACOCK: [An] *amazing* portrait of what was going on in America at the time. A film like the *Football* film, Jim Lipscomb's baby; to me, that says more—you know, how on earth would you justify, to the head of programming of public broadcasting, to spend the equivalent of $200,000 today recording a football game between two high schools that nobody ever heard of. How could you *possibly* justify that?! And, to me, that's one of the most revealing films ever made. It's a stunning film.

I remember Jim . . . [and] Drew came from the tradition of *Life* and was a reporter and knew what reporters do. And I suspect that you probably don't learn about reporting at the Columbia School of Journalism or any other school of journalism. Reporting has to do with "what is it like to be here." Good reporting. And [Drew] assembled . . . a group of ferreting weasels—no, that's two animals; ferret's enough—who knew how to dig in, who knew how to get involved, who knew—who sensed a story line.[24]

Blackie

INTERVIEWER: I think the question is . . . [does] successful documentary relate to the intensity of the situation and the intensity of the excitement of the audience?

DREW: I think that's true of certain documentaries, say the one on football, but if you look at *Blackie*, where's the intensity? It's in the inner working of what's going on inside the guy, and if you don't perceive any intensity then there isn't any.[25]

Harold Fredric Blackburn, "Blackie", is an intense but quiet man piloting trans-Atlantic jets between New York and Rome. Given Drew's background and interest in aviation, Blackie must have seemed an inherently interesting subject. But there was an extra twist in Blackie's story; he was being forced into retirement by airline regulations because of his age, and he was not happy about the change. Drew had become aware of Blackie when John Bainbridge wrote a profile for the *New Yorker* on the retiring pilot. A lifetime career in flying was coming to an end. "We made a few calls and found out he hadn't retired yet. In fact he didn't retire until Christmas Eve, which was his birthday. Say no more. I mean, that was the story. Ha."[26]

It seemed a promising topic; a sympathetic character, a bittersweet situation, and strong visual possibilities. Sequences of Blackburn piloting his 707 jet through storm clouds leaving Rome to a beautifully cloudless sky above thirty-thousand feet, and a later night landing in New York are among the most photogenic in any of Drew's films. But Drew and his associates were to discover, again, that stories are difficult to judge accurately from afar, and that the principles of candid television journalism that had so far been developed did not work well in every situation.

How [do] you shoot films in the cockpit of a 707 during instrument letdowns and night landings and takeoffs and so forth; well, we did that, we recorded what happened in the cockpit, we recorded Blackie at home on his farm in Pennsylvania, and when we went to put it all together, that story simply would not tell itself. That is, we had followed our theories to the utmost and recorded everything that happened and there was no way that film would tell itself.

A slight editorial problem. You get to the climax of putting this film together and it doesn't work according to your theories, so we had to face the fact that if it didn't work according to our theories it still had to work some other way, and we were forced into an extensive voice-over device, which was Blackie talking about his thoughts and feelings and history and so forth, and intertwining that with the pictures we had.[27]

Blackie was similar to an earlier Drew subject that had yielded somewhat similar results—Scott Crossfield, the "X-Pilot." Both were professionals, going about their daily routines without any outward sign of the emotional tensions that Drew sensed must accompany their activities for the cameras to focus on.

Later critics have generally treated *Blackie* as a minor film. One reason, curiously, may be that it lacked what many of those same critics came to criticize as a Drew trademark—a distinct and dramatic crisis for the principal subject.

The "Crisis Structure"

The Drew films are a synthesis of cinema verite techniques and fictional conceptions of character, action, and structure. . . . It is a grafting operation performed by maintaining the purity of filming methods and applying them in the service of particular theories of what these films ought to be about and how they should be put together. . . .

The Drew films . . . represent a personal vision in the same manner that fiction films can express the world view of their directors.[28]

As Drew's development of candid, non-intrusive filming became better known, and thus less "innovative", attention began to focus on questions of story and structure; how the filmic materials were used rather than how they had been obtained. Critic Stephen Mamber, among others, has analyzed Drew's almost unfailing use of a crisis moment as a principle structural element in his films.

The basic organizing principle behind a Drew film can usually be stated in the form of a success or failure question. Will John Kennedy win the election, or will Hubert Humphrey [in *Primary*]? Will Eddie

Sachs win the race [in *On the Pole*]? Will Paul Crump be saved from the electric chair [in *The Chair*, 1962]? Will the Kennedys' integration strategy work [in *Crisis: Behind a Presidential Commitment*, 1963]? This description of plot may sound overly simplified in that the same device can often be applied in explaining the structure of fiction films, plays, and novels, at the expense of ludicrously distorting the complex concerns of the work. (Why did Kane say "rosebud"? Will Hamlet avenge his father's death? Will Ahab find and destroy Moby Dick?) But the point is that this *is* a traditional fictional structure and not an inevitable conclusion of direct-cinema methods and intent. . . . As in fiction, the Drew films take advantage of devices that provide a skeleton to build upon.[29]

Given Drew's attention to storyfinding and the dramatic elements of structure that he found so important in the novel and short story, it is not surprising that he would chose to structure his reports as "stories," using whatever devices, fictional or otherwise, that he considered appropriate. What Mamber sees, however, is a potential conflict between the advances Drew had made in obtaining his source materials and the means used to structure them into stories. His examination focuses on the "crisis structure" that many critics have cited in Drew's work.

DREW: I've objected to the word "crisis" in the first place. So if I try to be smart about this I would change it to the "turning point," or the point of revelation or the crux of the matter, which does not have to be a head-on crisis. It has to be some place where the forces that have been building throughout the story come to some kind of resolution. Now, is that necessary? I say, yes, that is necessary to good storytelling. And if people can make—if people can tell stories in such a way that there is no revelation or turning point or crux, more power to them. I just haven't seen it done. And as for myself, I consider it a discipline to draw the lines until they meet and something happens.[30]

Drew is arguing that a skillfully structured approach to the presentation of cinema verite materials is both a mark of considerable discipline and a professional imperative. The conflict in views is, at one level, a reflection of the disagreement over proper and effective forms of dramatic expression that has gone on for a century and more, since the period of Flaubert and Zola.

It's really an attack of naturalism on realism. That is, naturalism being formless material, presented because the author says you should read it, and [realism] being something with a structure that says "you don't have to look at this, but this character is interesting," and then starts

involving you by letting that character lead you through some kind
of line of development. . . .

. . . The naturalistic novelists are novelists who write books that
don't have lines of development; they don't have a plot or climax or
whatever. The object is to present "material;" it corresponds, in
filmmaking, to screening the rushes. The realists, Flaubert, for instance, feel that if you tell an interesting tale, with interesting characters and something happens, that's a reason to enter a story.[31]

While Mamber clearly recognizes the pragmatic aspects of Drew's
choice—"obviously, his structure is . . . a familiar form that maintains
audience interest and responds to deeply felt human needs for story resolution and unity"—he also advises considerable caution in accepting the
drama that is presented on the screen: "Reality does not always coincide
with drama, and when it does we had better look twice."

MAMBER: Editing can be as much a form of "fictionalization" as
scripting or acting. It is often harder to spot, possibly insidious,
and sometimes scarcely credible. Because the integrity of the filming
situation is respected (in that no one is directed, no scenes are prepared), the opportunity to play down this aspect, to suggest by implication that the film must still be showing "what happened" no matter
how it has been edited, is tempting. Opening narration in the films
often plays up the shooting technique, emphasizing that it is a "true
story" (said at the start of *On the Pole*), that it "actually happened"
(*David*), that "it wasn't planned, it's for real" (*Petey and Johnny*), and
that it was made without "any acting" (*[On the Road to] Button Bay*).
It is, in fact, the sanctimonious repetition of the claim to undiluted
reality that wears thinnest in the narration and comes closest to un-
dermining the whole approach.[32]

Drew's concern that the audience be made aware of the important
difference between his *recorded* material and the *created* material of ordinary
television fiction programs is understandable, and his "sanctimonious repetition" of that difference is more apparent to a critic reviewing a group of
films over a rather short period of time than it would be to an audience
that may never have seen more than one of the films or, at best, may have
seen them at intervals of several weeks or months and probably interspersed
with a good deal of other television viewing. But Mamber's concern that
"editing can be as much a form of 'fictionalization' as scripting or acting"
emphasizes an often unrealized hazard of cinema verite films: there is an
important distinction between the nature of the original filming and the
nature of the eventual presentation that both cinema verite filmmakers
and their critics seem unwilling, or unable, to adequately address. The
conceptual struggle between the high-level accuracy and intimacy of cinema

verite filming and the structural requirements of a viewing audience trained in watching fictional presentations continues to this day; a fully acceptable combination of the two views has not been reached. But it is clear that the differences began to be seriously discussed—in fact, only became seriously discussable—after Drew's initial efforts in cinema verite had been completed.

But Mamber's criticisms came a decade and more after "The Living Camera" had provided Drew and his associates the challenge of wrestling with such issues in a workaday production situation. And at that time, there were clearly differing opinions as to how the newly developed techniques of candid television journalism were to be employed, views reflecting differences in organizational position and responsibility, professional background, and personal vision.

> DREW: The story was the important thing. And the things that made the story, the elements that made the story, were important. And diversions were not. And a lot of people loved their diversions. And the *discipline* of making a film that followed the story line is simply beyond a lot of the photographers. . . . And, yes, I'm the guy who feels the discipline and applies the discipline. . . . But, I have a problem with people who talk and talk that I wasn't going to the heart of the matter. I *know* I was going to the heart of the matter. And the people around me knew that.[33]

> PENNEBAKER: Drew and I really kind of came to some sort of—into some sort of conflict. Again, it was never very violent conflict, but I could see that . . . Drew was beginning to put together a kind of documentary commentary film; that it was like *Life* magazine. It would take an issue that would be fairly comprehensible to anybody— I mean, we were not looking for very sophisticated ideas and issues, but things that were pretty simple. You know; guy gets out of jail, what happens to him; drug rehabilitation center runs afoul of neighbors; that kind of thing. Things that the magazine thought it did well. . . . The constant preoccupation with a sort of "real world," but a kind of inactive [world]; that is, the solutions were always very grand and very noble, everything was kind of noble about them, and they—they didn't really want to get into reality; they wanted a kind of—it was kind of soap opera![34]

> DREW: See, I shoot these days, and I wouldn't dispute for a moment that what I see through the eyepiece in six hours of shooting during the day has more nuance and subtlety and complexity than what I'm ever going to put on the screen as an editor. . . . But, believe me, it's a strange feeling to sit in a room with photographers who are *living* every moment of their rushes.

> And you know that you are going to have to make that into an hour. And not only that, it's going to have to make sense on many

levels and so forth. And you just *know* that Pennebaker is going to hate you, and Leacock is going to be disappointed, but you hope that they might be thrilled by the results and—and, by God, most often they were! Or professed to be, at the time.[35]

SHUKER: I would just say that I would never criticize any of those other guys for feeling that way, because I saw Bob more than once have differences, and he was in charge so he overruled, and maybe there were some sequences that would have been better. On the other hand, the films did get paid for, and they did get on the air, usually. So that's part of a compromise. *Life* magazine, after all—in fact, all of Time, Inc.—said, "It's group journalism." And that's what Drew Associates was, for better or worse. It was group journalism. And it's hard for some people to swallow and therefore they went their own way.[36]

As the production of the films to fulfill the Time, Inc. order progressed and the earlier successes of *Primary*, *On the Pole*, and *Close Up!* faded, the focus of Drew's attention shifted increasingly from the possibilities of obtaining candid source materials to the practicalities of shaping those materials for television audiences. An earlier set of preconceptions had been recognized and resolved, as cameramen and field producers became able to record what actually happened instead of what should happen. But they were replaced by another, more powerful—and perhaps more accurate—set of preconceptions about how an audience expects to have material presented to it. The ability to explore and record human activity in new ways was being limited by the inability to effectively present new materials to "old" audiences.

Susan, Jawaharlal, and Karim

Among Drew and his associates, *Susan Starr*, *Nehru*, and *The Aga Kahn* are considered the least successful of the series of Time, Inc. films that were packaged as "The Living Camera". All were chosen to allow the camera to have access to a "crisis moment," or "turning point," in the lives of their principal subject; in all cases, the crisis is not powerful enough and neither is the individual portrayed, for various reasons.

Susan Starr

Susan Schwartz, renamed Susan Starr at the age of seven by her mother, was a finalist in the Dimitri Mitropoulos International Music Competition at New York's Metropolitan Opera House. The tension and excitement of the days leading up to the competition were clearly to be the central focus of the film, "the challenge of her life," but love intervened. Under considerable pressure from her manager-mother "to practice, and to be good and to be beautiful and to be smart and so forth," Susan shows a bit of independence in—politely—inviting another of the contestants to breakfast.

"You see them fall in love, because they aren't in love yet when she invites him to breakfast, and he arrives at breakfast, and he is there to see Susan, but he has to spend most of his time talking to Mother. But they hit it off enough that they decide to have dinner, and Mother invites herself along to dinner. And the boy's jaw drops."[37]

After the dinner-date, Susan plays, finishes third out of three finalists, and is seen dozing on the train back to Philadelphia to the accompaniment of her piano practice and film flashbacks of herself and the boy.

The narrator says, " 'Do you pronounce your name Susan or Suzanne?' Eight weeks and four days after Kenneth Amada asked Susan Starr that question [at their first breakfast meeting], they were married."[38]

Susan Starr is occasionally a warm and funny film, but Susan, with bouffant, mink coat, and a constant air of polite shyness, is not a character with the emotional intensity of an Eddie Sachs. Casting, Drew may have again discovered, was as important as "crisis" in the choice of cinema verite subjects with strong storytelling potential. Where *Life* magazine could manage with a few dramatic images and the storytelling ability of the final writer, candid television journalism demanded much more of the chosen subject, and of the producer who did the choosing.

The Prime Minister

"On the basis of [*Adventures on the New Frontier*], I wanted to make a film on heads of state and I went to Egypt and Russia and India in order to try to persuade the heads of state of those countries to allow us to live with them and shoot candid pictures and make a similar film."[39]

Robert Drew never lacked confidence when in search of a potential story. "You might call it a long-shot. But there have been a lot of long-shots. There'd never been a film on a U.S. president either before—an internal film—before we did. We were emboldened to try all kinds of people."[40]

Drew's plans were always more than wishful thinking, and his aggressiveness in attempting to develop a heads-of-state series is typical. Henry Cabot Lodge, Richard Nixon's vice-presidential running mate in 1960, had an office in the Time-Life Building; Drew met with Lodge and was put in contact with an Indian politician with ties to the prime minister of India. U.S. Ambassador to India John Kenneth Galbraith, who had been a minor character in *Adventures on the New Frontier*, was

shown the film and he helped make arrangements for a meeting with
Jawaharlal Nehru.

> [Nehru] marched into the room, and he was surprisingly small and
> surprisingly preoccupied-looking, and sort of said, "What do you
> want?" and I said, "I'd like to make a film about you at work." And
> he looked like he had just encountered something really disgusting.
> And I talked a little more, and sort of told him he had to look at this
> film. And we looked at the film—they darkened the room. When the
> film was over and the lights came up, he said yes. So I think he'd
> enjoyed watching Kennedy fool around in his office for a day or two.[41]

Nehru was prime minister of the most important third-world nation on
earth, and he was facing reelection: "I wanted to make the film during an
election campaign, where he had something to lose or something to win."
But the Indian election was not the same as the U.S. election two years
earlier; the issues were much more complex and vague than in America,
and an American television audience in 1962 had little understanding of
those complexities.

> In the case of Nehru, I thought we would have a film with a
> structure, mainly because he was facing an election campaign. And
> Leacock shot beautiful footage of everything, and we were really
> there with the man at breakfast, lunch, and dinner, and in his office
> working, and worrying about international affairs, and agonizing and
> so forth. And campaigning. We saw him almost overwhelmed by
> mobs of millions and so forth.
> So the material was very strong, except that it did not, in the end
> when we put it together—did not tell a story by itself, even with
> considerable narration. It would not have been a film which told
> itself. . . . It finally occurred to me that the most human thing we
> saw about Nehru occurred after [the campaigning], on the last day or
> two. After we had broken our agreement with him, which was to not
> ask questions.[42]

Drew's solution to the structural problems of *Nehru* was based on an
agreement made with Nehru that the crew would only observe his activities
and not ask questions. At the end of the three-week shooting period,
correspondent Shuker did, in violation of the agreement, and as planned,
ask questions. In the film, Shuker and Leacock introduce themselves and
describe the agreement; both narrate the events of the campaign; the
agreement is broken, and Nehru talks, in difficult, accented English, of
his philosophy and his life. It is an awkward and unwieldly device, at best.

The third part of Drew's plan to film heads-of-state produced only "an indirect reaction"; he traveled to Moscow and, through the contacts of the Time, Inc. correspondent there, made contact with Nikita Khruschev's chief of public information, whose name Drew recalls as Karlomov(?).

"I showed the film to a succession of Russian people. And the final one was Karlomov, who came to dinner and stayed late and challenged me to a drinking duel, and showed a lot of interest in everything. He went off with the film, and the film reappeared, and there was no answer then, and I left the Soviet Union, and there never was an answer."[43]

Drew's "long-shot" at the three most influential men in the world was only partially successful: *Adventures on the New Frontier* was more of a trial run for a later film; *Nehru* was a limited look at the complexities of political power on the Indian subcontinent; and from Russia, "there never was an answer." But that Drew's conceptual reach could often exceed his operational grasp was perhaps a prerequisite to any sort of substantial progress that might take place during this developmental phase of cinema verite.

The Aga Kahn

Karim Aga Kahn was twenty-five, Harvard educated, "a direct blood descendant of Mohammed," an Olympic ski racer, and imam to the largest group of Muslims in the world. He was also a subject of "The Living Camera" for six months, facing a series of the Olympic ski trials (he finishes forty-eigth of ninety-five in the finals); a massive reorganization of Muslim-controlled business enterprises in Africa, the Middle East, and Asia to meet the challenges of Western business methods; and a resolution of the demands of the conflicting heritages of his father, Ali Kahn, "the dashing sportsman of the West," and his grandfather, the last Aga Kahn, "a rich and powerful imam . . . of the East."

But, somehow, it is hard to care. Karim's conflicts are real, but the Aga Kahn is a reserved and private man, and a curious choice for "The Living Camera." Wealth and power are certainly important topics; the religious leader of millions of followers is a person of great potential influence, and therefore of great potential interest to both followers and outsiders. But the requirements of cinema verite are not that the subjects be important but that they be interesting and open. The flaws in *The Aga Kahn* are not with the idea of showing the activities of a rich and powerful man, but in the characteristics of the man apart from his wealth and power and, most importantly, his unwillingness to share those characteristics with a camera team. Drew's choice of the Aga Kahn as a subject may have been a likely one—for *Life* magazine.

Shooting Jane

Pennebaker said, "We went from *David*, where we might shoot three or four rolls in a day—I think in the whole film we maybe shot twenty-five thousand feet—to *Jane*, where we probably shot a hundred thousand. . . . For us, that's incredible."[44]

Principally the work of Pennebaker and Hope Ryden, Drew Associates's only female correspondent, *Jane* is an example of the enormous effort, physical and conceptual, that cinema verite filmmaking often involved.

> DREW: *Jane* is an example of a story in which we were covering people who were leading a full, rich life. Jane Fonda got up at nine o'clock in the morning and spent a whole long hard day at work being an actress or rehearsing and so forth, and went to bed at one or two in the morning. And Penny and Hope without an assistant were shooting, were with her continuously.
>
> Then they had, from say one or two in the morning till seven or eight the next morning to charge their batteries, literally—the batteries of their camera—repair their equipment, reload their magazines, and think through what they would go after the next day, how the story was going, what mode the character was in, and so forth. So there was a kind of generalship that had to take place in whatever hours you could get away from the story, to think through the tactics and strategy for the next day or for the whole length of the film.
>
> Now Hope was doing that. That was her responsibility, she was good at it, and she was doing that. . . .
>
> But Penny was also thinking, so she had to stay in touch with Penny's thinking, and they had to work it out.[45]

Nominally the story of how a new play is brought to Broadway, it is quickly apparent that the real center of the story is Jane Fonda, then only a fledgling actress with a famous father. *Jane* is the experiences of Jane, from rehearsals to opening night, from a dressing-room kiss by her director boyfriend to the eventual reading of the newpaper reviews. And the task of exploring, and adequately recording, the complex process that was taking place became a test of the skills and wills of both Ryden and Pennebaker.

> PENNEBAKER: We were competing with [each other] trying to make two different kinds of films. And I was convinced that we were losing the real film and getting some kind of—I don't know, kind of a—I don't know. Again, we hadn't looked at stuff. We were just guessing at what seemed to me to be going down, but . . . I found myself worrying much too much about the quality of the picture, how pretty it was, and things that I think were not really part of it.

But I guess in a way I was also trying to prove that we could make this thing absolutely theatrical. I mean, the one thing that *Jane* proved to me was that theatricality was absolutely possible with this technique. Which up to then was uncertain. . . .

Hope and I were really going different directions then on that film. I think Hope was coming at it the way a journalist would a story. She was really ready to settle for much less. I think I was trying to make, you know, a million dollar movie out of it.[46]

The "generalship" of the production, as Drew termed it, was ostensibly in the hands of Ryden, as correspondent; she had made the contacts with Jane Fonda and others associated with the play, she had gotten the topic assigned for production, and she had gotten Pennebaker "up to bat." But *Jane* is, in its best moments, a film of such personal intensity that it could not be "produced" by a person abstracted from the filming—and especially the *photography*—process. The risks and uncertainties of unscripted cinema verite production were in full force in *Jane*.

PENNEBAKER: It was always like agony, you know. You didn't want to shoot all the film up, and every day seemed like every other day, kind of hopelessly—nothing seemed to organize. I mean, when you see the movie after a while, you assume that the whole process was as organized as the movie got to be, but, of course, it wasn't at all. That movie is fiction, in a way, distilled out of whatever we did get. But it's much more complicated, had many more setbacks and peculiar things going on. Which, in a way, were interesting, and maybe more interesting than the movie we made.[47]

As the cameraman, Pennebaker was making the multitude of small decisions that would record the texture and detail that *Jane* would later come to depend on: "those long, long runs on Jane staring at herself in the mirror—those are Pennebaker's sensibility." And that shooting, always conditioned by the ambiguities of an uncertain story developing in an unknown way, was a constant balance between the necessity to produce a satisfactory story continuity out of what *appeared* to be happening and the equal need to not lose sight of what *might* be happening. Satisfactory control of limited filmic resources depended on both planning and non-planning, on an ever-changing conceptual design for the evolving story and on the desire not to force pre-conceived directions into the flow of the story.

PENNEBAKER: You had a lot of little signals going on in your head about what—what was germane and what you were kind of after, and what you believed was happening. But at the same time you had this incredible need, absolute demand, to not be preconditioned, so that when things happened that you didn't expect, you could kind of move away with them and find out. And in the end, those were always the more interesting things. The things you [discovered] as you went. And so, you had to teach yourself *not* to get preconditioned, but at the same time it was very hard not to go in without having some kind of pre-conceptual idea. So, you were caught between these two opposite poles and it was like stretching yourself out, to be alert on both ends.[48]

The capabilities of Drew's innovations in television journalism had matured a great deal since *Primary* and *On the Pole*. But, increasingly, the sophisticated skills brought with them both the awareness of new possibilities, and new problems. Improved means of storytelling had not kept pace with improvements in observing and recording the "real world"; to some of Drew's associates, the new source material was being shaped to meet the demands of old forms. A small case in point is the handling of Jane Fonda's reactions to the play's reviews.

> LEACOCK: When Jane Fonda read the reviews . . . of the play, which were devastating. . . . her first reaction was, as I recall, was, "Who's he, what does he know about theater!" Pop, pop, pop, pop, pop. At the same time absolutely mortified by what he said. And later, a different reaction, more serious one. And to put in both was confusing, and somehow we just ended up with the later reaction. Instead of the flip, "What does he know!" Blah, blah, blah. And it's always bothered me that we really didn't deal with the conflict. And I think this is true of any editing, any film. You always get the pressures, and this is not just Bob, this is the pressure of the industry.[49]
> PENNEBAKER: We'd figured out how to get complicated stories, and really felt them and that what the problem was in doing it was not— it was no longer technical, it was now much more of a problem of understanding what you were after. And how you had to get it. . . .
> And so we were beginning to understand the *process* to a very detailed degree. And yet what we saw was that the requirements of it didn't—weren't up to that. That television didn't really need that. Or want it. And so we were beginning to have some doubts about where Drew was going with it.[50]

As the development of cinema verite progressed, it was constantly Drew's role to be sensitive both to the talents and interests of his staff and to the capacities of the television audience. And the conflicts that Drew was called upon to resolve occurred not only as the result of differences between the attitudes of his staff and the "outside world" but also between the views of individual staff members.

DREW: Hope [Ryden] cut *Jane*. Penny was in an uproar. They had fallen out; I mean, there was a personal side to this that I didn't know about at the time. During the shooting of the film, they'd been the best friends you can imagine. During the editing of the film, they became the most distant associates you can imagine. And Hope was not too sensitive to Penny's feelings, and she cut a film that was a little stiff. All I can say is "stiff". And I knew it was stiff. And I was holding my peace until I saw where and how I thought it ought to be fixed.

    Leacock came storming into the room one day and said, "That film has to be fixed!" I said, "Yeah. Okay. Well." "And it has to be fixed with Penny." And I thought about that and I waited a day, and we talked again and I said, "Okay, we'll do it with Penny." Which meant that I was going to have Hope as a tiger on the other side and I'd have to keep her out of the room and so forth. So we did. We—*we*; the three of us, sat there.[51]

Professional, and personal, differences often influenced the final outcome of a particular film, and Drew's control at that level was clearly limited. The complex process of both shaping an entire film and of making judgments about particular scenes was always partly commercial, partly aesthetic, and partly personal.

    Now Jane is sitting in the dressing room, near the end, in a long, long scene after she's realized that the play's a flop and she's probably realized that her lover was not a lover. And she's probably realized that she sees herself at a dead end of some kind.

    And she sits in the room, and just looks in the mirror. And it's one of the most wonderful scenes in any film, I think. And it runs a little long. But Penny thinks it runs a lot short. And that it should go on longer and longer and we should have just left it and left it. Okay. At some point, someone had to decide; I decided that it had run long enough. At the point where I cut it, which is what you see in the film. . . .

    . . . Penny passionately wanted that scene to run for—I don't know how long—minutes, maybe. Leacock knew that scene shouldn't run that long; but he left it to me to tell Penny! You know, I mean, friends—. But things do get complicated.[52]

Paul and the Chair

The most important, and most widely known, of the "Living Camera" films was the last; it attracted the attention of critics worldwide, and it was assigned for production on the basis of a 10-minute phone call.

I had sent Shuker to Chicago on some kind of a story search. He called me from a pay phone and said "I have a story. It's a condemned man, and the warden is his best friend, and he's asked [the warden] to pull the switch. There's gonna be . . . a one-day trial, with nine judges, to determine whether or not to recommend to the governor that this man be saved from the chair or be electrocuted. The [man's] lawyer is a guy named Don Moore and he's frantically working on this. And his opponent is Assistant State's Attorney [and later governor] Jim Thompson and he's determined to electrocute this guy, and it's a good story. . . ." So I agreed to the whole scheme, and started dispatching people to Chicago.[53]

Drew's trust in Shuker's judgment turned out to be well-founded. By having the camera teams in position, Shuker was able to take advantage of developments that could not have been anticipated and would have been lost with more conventional assignment and shooting practices. Not only was "the sense of being there" important; for Drew and for cinema verite, *being there* was.

I think we'd been shooting one day . . . [and prominent New York trial lawyer] Louis Nizer suddenly popped up. And . . . Nizer really took over Moore's job and developed another line of defense, which was to simply flood the judges with positive statements about what had happened to the character of Paul Crump, the convicted murderer and the man who was about to go to the chair—good things, good developments in his character that had happened since he had been in jail. And therefore he shouldn't be electrocuted.[54]

Although the resulting film was once titled *Paul* in conformance with the use of the names of subjects as the titles in "The Living Camera" series, it is almost always referred to by its alternate title, *The Chair*. Indeed "the chair" at the Cook County Jail in Chicago is a dramatic character in the film: Warden Jack Johnson, "in charge of all executions," leads the camera on a two-minute-and-thirty-second trip from his office, down prison hallways, through the prison chapel, through clanging prison doors opened to his practiced knock, to "the death chamber" and the chair. Paul Crump, ostensibly the center of attention in a case that may become a "turning point in legal history"—no governor had ever before commuted a death sentence on the grounds of rehabilitation—is seen only three times, very briefly and in almost-public situations where little of substance is revealed about him.

The film actually centers on Crump's volunteer attorney, Donald Page Moore. It is Moore's efforts to enlist support for Crump's cause, his maneuverings with the Chicago newspapers and the city's religious hierarchy to present a picture of positive rehabilitation, his presentation to the state's parole board in a jammed temporary courtroom, and his deeply personal reactions to specific events along the way that provide the fascination, and insight, of *The Chair*.

The various shifts in storytelling focus—from the presumed hero, Paul; the actual-but-unacknowledged hero, Don Moore; segments involving the warden, Louis Nizer, the State's Attorney, and the commutation argument before the parole board; and the chair—created a series of continuity tensions that some critics and audiences found confusing and disappointing. Attorney Moore, at work in his office, is clearly the most interesting and revealing as he works on final preparations for his case. Some moments are those where cinema verite excels: Moore on the phone trying to line up witnesses to support Crump, saying "I need a rabbi . . . get me a big shot . . . I'll put him on after the monsignor"; he closes the call with, "I'm deeply grateful, and I hope you'll pray for us. I mean it," hangs up the phone and exclaims "Old fraud!" And in one of the film's most-cited moments, Moore receives a call informing him that Archbishop Albert Meyer of Chicago will issue a statement of support for Crump, and afterwards cries, his head held in his hands.

The contrasts between intense emotion, clever manipulation, and calm professionalism are potentially profound revealings of the character of Donald Page Moore. They illustrate the power of cinema verite as an approach to documentary filmmaking, and the power of a crisis situation to provide the elements of good storytelling. In almost any other context, Don Moore, the hard/soft, tough/weeping defense attorney, would be either laughable or cynical. When the moment is right, and the camera's access to the subject adequate, cinema verite can produce sequences of unparalleled insight; without those conditions, however, the method struggles.

Paul Crump is seen more as an object, being acted upon, than as a central subject. Only near the end of the film, after the commutation—to 199 years—when Crump is brought before a crowded news conference, complete with anxious photographers, is there a moment of insight: "Hold it a second! . . . Paul, will you look this way here!?" Crump makes a statement: "I thank God [Reporter: "A little louder!"] and Governor Kerner . . . I thank hundreds and hundreds of people, little kids and things, all over the country, who['ve] been—." He falters, overcome, it appears, by the enormity of the moment and the inability of the statement he is making to these crowding strangers to express his feelings. A photographer breaks in: "Paul, look over here at me and smile for me here, will you, Paul!!"

For Drew and his associates who had filmed and preserved that segment of human interaction—the stumbling Paul, the insensitive photographer—it was an example of cinema verite at its best; a marvelously revealing moment. Leacock says: "I think mostly we succeeded in capturing moments. Making whole films is another problem. . . . Most of the films have wonderful moments. It's hard to put them together as things that satisfy the need that television seems to have for completed wholes."[55]

Capturing the material became nearly as interesting as the film itself. Moments of uncertainty multiplied over the shooting period. At any turn, the prospect of a great story, and the resources already put into developing it, might be lost.

> LEACOCK: Bob and I moved into the lawyer's office. And he was convinced that we wanted to interview him. And he was delighted. And so I went in and he said, "What can I do for you?" and I think we said something like, "Nothing." We put the camera down, we went out for coffee; we came back, we sat around, he was still trying to please us, and he finally decided we were crazy. We didn't ask him anything, we didn't do anything, we just left the office. And finally he said "To hell with these people!" and went ahead and did what he was doing. And then we started to film.[56]

> PENNEBAKER: In the middle of it all, [Louis] Nizer comes sneaking in secretly, and there was a reporter out in Chicago who told us this information in a bar one night. He said, "Do you know Louis Nizer's going to be on it?" I said, "How do you know that?" He said, "I just know. And he's staying in this hotel and he's in this room. If you go there, you'll find him. He's not under that name in the hotel."
>
> So we went and knocked on the door and sure enough, here he was.
>
> For us it was a constant series of untangling this mystery which surrounded all this filming.[57]

> DREW: We were together every evening, and it was like war. You'd go out and fight your battle and come back and replan your strategy and find out who got what and how the characters are doing and are there any new openings to be covered and so forth. . . . But things were occurring simultaneously during the day that one team couldn't inform another one about.[58]

> LEACOCK: And we didn't know that we could get into the courtroom; Shuker was very much involved in that. Getting permission to get into the courtroom was unbelieveable; supposing we were locked out?[59]

> DREW: Cameras were not allowed [in the hearing room.] Somebody, some lawyer, was going to make a plea in the beginning that the court be declared open to cameras. So I think we had three or four teams

in the room with hidden cameras—that is, they were in suitcases and recorders were hidden in briefcases and so forth, so that if it was declared legal, we could unpack the stuff and start shooting. And as I recall, there was no resolution of that. Therefore, I think, it was illegal. And we did start shooting, however.[60]

LEACOCK: We had to face the probability of his being executed. What sort of film is that; it's a different movie. And we had to figure out what the fuck we were going to do; we were going to try to smuggle a camera to the death chamber. I think.[61]

DREW: I had no doubt that we're going to end up with a film; that was easy. *Primary* was tough, and *Eddie* was tough. . . . But by the time we got to *The Chair*, that pressure had diminished a little. Just because we knew the cameras worked; we could shoot with 400' loads, I knew which cameraman I could trust and which I couldn't and which to put where. . . . Now the other pressures, to make that work in the broadcasting world, was important to the next film, but it wasn't crucially important to that film.[62]

LEACOCK: Bob was under such strain that he finally left [Chicago]; I think he was under such strain, he finally couldn't see out of one eye . . . and he pulled out, the strain was so tremendous. And I ended up shooting with somebody else. Just the strain of getting at the— Bob was always under these terrible pressures; so was I, actually, a lot of it. We felt—it's a killer. This is an insane way to make a movie. What happens if you don't get it? . . .

And this was true of Flaherty, too. And I think it killed Flaherty. And sometimes I thought it was going to kill Drew. Sometimes I think it's going to kill me. [Laughs] You're out there! You're a hundred-thousand dollars—or whatever it is, a million. What are you doing farting around, there's no movie here. And there was the football game—but even then, "So what?" It's a football game; is there a movie there? Flaherty in Louisiana; he spent six months filming goddamn alligators! I said, "What are we doing?!" Shooting fucking alligators! Who gives a shit! How are you going to make a movie out of it? And it's terrifying. . . .[63]

By the time Paul Crump was lead away down a jail hallway to be transferred to the Illinois prison system "for the rest of his natural life," Drew and his associates had the material necessary to construct an important film. But at that point the adventurous uncertainties of shooting were replaced by the conceptual differences of editing. *The Chair* is a complex story in the telling, including as it must, the material on Paul Crump and the legal background for Crump's unique appeal. It must also include the multi-dimensional relationship between Don Moore, the young defense attorney handling a big case; Louis Nizer, the famous outsider with a dramatic change in strategy; and Jim Thompson, the confident prosecutor with a clear eye for the publicity of the case. Also, the warden tests his equipment in readiness for the probable execution; the lengthy and complicated court hearing; and intermittently throughout the film, serving as a symbol of the complex controversies that continually surround capital punishment, the chair itself, checked and ready, standing almost too plain and neutral in the center of "the death chamber."

All this material is replete with information, detail, and nuance; it is also fragmented, complicated, difficult to follow, and *very* long! Much of the material, but the parole board hearing especially, suffers from indistinct sound, poor camera position and/or lighting, and extensive compression in editing. And yet, *The Chair* remains one of the most powerful of Drew's films, the fragmentation and excessive informational detail and technical flaws overwhelmed by the fascination of the will-he-or-won't-he, "crisis structure" story of Paul Crump and the Cook County Jail's electric chair.

> PENNEBAKER: The problem that Ricky and I had, particularly with *The Chair*, was . . . it was a difficult, it was a complicated story. It wasn't: "There's a guy on Death Row about to burn," but that Nizer was out there, under an assumed name, to save him! And [Moore] didn't want Nizer to be out there saving him, even if it saved him! I mean, the story was really a marvelous and complicated story. And Drew, I think, was moved to try to not make it so complicated; to make it more simple. And to—so that people would understand it and go for the pathos in Crump getting spared.[64]

"In this case I got the blame. I mean, I really edited the film." Drew has taken full responsibility for *The Chair*, especially its final, edited, shape. And the criticisms that have been leveled at the film have centered on two of Drew's editorial choices, his portrayals of the two main characters—Don Moore, and the chair.

> NARRATOR: The decision is coming today. The Parole Board is about to make its secret recommendations to the governor. At the county jail, Paul Crump waits, twenty feet from the chair. As soon as the governor makes his decision, he will phone Warden Johnson. But the warden must proceed with the execution schedule: practice drills, with the chair, so the execution will go smoothly.[65]

At sixty-three minutes into the seventy-five-minute film, this narration opens the final section of *The Chair*. Pieced together from segments shot before, during, and after the actual deliberation-and-decision day, the final twelve minutes of the film is more "mood" than strict journalism, a collage of scenes and segments designed to bridge the gap between the parole board hearing and the governor's announcement—or, as some critics have charged, to build the tension and "hype" the ending.

> DREW: I think that there's a certain part of the film where I unhinged it from reality and swung it into a kind of orbital, sonic, visual, kaleidoscopic—not kaleidoscopic, but . . . I spun it—when I felt emotionally—when I hit a sort of emotional pitch in that film, I took it from the literal way it had been progressing and sort of swung it into a more fluid, impressionistic mold. And I did find critics disagreeing with that and accusing us of hyping it and so forth. But that's the way I felt so that's the way I edited it. . . . I don't think it departs from realistic story editing to become overly dramatic. The things that might seem overly dramatic are actually dramatic. The sound that door makes in the death chamber and the way that chair looks when you're thinking about Paul Crump frying in it and all that stuff—the juxtapositions there—I think they're all valid and true and dramatic by themselves.[66]

"The sound of that door," as the warden makes his way through the jail's hallways on his way to the death chamber, became, in the way it was used, a source of critical contention about *The Chair*. In the final eight minutes of the closing section, the portion Drew refers to as "unhinged," the warden's trip to the chair and his rehearsal of his staff in the etiquette of an execution became a motif around which the actions of other characters are made to revolve. Paul Crump sits silently in his cell; Don Moore talks to a reporter; the warden rehearses; a TV station reports that the governor has made a decision and will announce it after lunch; cameras are set up in the warden's office for the inevitable news conference; and Moore gets a positive tip from a reporter—"recommendation: commutation"—and then a negative one—"let's keep our fingers crossed." The warden rehearses; Jim Thompson, the prosecutor, plays golf (a scene used earlier); Don Moore bowls (a scene used earlier); the warden sits in his office (a scene used earlier); Paul Crump sits in his cell (a scene used earlier); Don Moore listens to a radio in his office (seen earlier); the news conference cameras are ready and waiting (the end of the earlier action); and the warden's secretary announces, "Warden, Governor Kerner's calling!"

A nonliteral use of source material, including flashbacks, is not uncommon in documentaries as well as in commercial, industrial, experimental, artistic, and even fiction films. But not often in straight journalism. And to compound the matter, the footage of the warden and the chair in the "unhinged" section is described as a "practice drill" for a possible execution. Leacock says that it was filmed as much as a month after Paul Crump's death sentence had been commuted: "the scenes of walking down the corridor and things . . . were shot a month after the whole incident was over, in order to conform to the 'will he or won't he [be saved from execution]' thing."[67] Drew does not see the delayed shooting as a serious problem.

> Even if it were shot a month later, it was a very legitimate use of film and film recording to enter the prison and look at the electric chair. This film is called *The Chair*; a picture of the electric chair. (pause) I don't care exactly when it was shot. I do care what happened in the progression of the trial, but I don't care when I see the electric chair. . . . I *don't* recall sending somebody back a month later to shoot it. And I don't say that couldn't have been done—I *would* have done that.[68]

Those who consider a more literal presentation of events to be one of the underlying strengths of cinema verite are understandably uneasy with Drew's willingness to reenact material necessary to support his storyline. The scenes of the electric chair are not simply photographs illustrating its existence; they are, especially in the "unhinged" section, scenes with a high emotional content, presented at a point in the story line that implies that the warden's rehearsal is the real thing, and that the execution of Paul Crump is an imminent possibility. Many serious journalists would consider the use of staged material for so important a storytelling function, without any qualifying information being supplied to the audience, to be unethical. Drew, in his efforts to create a story that would reflect the tensions and apprehensions he observed at the time, clearly would not agree.

"All films made today are made up of pictures shot at different times and different places and put together. And if I didn't get a picture of the electric chair in the exact sequence in which the film needed an electric chair, that doesn't mean 'staged.' The chair was there and we photographed a chair and it doesn't mean re-enacted. . . . You can fault me for putting it in where I did, but not for staging or recreating."[69]

The second series of editing choices that has drawn significant criticism are those involving Don Moore. Those criticisms are in two principal areas; first, that Moore was acting because of the presence of the camera and, second, that the story's emphasis on Moore detracts from the more important story of Paul Crump.

The suggestions that Moore is acting center on the point in the film where he cries in response to Archbishop Meyer's initial support for Paul Crump's case, support Moore had evidently lobbied hard for.

> One could argue that we shouldn't see drama in real life. We shouldn't see anybody cry, and we shouldn't see anybody care very much. But those particular people we did see cry and care. . . .

... You sometimes run into people who are at the end of a long battle, and you can tell that they're embattled, and you can tell that they've been affected by the battle emotionally. And I felt that I was seeing a man who'd flown maybe forty out of the fifty missions in his war. And I was surprised when he was emotionally overcome at the— when the archbishop agreed to intercede in Paul Crump's behalf. But I could empathize with it and see it, and I didn't distrust him.[70]

In this case, Drew was the field correspondent, recording sound with Leacock as Moore's "long battle" unfolded. Perhaps it is better to trust the judgment of those with immediate knowledge of a situation, at least insofar as the credibility of their performance justifies trust, than to infer judgment from afar.

The final criticisms of the story balance between Moore and Crump are ones that Drew could easily answer. "I never thought of the film as having any possibility of being just a film of Paul Crump or just a film of Don Moore. It was a film about a man trying to save another man from the electric chair in the face of a trial, so I expected to see the lawyers on both sides and the man who was the object of the thing, his jailor, and the judges, and what they said. So it was a story of characters caught up in a process."[71]

Drew, the journalist, was intent upon the broad story of an attempt to make legal history, as well as upon the personal struggles of those involved. The result was a series of editing judgments that can be disputed on both storytelling and accuracy grounds, but it was Drew's responsibility, as executive producer, to make the choices he thought best for *The Chair*, "The Living Camera," and for the system of candid television journalism he was working to develop.

19

The Critics

"There is a film world. That is, there is a film culture, with its publications and with its critics. . . . On the television side, I don't see that. There is no continuity and there is no "world"; there's stuff that appears in the paper occasionally and it's gone. So, there was somebody there to recognize what we were doing, you know, on the film side."[1]

The editors of the most important film journals—*Film Quarterly, Film Culture, Sight and Sound*, and *Cahiers du Cinema*—had begun to notice the changes taking place in the field of documentary. Drew and the fruits of his innovation would get a careful, extensive, and often sharply critical examination from these and other publications whose interest was principally in *film*—as an artistic, aesthetic, or communications exercise to be judged quite apart from commercial success or failure.

Documentary had been a subject of critical concern since John Grierson's earliest reviews of Robert Flaherty's *Moana* (1926),[2] but documentary had never competed successfully with fiction films for the bulk of critical attention, partly because there were so few documentary films made. But films that departed in significant ways from the familiar Hollywood forms occasionally received critical notice. In retrospect, some of those criticisms seem backward-looking and widely off the mark in terms of recognizing the possibilities revealed by Drew's innovations. But they were part of the process by which critics and, through them, audiences were trying to recognize and understand those innovations. Drew's efforts demanded different perceptual patterns on the part of the viewer to be fully effective; the critics, at their best, were trying to identify and foster those patterns.

"Free Cinema"

Among the forerunners of cinema verite were several short films that came to be grouped together as "Free Cinema." Funded by the British Film Institute as "experiments by young talent . . . unlikely to find sponsorship under ordinary commercial conditions," the films used the equipment and techniques of conventional fiction filmmaking in unconventional ways—to observe, rather than to create, human activities.

Nice Time (1956), which watched a Saturday night crowd in London's Picadilly Circus; *Momma Don't Allow* (1956), an evening of dancing at a jazz club; *Together* (1956), a partly observed, partly directed film of two deaf mutes at home and at work; *O Dreamland* (1953), a sardonic editing exercise contrasting amusement park attractions and attractees; and *Every Day Except Christmas* (1957), quick portraits of workers in the Covent Garden Market, share a common element: they recorded activities that were mostly naturally occurring and unrehearsed, although it is clear that the subjects knew they were being filmed and that the camera's mobility and flexibility were extremely limited. Lewis Jacobs, among other critics of the time, was intrigued, if not greatly impressed.

> [In *Momma Don't Allow*,] the camera was a casual spectator, focusing upon the passing moment and letting it speak for itself. The people—the musicians and dancers, the shy, the bold, the slummers—were pleasantly observed but there was a singular note of passivity in the treatment. . . . The result was objectivity to the point of remoteness. . . .
>
> The cold objective treatment of the characters [in *Together*] tended to oversimplify them. They appeared to be aloof, indifferent to their own dilemma. In the filmmakers' ruthless attempt to avoid any narrative or dramatic structure which might have emotionalized the incidents, the scenes became drawn out and monotonous, the tempo tedious; the sequences lacked climax, often ending abruptly.[3]

Jacobs saw Free Cinema as an interesting but minor variation on conventional feature filmmaking, as important for its independent financing as for its attempts to render reality. The openness of form—or formlessness, as some critics saw it—was troubling, and the significance of the observational capacities of the camera went largely unnoticed.

As for the makers of the Free Cinema films, none displayed any lasting interest in their semi-documentary efforts. Among them, Alain Tanner, Tony Richardson, Karel Reisz, and Lindsay Anderson went on to successful careers in fiction films, establishing in the process an acceptable route into that field: fund, direct, and manage a short film, usually a documentary, in order to prove yourself able to handle a full-scale feature production.

Pre-Verite

The work of the Free Cinema group in London got favorable treatment from critics Colin Young and A. Martin Zweiback as they reported on the fifth Robert Flaherty Film Seminar of 1958. The Flaherty Seminar had become a principal showcase for documentary films and filmmakers, establishing a tradition that has lasted to the present day. But the attention of Young and Zweiback was directed more toward other names that were to have a longer association with cinema verite: John Marshall, Robert Gardner, Michael Brault, and Jean Rouch. Marshall's *The Hunters* (1958), an anthropological study of the Kalahari Bushmen that Gardner assisted in finishing, was praised for "the scientist's method and the poet's vision."[4] Brault, who was later a principal cameraman on the germinal French *cinéma vérité* film *Chronique d'un Été (Chronicle of a Summer*, 1960), showed several films from the National Film Board of Canada. The NFBC was developing both the equipment and a filmmaking philosophy that resulted in a form of cinema verite that was parallel to the work of the two better-known practitioners, Drew and French anthropologist-filmmaker Jean Rouch.

Young and Zweiback devoted most of their attention to Rouch and his "most remarkable films." *Les Fils de l'Eau (Children of the River), Moi, Un Noir (I, A Negro*, later translated *I, A Black*, 1958), and *Les Maîtres Fous (The Mad Priests*, 1955), winner of the first prize at the Venice documentary festival in 1957, were shown and provided the basis for extended comments on Rouch's working methods, especially his use of a hand-held, spring-wound camera and the sound tracks he postrecorded with his West African subjects as they screened the footage of themselves. The critics examined "the extremely odd films" of tribal customs and activities presented in quite direct and unvarnished fashion, and noted a pending dilemma that future cinema verite filmmakers would face—and that Rouch was determined to ignore.

> Audiences seeing his films outside the somewhat rarefied and uncommonly sympathetic atmosphere of a Flaherty Seminar will often be disappointed and find his films obscure, repetitive, and poorly formed.
>
> Rouch, however, is primarily a humanitarian and in conventional terms only secondarily a filmmaker. And if the conventional expectations of film audiences or producers interfere with his work, he feels it is they who must give way, not he.[5]

Young and Zweiback concluded that "we must reconsider the traditional image of the documentary." It was an indication of the future direction of both filmmaking and criticism in the documentary field, but the critics would have to await the lead of the filmmakers.

Recognition

Callenbach, 1961

By 1961, Drew's innovations were beginning to attract the attention of "film" critics. Ernest Callenbach, editor of *Film Quarterly*, examined the early Drew films shortly after their completion. *Yanki No!*, *Primary*, and *On the Pole* found favor with him, although he was capable of sharply critical comments. "Little by little, we realize that [Eddie Sachs] is phony and a fool; and [*On the Pole*], while remaining scrupulously documentary, becomes a kind of deadpan satire on American culture."[6]

But Callenbach's most important comments are those of near-recognition of the significance of Drew's accomplishments. After describing the action in *On the Pole*, he offers this assessment:

> Thus summarized, *On the Pole* sounds like a documentary anyone might have made. What cannot be described is the casual yet powerful manner in which Leacock gets close to the driver, his fellows, and his wife. The observation is as acute as that of a fiction film or a novel. It is as if the film were entirely shot by candid cameras. . . . This is an immensely intriguing kind of break-through. For documentary as practiced in the classic manner has inevitably boggled at the impossibility of getting people to be themselves. . . . Leacock escapes all these restraints, and manages to catch the human continuity and the moments of candor, hesitation, embarrassment, revelation as they occur. This is better than all but the highest acting.[7]

"The observation is as acute as that of a fiction film"; "this is better than all but the highest acting." Callenbach had not yet fully caught the direction that Drew and cinema verite were taking; his reference points were still firmly lodged in the fiction film world. Documentary meant Ed Murrow, "bright lights . . . an imposing camera rig, and . . . lots of imposing narration." Drew's innovations were only partially recognized.

More importantly, Drew's innovations were barely recognized as his. An opening editorial note cites "Three TV films produced for Time, Inc. by Robert Drew and made by Ricky Leacock," but Callenbach's text mentions Drew not at all. Leacock was listed as filmmaker in the credits on each of the films; Drew was listed as executive producer. Drew's use of the term "filmmaker" and the critics' apparent lack of familiarity with the "producer" as the controlling force in television production may have contributed to Callenbach's misattributions. It was among the first of a long series of regretable and troublesome errors in this regard.

Marcorelles, 1962

Louis Marcorelles, a frequent contributor to the influential French magazine *Cahiers du Cinema*, toured the U.S. and Canada, lecturing and seeing films. The importance of the Drew-Leacock-Pennebaker innovations in his mind can be measured with a ruler; they received as much space as the other major point-of-interest for the touring critic—Hollywood.

Marcorelles had been alerted to the "Drew-Leacock team" when three films—*Primary*, *On the Pole*, and *Yanki No!*— were shown in a small Paris theater a year before his trip. His visit with Leacock left him impressed with the attempt "to create a new form of filmed journalism"; *Primary* and *Eddie* (more likely *On the Pole*, the earlier version of *Eddie*) "[afford] us new insight into the individual and his most private motivations."

> The revolution could be as important to the future of the cinema as Brecht and the Berliner Ensemble . . . were to the theatre. Truth no longer lies in seeming to give a "good performance," a star turn, but in seizing the individual unawares, rather as you may discover the real face of a woman in the early morning on the pillow beside you. The camera which captures people in their natural habitat, situating them exactly by means of synchronized sound and image, has made inacceptable much that used to be taken for granted.[8]

Marcorelles is attentive to the strength and the weaknesses of Leacock's method "which, at its best, presents fragments of exceptional intensity, but which rarely manages to sustain a character for any length of time." But Marcorelles is not primarily concerned with "filmed journalism"; his interest is in "helping to shatter the pseudo-realist connections of Hollywood," and he views the Drew-Leacock methods as contributing to that goal.

> The quest for absolute reality which [Leacock's] technique assumes mercilessly shows up any trickery in the scenario—or rather the subject. But sooner or later the element of "myth-making" in the films will have to be admitted for what it is—one way, among others, of creating fiction. Once it has been acknowledged that objective cinema cannot exist, the value of the Drew-Leacock methods will emerge more clearly. By bringing us closer to people, they will have shown us that there are more profound, more secret truths than either theatre

or literature knew of, and on which the cinema will be able to draw to dig still deeper.[9]

Marcorelles' observations preview a fundamental theoretical dilemma that Drew's developments in candid television journalism first allowed to be posed: how to accurately integrate recordings of real events into the theory and practice of a medium so firmly based on the use of fictional, or at least narrative, devices. Is it necessary to agree, without qualification, that "objective cinema cannot exist"? Does the product of Drew's innovation "have to be admitted," in Marcorelles's words, "for what it is—one way . . . of creating fiction?" Is the presumption in favor of narrative formulations unchallengeable? These questions, in many variations, continue to arise, and to go incompletely answered, to the present day. What is significant is that until Drew had acted, these questions could not even be realistically raised, let alone addressed. Drew's efforts had fundamentally changed both the practice and theory of film—documentary primarily, but the fiction film as well—and the questions and challenges he presented were not to be settled satisfactorily in the short term, if ever.

Lyon, France, 1963

In the winter of 1963, Radio Television Française sponsored *Marche International des Programmes et Equipements de Television*, a three-day conference in Lyon "to discuss the technical and moral questions arising from this new method," cinema verite. The conference also produced the first formal confrontation between two ideologically separate forms of documentary that have, unfortunately, been indiscriminately lumped together as cinema verite: the more-accurately described *"cinéma vérité"* of Rouch and the "direct cinema" or "candid television journalism" of Drew.[10]

Cameron and Shivas

Ian Cameron and Mark Shivas were first into print with a report on the conference, interviews with important participants, and evaluations of the new methods.

> The new equipment filled such an obvious need that it is surprising that it was not developed earlier. You can now film actuality without "arranging" anything. What you film and record may be the "true" situation. But by the montage of the "true" raw material, you can do any number of things: two differently edited sequences of the "true" material may produce utterly different results, and both results may appear to be true. Among some of the technicians at Lyon a blinkered approach to the new possibilities was evident, the result of an inadequate appraisal of their medium: because they could now record actual

events and sounds, they believed that anything else, including any sort of rehearsal or post-synchronization, was immoral and unworthy of a showing at a conference on Cinema-Verite. If the material was not spontaneous, they said, how could it be true?[11]

Shivas reviews briefly the films of Leacock and Drew, describing their methods, and noting, as Drew and his associates had begun to realize, that "if there is no ready-made dramatic structure . . . this kind of reportage may find itself in trouble." He then turns to "a totally different type of filmmaking" that was developed by ethnographer Jean Rouch: where Drew inquires by watching, Rouch inquires by interviewing.

> For Rouch the camera [in *Chronique d'un Été*] acts as a catalyst, bringing out hidden emotions, encouraging frank discussion. By considering [the subjects] important enough to be filmed, by giving them an outlet for their emotions, he makes them aware of themselves, begin to consider their daily lives, their attitudes to their surroundings. What occurs as a result of the camera's presence is more important to him than what happens in front of the camera.[12]

But the central focus of Shivas's report is not on the improved means of recording uncontrolled human activity that had been presented to the conference but on how these new means can be adapted to more traditional ends. Shivas targets his strongest critical praise on a feature film, Jacques Rozier's *Adieu Philippine*, "the Nouvelle Vague's finest achievement to date."

> [Rozier] uses many of the methods used by other exponents of Cinema-Verite; like Rouch he sets a pattern for his characters to follow, but here it is entirely fictional. Like Leacock's camera, Rozier's seems to be accepted unself-consciously and to be neither controlling the action or making a comment on the characters. The natural performances and settings, and Rozier's use of music to stress the symbolic and lyrical passages, produce a feeling of reality stronger than many of the murky, awkwardly-focused reportages shown at Lyon. His improvisation produces a result as "true" as anything springing from directly recorded life.[13]

Shivas and Cameron drew no conclusions about the range of films presented at Lyon, although they appeared to see cinema verite as a sidelight to the principal concern of the "film world," the feature film. "Reportage" was not highly regarded, and television was not mentioned.

Marcorelles

Louis Marcorelles, writing of the same conference, places the films in a somewhat broader context, recognizing "the major role played by television in the evolution of new cinematic techniques, and television's own failure to draw the kind of aesthetic conclusions which these techniques lead to."[14] He has both praise and criticism for cinema verite, but his commitment to the forms he is more familiar with is plain.

"When this search for truth admits the need for subjectivity, when the fiction film recaptures its rights over this territory, taking from cinema verite its directness, its ability to involve us with people on its special level of intimacy, then, one feels, the mission of this innovatory cinema will have been accomplished."[15]

Marcorelles' criticisms range from those that Drew and his associates were familiar with from their own internal discussions—"how far the simpler human truths [in *The Chair*] have been sacrificed in the editing to the more facetious elements of Hollywood-style suspense"—to some criticisms that Drew would dismiss as examples of the "word-logic" he was working to avoid—"there is no suggestion in [*Jane*] of any criticism of that whole great myth of American show business." Marcorelles also notes one of the important differences between the "cinema of immediacy" as practiced by Leacock and as practiced by Rouch. "The evident hostility between their points of view suggested not merely an incompatibility between two different ways of looking at things, but even in a sense between two rival forms of civilization, the French and the Anglo-Saxon."[16]

And Marcorelles is the first to focus on an increasingly troublesome factor in the more enduring critical articles on cinema verite: the question of accuracy in crediting responsibility and achievement in the films of Drew Associates.

> One ought to note, too, the essential part played by Robert Drew in the final editing of these films; the ultimate decisions and responsibilities are his. Some Sherlock Holmes of film criticism may one day be able to elucidate the different parts played in the partnership by Robert Drew, one-time reporter for *Life*, and Richard Leacock, the passionate cineaste. And his starting-point might be that Drew always talks of their work as screen journalism while Leacock never uses the term.[17]

Three Views, 1964

In 1964, *Film Quarterly* presented "Three Views on Cinema-Verite," the most comprehensive critical summing-up of the work of Drew and his associates and other principal filmmakers working in cinema verite. It was the best analytical examination of cinema verite, as it was then understood, to appear. All of the Drew films involving Leacock, Pennebaker, and Shuker had been completed; the related efforts of the Maysles brothers,

Rouch, Chris Marker, and Mario Ruspoli were available for consideration; and the concept of cinema verite had not yet been broadened and complicated by the films of Frederick Wiseman, the ethnographers (Napoleon Chagnon and Timothy Asch, Hillary Harris, and David and Judith MacDougall), and the advocates (Julia Reichert and James Klein, Barbara Kopple and Hart Perry, and Michael Rubbo[18]). It was an optimal point in time to consider the initial development of cinema verite in America, and the issues of accuracy, storytelling, objectivity, and truth.

Young

> In attempting to get at the *truth* of a situation, the preconceived script is disallowed, the filmmaker does not *direct* (in the sense of controlling what is in front of the camera), and the editing process is faithful to the actual event—its continuity, its relationships, its entire character. No one, I maintain, really expects to find such a thing as the "objective statement," although some of the new documentary filmmakers sometimes permit themselves to talk as if that's what their films were concerned with. . . .
>
> This, then, could more accurately be called the cinema of common sense, the naturalist cinema—Louis Marcorelles prefers "direct cinema," Drew Associates have dubbed their program "The Living Camera." It can readily be distinguished from the conventional cinema which deals, and revels, in contrivance—the immaculate control which a filmmaker can exercise on his material so as to present to an audience his very personal vision of it.[19]

Colin Young, in "Cinema of Common Sense," provides this succinct description that moves criticism beyond the technical advantages of the new light cameras to the substance of the cinema verite approach—the way in which the filmmaker records, and later presents, his or her subject.

> In editing [*Nehru*], Leacock has said they found themselves without any dramatic material, without the usual elements of narrative conflict. They had just faithfully followed and recorded the work of an extraordinary man over a short period. But in looking for some thread to tie together the various parts they concluded that the key was in the promise they had made to Nehru—a promise they had, in the end, broken. . . . They keep pointing to this sequence, building it up, and then finishing the film with it. Unfortunately it is a complete fizzle. . . .
>
> These errors of judgment are a holdover from the conservative classical drama. They ought to be totally unnecessary. It ought to be enough to spend fifteen days with Nehru . . ., so long as the filmmaker

is telling us something we did not know before, and probably could not know very readily by any other means.[20]

Young's criticism provides an interesting point to ponder: Drew's innovative field materials are combined, in *Nehru*, into a story that is seen as "conservative classical drama". The growing tension between innovation and convention, between the ability to generate never-before-seen raw materials and the presumed need to shape those materials to meet the expectations of the audience, was a dilemma that was not to be fully resolved by Drew, nor by any of the others who were to follow his lead.

Young's work is primarily directed toward suggesting that critics must adopt a more open and tolerant attitude toward cinema verite as a new form, rather than applying the standards developed for older, fictional forms: "The cinema has moved forward. The critics want to hold it back. . . . The idealist critics should not run away when they meet an empirical filmmaker. He is neither obscene nor dangerous. He is merely exploring a part of the cinema—the part [Siegfried] Kracauer claimed (falsely) is the whole."[21]

Graham

"*Cinéma Vérité* in France," is primarily concerned with the meaning of "cinema verite," not only in the definitional sense but also at the operational and critical levels. Peter Graham points out that the phrase is derived from Dziga-Vertov's term, "kino-pravda," and was "dug out" for use in the publicity for Rouch's *Chronique d'un Été*.

But Graham is most concerned with objectivity and honesty: "the film-maker cannot be objective and must mould reality according to his personal beliefs." It was an early statement in the long and inconclusive controversy over "objectivity" that has dogged critical discussion of cinema verite for over thirty years. Graham correctly identifies the source of the "objectivity" dilemma: the high level of authenticity that film has with audiences. He is on guard against any claims of "objectivity"; film's "reality" is only a means to the filmmaker's ends.

"If film is an art, its purpose is not merely to record, but to select, organize, and alchemize what is recorded. . . . Although the camera can be absolutely true to an event in its external manifestation (actions, words, gestures) it can never, alone, be true to the meaning of that event, which is always dependent upon the selection and arrangement of the context."[22]

Graham's criticisms reflect his personal reactions to the films he examines, somewhat at odds with Young's broader concern with the progress of documentary criticism. He dislikes Rouch: "none of [his] films reaches a higher level than interesting experimentation." And he finds in Drew-Leacock, the Maysles brothers, and Chris Marker—three quite dissimilar approaches to "objectivity"—"the two essential qualities of the good cinema verite . . . film, artistic honesty and the courage of one's convictions." Graham's criticisms may be idiosyncratic, but he is clear about his main point: "Marker, the Maysles, and Drew and Leacock . . . present not *the* truth, but *their* truth. The term 'cinema verite,' by postulating some absolute truth, is only a monumental red herring. The sooner it is buried and forgotten, the better."[23]

Breitrose

Henry Breitrose, in "On the Search for the Real Nitty-Gritty: Problems and Possibilities in *Cinéma-Vérité*," deals almost exclusively with the Drew films. In *Nehru*, "nothing happens." *On the Pole* "tell[s] us more about . . . Eddie Sachs than he can verbalize; . . . his actions are more eloquent than his verbal statements." A segment of *David* "screams to the audience 'Isn't this poetic and moving!'" In *Mooney vs. Fowle*, "The 'Living Camera' technique becomes doubly complex, doubly promising, and doubly disappointing" because "the parallelism [between the two coaches] doesn't really work."[24]

The criticisms are as valid as any, perhaps, but they are mostly source material for the major point Breitrose makes.

> Ultimately, critical judgment about the "Living Camera" films becomes trapped into dependence on the nature of the subject. The films, generally, are as good as their subjects are interesting. But "interesting" implies only a kind of pragmatic tautology. Subjects "work" in "Living Camera" if they have within them enough structure so that the film itself takes on a natural rather than an enforced continuity, such as that of traditional dramatic conflict. The problem is really whether the subject fits the form, which is the reverse of looking at the form-content relationship from the more traditional and perhaps more sensible point of view of fitting the treatment to the subject.[25]

Breitrose's final concern is to offer a caution to those, both critics and filmmakers, whose fullness of understanding of cinema verite—or candid television journalism—is less than their enthusiasm for what is newest in film technique.

> What seems to have happened is that important technological advances in filmmaking have become, for some, a magic key to the truth of the world. All of the nonsense about the filmmaker, armed with camera and recorder, being able to . . . find the real nature of

the world appears to be a suitably elaborate rationale for the fact that some of the films made in this style cannot do justice to their subjects. Objectivity, in film, remains as big a myth as it ever was. An enormously promising way of treating certain kinds of subjects, i.e., those with strong internal structure, in which optimal spontaneity can reveal meaning hitherto inaccessible, is well on its way to becoming a mystique of technological existentialism with appropriate overtones of Zen nonpreconception.[26]

Reactions

The cinema verite filmmaker is a special kind of film journalist who is trying to record what really happens more truly than a reporter taking notes. He turns the camera on because he thinks something important or beautiful, sad or funny is happening before him and he wants to share that vision with the viewer. If there is a story, it is not one he created, but rather one that he placed himself in the way of watching, a real-life drama.

None of this means that the filmmaker necessarily forfeits his point of view, and most of this talk about objectivity is beside the point. Probably no cinema verite filmmakers including the Maysles, think that they are totally objective, and those critics who enjoy blasting at the impossibility of complete objectivity are bravely destroying strawmen.[27]

James Lipscomb, one of Drew's associates, responded to the "Three Views of *Cinéma-Vérité*" expressed by Young, Graham, and Breitrose in one of the very few formal responses Drew Associates made to the critics. Lipscomb corrects some factual errors regarding *Susan Starr* and *Mooney vs. Fowle* and makes an attempt to address the problem of misattribution of the "Drew-Leacock" films, a situation "probably more embarrassing to Ricky Leacock than to anyone else."

Robert Drew founded the Company [Drew Associates] and its films carry the name of the Company. Leacock has been a photographer, editor and producer on some (not all) of the films as a part of a team. . . . Leacock is a great talent and friend and deserves recognition, but in fairness to others involved, the following facts should be noted.

Of the ten films co-produced by Drew Associates and Time, Inc., Donald Pennebaker . . . was principal cameraman on more of the films than Leacock. Gregory Shuker was producer on more of the films than Leacock and others edited larger portions than he. . . .

All but two of these films were produced by teams headed by

filmmakers other than Leacock. Leacock's contribution was important . . . but these films are not in any sense "Drew-Leacock" films.[28]

LEACOCK: I don't know how that happened. It's very hard, once these
things happen, to undo them. I've probably had more of the films
attributed to me than anybody else, films I've never had anything to
do with. . . .
It's very hard to get it unattributed.[29]

Drew, at the time, was unconcerned about the crediting of his organization's work by "film" reviewers.

To me it was all grist for the mill and good for the project. In later
years, when people begin to treat that stuff as history, then it bothered
me because that wasn't the way it was, but . . . it didn't bother me
at all then. I was trying to promote . . . our revolution any way I
could. And strengthen any individual in the organization any way I
could. . . . When it did bother me was years later, when I saw books
being—history being written in a cockeyed manner.[30]

The misattributions continue to exist in "the literature"; the corrections
by Drew's associates and other critics have never managed to catch up with
the initial errors. It remains a problem for later readers, but it was not an
immediate concern of Drew's; in fact, he cannot recall having seen any of
the significant articles. But he can recall, forcefully, his reactions to the
French version of *cinéma vérité*.

DREW: I considered that they were absolutely in the Dark Ages. I mean,
it was Jean Rouch who would walk up to people in the street with a
microphone and ask them provoking questions, and people considered
that that was in the same league with what we were doing. . . .
We were trying to show things as they happened. They were out
there provoking things and being artists, and doing other things,
but—*Chronique d'un Été* was a directed film. It was a very good
rendition of life in the provinces. But it wasn't really real—it was
directed real.[31]
LEACOCK: It was in France that you got the discussions; . . . just
incredible levels of intellectual interest in what was happening. Some
violently disagreeing, some hating it, some loving it. But at least they
reacted! I mean, here, nobody'd give a hoot in hell. You go to NBC;
they never heard of us! Couldn't care less. And with the exception of
a couple of remarkable people at ABC.
But no intellectual furor here. It's an irony to me! We could *do* it
here, but nobody was particularly interested, in a sense. In France,
they couldn't do it, but they were tremendously interested.[32]
SHUKER: Historically, the phrase "*cinéma vérité*," which is French,

came out of a tradition in France of basically talking-heads. . . . where you just had people staring right at the camera, or slightly off the lens, talking to the interviewer, whoever it was and the interviewer was cut out [in editing]. And the idea was that you were getting at the "truth" by these long, probing interviews. And the people's response was all that mattered. . . .

And I've always thought, in an affectionate way, how French that is: a people so in love with their language and their logic . . . that the ultimate action, in a funny way, in French context, is talking. And therefore that was an effort at getting at "the truth." The "verite" was words. Logic happening right in front of your face; you know, you the viewer seeing it happen in another person's face, watching a mind open up and grope and so forth.

Now that's French.[33]

The views of serious critics, American and foreign, meant little to Drew and his associates, in the short-run. And if they had continued to produce innovations and breakthroughs, the early criticisms would have been superceded in the longer run. But as the pace of innovation slowed and the problems facing the developers of cinema verite became less technological and more presentational, as the internal makeup of Drew Associates changed, and as the number of significant players and workable production strategies in the documentary field increased, these early critical evaluations became the principal ones. They are segments of "the literature" that are regarded not so much as fragmentary records of the development of cinema verite but as the final critical summary on a documentary philosophy now accessible only though these records. The resulting effects of these criticisms for Pennebaker, Leacock, Drew, and others—and for the long-term viability of the concept of cinema verite, or candid television journalism—have likely been greater than anyone at the time realized.

20

Drew Associates, 3

The idea was to do a series of personal dramas, . . . and it was to be a discrete series which would go on the air, broadcast one a week or in some succession. The hope was that [if] we could put, say, a dozen of these on the air in succession, we might change some of the ground rules on which journalism was viewed and produced. And the idea was that they would go on the air on a network, nationally broadcast to the big audience. And I still believe that if that had happened, that they might have had something of the impact that we imagined or envisioned. But that didn't happen.[1]

The core element of Drew's dream didn't happen. The hoped-for test of candid television journalism as an integrated series of network programs, broadcast in a regular pattern, with full promotion and publicity support, the test that would educate the audience and revolutionize the practice of television journalism, never came off. Time, Inc. had, after the initial falling-out with ABC in 1961, ordered two million dollars in new productions without any network contract for the series.

"It was [Wes] Pullen's decision to make the order. But . . . if you are involved in a disaster you can't disassociate yourself from it, and I could see one coming two years before it actually became that. You simply cannot make two million dollars worth of films and not have any place to show them."[2]

Drew and his associates had labored long and hard and had grown to eighty-plus people. Some films were critical successes, some were complicated and uncertain, almost all were interesting and important early experiments in cinema verite. But they were not seen, except in syndication, at odd times in odd places, unpublicized and mostly ignored.

Critically, the films were winning all kinds of awards and so forth. Breaking new ground. But the reason we made them was to try to establish a form of reporting which would pull audiences and pay for itself. So when Time, Inc. failed to sell them and the contract went out, then that was the death of that idea—of trying that idea out. And the films were left—God, they were left to half-assed syndication and half-assed promotion and it was a kind of a massacre.[3]

Without an outlet on a major network, the Drew productions, packaged as "The Living Camera," were syndicated to the Time-Life and RKO-General stations, among others. And in the labyrinthian accounting systems of Time-Life Broadcasting, the films actually made back their costs over a period of years. But a ledger balance was not what Drew, or candid television journalism, needed. Drew was searching for another breakthrough great enough to shake the foundations of his profession. The earlier breakthroughs—*Primary*, the equipment developments, *On the Pole*, the discovery of how to "see into" a subject, *Yanki No!*, the recognition of the importance of "the story," *The Chair*—all had been the result of enormous mental, physical, and institutional exertions, and had not been sufficient. What Drew was lacking was the hardest type of breakthrough—commercial success.

PENNEBAKER: In order to put the money together to finance Drew's operation, it was done through the side of the magazine [Time-Life Broadcasting] which was their investment [side]. So, in a way, it had to really succeed. . . .
    . . . They were taking money out of the magazine and reinvesting it in Bolivian tin mines and oil wells and buildings in Geneva and in various enterprises. So it was looked on as heavy investment money, and [Drew Associates] was kind of looked on as an investment, and they wanted it to pay back fast. Have it pay back in real money.
    And on the face of that, Drew's problem was that—what he hadn't faced was that television companies were not really too sympathetic to this. They didn't want to be making money for Time-Life. They wanted to make money for themselves.
    And the only thing that you could ever dangle in front of them was the name, *Life* magazine, maybe and some of the editorial input. But *Life* wasn't interested in putting in editorial input.
    And it became clear to me because, in fact, we were outside. . . .
    None of the [investment] people were really coming into it, nor [were they] interested in it.[4]
SHUKER: On a journalistic level . . . there were two patrons; one was Andrew Heiskell, who was the publisher of *Life* when this thing started and then he became chairman of Time, Inc., I think chairman of the board. But Heiskell was a journalist, he was science editor at

Life before he [moved to] the business side. . . . Heiskell understood it, and was the champion of it. And a man named Roy Larsen, who was a real elder statesman of that company, . . . he came up through the business side. But both Heiskell and Larsen were great believers in this because they saw it as a journalistic breakthrough. . . . But I think Heiskell was probably the first person to understand . . . the changing nature of the television marketplace, and Heiskell was probably the guy, in the end, who pulled the plug. And as a person who suffered from the plug being pulled, I certainly would never, ever, criticize Heiskell because that was his job as chairman, and a sensitive man, and I have great regard for him, great respect for him. . . .

But I think that Time, Inc. probably gave the company a fair shot, and good support, and when it was over, it was over.[5]

Time, Inc. did not renew its production contract with Drew Associates, and the lack of a strong prospect for commercial success was a fundamental reason. Drew's motivations and those of his principal associates, which propelled and sustained them in their sometimes uncertain developmental efforts, were highly personal. But as is often the case, personal goals and motivations had to make way for institutional realities.

PENNEBAKER: My sense of Drew was that he was a frustrated playwright. Maybe a writer, but I think more a playwright. Who was always fascinated by the power that playwrights had over audiences. . . . I don't think he wanted to write "plays," in the old stylized sense of what we think of as plays, but it was the writing-type quality—it was the putting together and the construction of scenes that have dramatic intensity and have confrontation with character and, you know, this kind of thing, that really appealed to him. And I think he got caught up in what Ricky and I were doing. . . .

I think that was where the struggle was, you know, in Drew himself. He had a real problem in trying to satisfy what he knew he was on the hook for, for *Life*; *Life* didn't care about "plays." It cared about getting their six- or two-million dollars, or whatever he'd taken, back. I think he was interested in both things. And they were incompatible. . . .

Which is why I say, we felt sympathetic for Bob, but I never wanted to trade places with him![6]

LEACOCK: Penny and I quit. We didn't want to go to ABC and shoot news. We were faced by a terrible dilemma.

Bob sent me—and I don't know why, I'll never understand, me, with my attitude toward money—he sent me to Canada, to the National Film Board, to do a study—cost accounting—about what it would mean . . . to do twelve a year, 23 a year, 24, whatever it is, and what it would mean in terms of money. . . .

And I know that Pennebaker and I got *terribly* depressed at the idea of doing this, because more and more they were bringing in professional editors; we were best at shooting, it was easier to find editors, supposedly, than shooting people, supposedly. More and more, we were becoming like *Life* photographers; just story, story, story. That didn't seem like a helluva lot of fun.[7]

Even before the end of the Time, Inc. contract, the initial configuration of Drew Associates was beginning to come unstuck. The differing viewpoints of managing editor and subordinates, and perhaps more importantly, of cameraman-observers and correspondent-producers, had always been sources of tension. Initially, the tension may have been creative, helping to generate the flexibility and adaptability needed to develop a new mode of journalistic inquiry and presentation. But tension prolonged, as modes of operation became more structured and less intuitive, could be abrasive, or destructive. The necessary settling of a developmental organization into the more practical and manageable routines of a production organization inevitably changed the emotional climate that had prevailed earlier.

But Pennebaker and Leacock did not leave Drew Associates immediately at the end of the Time, Inc. contract. They may have decided that they would not follow Drew into shooting news documentaries for ABC—one possibility—but they were still there as the organization wound down: "What we did was close down production and lay off everybody. That is, lay off large chunks of our staff. Keep the key dozen or so associates together while we went out to sell—to find a new sponsor."

And in the flurry of activity that accompanied the end of the Time, Inc. relationship, there germinated the final project in which Drew, Shuker, Leacock, and Pennebaker collaborated as Drew Associates. Born in the crisis atmosphere of that period, it became the most journalistically daring, the most intellectually difficult, and the most heavily criticized of all their efforts.

"It was touch and go. We didn't know. We had our agreement with Time, Inc. that called for certain payments to us for a few months after any termination, so we lived on that until that ran out. And at that point, honestly, within a day of that running out, ABC picked up *Crisis*."[8]

21

The Crisis

"Tom Moore [vice-president for programming] called to say that ABC would like to buy the program. That was nice because we had just run out of money and I was about to call back our teams, call off the film, and in fact, call off the company."[1]

Without the financial backing of Time, Inc., Drew Associates faced a very bleak if not impossible future. But in the midst of internal crisis—the possible dissolution of Drew Associates—an opportunity appeared that led to the production of the most significant, if not the most critically successful, of Drew's films. It came about largely because of the long-range planning and vision of Robert Drew, the talents of his associates, and a measure of luck. It would result in a one-of-a-kind, impossible-to-do-again film that would demonstrate the possibilities inherent in Drew's approach to candid television journalism. It would also issue a dramatic professional challenge to the then-prevalent reporting methods of television network journalism. The crisis within Drew Associates, financial and attitudinal, helped stimulate the development of *Crisis: Behind a Presidential Commitment*, and resulted in a significant crisis for candid television journalism.

Nurturing a Crisis

As recalled by Drew and his associates, the story of *Crisis* is a story of both good luck and good planning. It is a series of circumstances that could not have been accurately predicted, but which were broadly anticipated. In fact, the real groundwork for *Crisis* had been done two and three years earlier in Wisconsin, Africa, West Virginia, and Washington.

168

SHUKER: When Kennedy was elected, I know that Bob talked to Pierre Salinger at some length about the subject of this Presidency being documented from the inside, as best it could be, in a way that had never been done before. . . .

Adventures on the New Frontier was an effort, I think, to show good faith, in a way; that that film set out to record some aspect of foreign policy stuff, in Africa, and there was an Appalachian ingredient, and the inauguration itself. . . . By the time the *Crisis* film was in the planning stage, it was almost like a parallel development. I mean, Bob Drew had never stopped talking with Pierre, at least, I know, over the two years interim between those two films.[2]

Drew's contacts with Salinger included calling and visiting the press secretary several times to suggest potential crises that seemed suitable; "Too tender" was the reply that continued to come back. "The problem with the subjects I was interested in is that they were international." Drew would have to be patient until an appropriate domestic crisis occured.

SHUKER: How it came about was [that] in the fall of 1962 there had been, in the [United States] government, two crises in a row: One was the Cuban missile crisis and the other was the University of Mississippi—with James Meredith—integration crisis, where there was a death, or a couple, you know. And the White House had set up a thing called the ExCom—Executive Committee—which included the President and his brother, the Attorney General, and so forth. And at the time, the [U.S. Information Agency] was represented on that with [Edward R.] Murrow. But Murrow, unfortunately, was dying of cancer; so his deputy, Don Wilson, who had been the *Life* bureau chief in Washington, . . . was, basically, on the inner circles of government.

And I remember, after those two particular crises had ended, in the very early months of '63, talking with Don Wilson in the Time-Life Building, where he often appeared, since he was on loan to the government from Time, Inc., saying "My God, the next time something like that happens, it would be wonderful if you guys were in there, because we should have a record of how a crisis gets handled."[3]

Drew's efforts to lay the groundwork, to develop the contacts and the trust that would be necessary, were about to pay off. When the moment came Drew and his associates were ready.

SHUKER: [In early 1963] there was a story in the [New York] *Times* saying that two black students were going to integrate the University of Alabama, and they had decided to do it in the summer session, in order to keep the crowds sort of at a minimum, and to try to avoid another Mississippi. And that Gov. George Wallace, who was then relatively newly-elected, was gonna stand in the door and keep them out. And that the Justice Department was equally determined to get them in, but without any bloodshed. I thought. "This is IT! This is what we've been waiting for!"[4]

DREW: I told Salinger it was time to get our team in to the President, and he agreed. . . . This is what we were looking forward to from before [Kennedy] took office.[5]

SHUKER: And I had [an] approach, which was through Don Wilson, who was a great buddy of Bob Kennedy's—I said, "Listen, he's gonna be the key guy here. He's the Attorney General. And we have just finished a film about a fighting young lawyer, called *The Chair*. And let me show *The Chair* to Robert Kennedy. And tell him that this is what we want to do. Let me appeal to him as the fighting young lawyer!" Meaning [Don Moore] in *The Chair*.

So Don Wilson set up a screening down in the USIA screening room, and I went down with that film, and showed it to Bob Kennedy. And he asked to keep the print, and over the weekend he took it to the White House and showed it to the President. And they loved it![6]

As a result of the weekend screening, and against the background of familiarity with Drew, his associates, and their methods, the Kennedy brothers were convinced. And with that commitment, the remaining actors in the upcoming drama could be approached. Shuker recalls that "Jim Lipscomb went off to Montgomery, Alabama, and confronted Wallace and got the permission, cause 'Goddammit!' says Wallace, 'I'm not gonna let the Kennedys get away with that.' Meanwhile, Hope Ryden had gone off to talk to the NAACP legal fund, which was kind of shepherding the black kids."[7]

Leacock was later assigned to Deputy Attorney General Nicholas Katzenbach, Robert Kennedy's principal aide in Alabama, as an historic confrontation between the power of the federal government and the state's rights of Alabama—between traditional racial patterns and the coming of change, between Wallace and the Kennedys—began to coalesce. But with opportunity came risk, and Drew Associates, without the backing of Time, Inc., was in a decidedly uncomfortable financial position.

SHUKER: We had this remarkable movie that we were about to shoot and could not sell it going in, up front; the networks didn't want to touch it. And so—I remember this quite vividly—we took, from Time, Inc., . . . what amounted to, as I remember it, like the last two months of the rent money, July and August rent money, and other overhead money—the phone and so forth—and physically put that money into buying raw stock and processing it. Gambling that we could sell that film after it was shot.[8]

Pennebaker and Shuker were the first team out in the field, gingerly testing the access they had been promised. Almost immediately, Shuker sensed that "we were getting awfully close," and that the opportunity to cover presidential decision-making in the midst of genuine crisis was a very real one. "Bob Kennedy was easy, in the sense that nobody had ever done anything like this with him, unlike his brother, and I think he was—I think he enjoyed it. . . . He enjoyed being the center of attention. The President made it very obvious that he *wanted* his brother to be the main center of attention in this, because he wanted the emphasis on this whole thing to shift off the White House onto the Justice Department."[9]

The atmosphere at the Justice Department was relaxed—Shuker and Pennebaker played touch football with Robert Kennedy and his staff on the lawn along Constitution Avenue: "What you're supposed to do with the Kennedys, right?!"—but the issue was important, and the stakes high.

> SHUKER: Basically, here was this crisis coming up; the President was pretty well decided to use it as a vehicle to launch a—to take off from and make a major policy speech about civil rights, as a moral issue. . . . And at the time, there was some major civil rights legislation up on [Capital] Hill [in] different places, in different committees, in the House and the Senate. . . . Everett Dirksen, who was this big, heavy, Republican senator at the time, was obviously in the opposition party, and Lyndon Johnson, who was the vice-president, and a Southerner, was in the position of having to very delicately steer this legislation around up there on the Hill.
> So what was basically being talked about had to do with how far could they go, making a—one, a strong speech, and two, a strong presence on the day the kids walked in [to the University of Alabama]. How would that effect the legislation up on Capital Hill. And they were very sensitive about Everett Dirksen being able to cause trouble if they didn't, you know, treat that delicately. And that Lyndon Johnson was very much opposed to anything; he wanted to keep the whole thing as down as possible, including not making a speech.[10]

The stakes, and risks—political, moral, and historic—were high, and rising, as the date for the "Negro" students to enroll at the University of Alabama grew nearer. The Kennedy brothers did not want a repeat of the rioting and deaths that had accompanied James Meredith's enrollment at the University of Mississippi the preceding fall. So, as the jockeying for political and publicity position continued between Governor Wallace and the Kennedys, a series of key decisions were being considered: would the enrollment of the students be carried out as planned, and how; would Governor Wallace's threat to "stand in the school-house door" be handled with force, forebearance, or evasion; would the Alabama National Guard be placed under federal control, and in what strength and what reasons would be given? The time for decisions was drawing closer, and while those decisions would eventually be made by only one man, the President of the United States, he would first hear the counsel of his chief advisors, in meetings in the Oval Office of the White House. If cinema verite were to show the real process of decisionmaking in any significant way, those meetings would be vital.

> PENNEBAKER: We couldn't get in at first. We went to [President Kennedy's press secretary] Pierre [Salinger] and Pierre had said that . . . he would arrange it and to call him up if we had any trouble. Then he disappeared. Couldn't get him. . . . Greg and I went to Bobby and said, we can't get in. And . . . he kind of smiled, and he obviously knew more than we knew. And we told him I'd called Pierre and couldn't get him, and whoever it was had given express orders we weren't to be allowed in. There was no mistake, they said. "We don't want Pennebaker in the White House shooting." We didn't know who did it, but [Bobby] did.
>
> So he took us over in the limo and let us off at the back door. So we were in the office, and I remember I was sitting in the—and when we came in, [President] Kennedy remembered me because I'd spent a week filming there the year before [on *Adventures on the New Frontier*] . . . and then I also had met him on *Primary*, so he kind of remembered who I was.
>
> He had a big smile on his face, and he sat down and he told a joke, you know, and I kept looking around and seeing, you know, it seemed peculiar to me that he was making this big effort just on our behalf.
>
> And in walks [presidential advisor Theodore] Sorenson, and Sorenson's jaw practically fell off when he saw us there. And I realized Sorenson was the one who was keeping us out. And I hadn't realized till then. And Sorenson looked at me like bullets. I'm telling you, I was really getting nervous.
>
> And Kennedy was watching it all and kind of smiling, you know, so I figured, okay, this is the game, you know. I'm in here as a token filmmaker of some sort.[11]

Pennebaker faced a rare opportunity—and challenge. The men—the Kennedy brothers; Sorenson; Lawrence O'Brien; Kenneth O'Donnell; Ramsey Clark; Burke Marshall, Robert Kennedy's assistant—gathered informally in an almost-too-spacious office, talking conversationally about two widely differing strategies toward an issue of significant national consequence.[12]

> PENNEBAKER: There was Kennedy, who envisioned another Oxford, you know, in which several people had been killed; there was the question of bringing the Guard in, should they nationalize 20,000 men under General [Clayton] Abrams; and there was two different factions within the White House. The one faction was Ken O'Donnell and [Theodore Sorenson] who was his immediate assistant. . . . But the problem was that Bobby [Kennedy] and Burke [Marshall] were both determined that the President should give this speech on civil rights, and make known his position on civil rights; his feelings, his mood on civil rights. Everyone else in the White House said, "If you do that, you'll blow the whole legislation [program] coming up in the fall, because you're gonna alienate a whole lot of Southerners, who you don't need to alienate, and in the end, its the legislation that's gonna make the difference." And Bobby, I think to his credit, said, "Well, that *might* be, and that's a kind of cynical view of it, but if you don't tell people where you're at, they're not gonna know who you are." And in the end, Kennedy was persuaded to make the speech. But the process leading up to that was very hairy. . . .
>
> It was a very hard thing to film. And I was there kind of—I mean, I wasn't sure whether I was gonna get tossed out or not. But Kennedy kind of let me be there, and nobody else could throw me out! And they had to go ahead as if I weren't there.[13]

As the unfolding confrontation progressed, tensions began to grow and uncertainties became more immediate. And at the edge of decision-making, observers of internal conflicts and uncertainties, stood the documentary team of Gregory Shuker and Donn Alan Pennebaker.

> PENNEBAKER: It's an extraordinary ten minutes in the Oval Office, of those guys wandering around trying to figure out what the hell to do. I mean, they're really scared. The President sitting there trying to figure out, you know, and realizing that that group of people was split down the middle. There was Burke Marshall and Bobby Kennedy on one side and all the rest of them on the other, and any decision he made was really going to be—was going to have a big effect on those people in some way, that I didn't fully comprehend.
>
> But the pressure was tremendous and everybody was very uptight about me filming it and being there, and that the President wanted me there, I guess, but—I mean, I felt that he felt that that was— should come out of it. So I filmed that.[14]

Pennebaker's opportunity/challenge would demand the use of his entire filmmaking background and experience. He was well equipped, but the challenge of the moment for Pennebaker was to sense the mood of one man toward the process that was underway: to understand, as best he could in the tangle of motives and agendas present in the Oval Office, how John Kennedy perceived the shooting of the presidency.

> PENNEBAKER: You had this little problem, that you had to be careful when you shot, because if you started to film something that he didn't want you to film, he was going to say, don't film this. Actually, he never said that to me ever. But that was the thing waiting for you, the little lion waiting in the bush.
>
> And then, how do you start again? When do you decide that it's okay to start, because he isn't going to say, now you can start. I mean, he sort of forgets you, you know. Once he's turned you off, he's put the problem aside.[15]

> LEACOCK: [Penny] would notice that the President would keep glancing at the camera. And then he would stop. Because if he didn't, he knew that within minutes the President was going to say, "Stop." *Then* you have the problem of starting again. You have to get a Presidential permission, to start again. If he stopped before the President stopped him, then he could decide when to start again. Okay, you're going to miss a whole lot of stuff, but you've got the power to start again. It can get hairy.[16]

And if the risks in shooting a president were great, so were the rewards for success.

> PENNEBAKER: It was like going out on some type of adventure. It would be like going looking for sunken treasure. You're under tremendous pressure, you can't fuck up, everything is very hyped. You're getting things that you *know* you're getting for the first time; that is, nobody's ever done them before. So you have an extraordinary kind of feeling of climbing mountains.[17]

They were dedicated professionals, perhaps, but the uncertainties and excitement of the struggle for a story of such magnitude had marked effects on the filmmakers. Later in the shooting, as the key confrontation of state and federal forces was drawing closer, Ricky Leacock photographed the same action as Pennebaker did—at a distance of 775 miles.

> LEACOCK: I was shooting in Tuscaloosa, with Katzenbach. I hoped that Penny and Greg were with Bobby Kennedy; I had no idea then. I had no idea that somebody else was shooting on the other end of Katzenbach's phone call to Kennedy. I couldn't understand anything

that was being said. It was all "Uh Huh. Uh Huh." It wasn't until we got back to New York, sunk it up, and set up two projectors—God, we had both sides of the conversation! Whooo! That was one of the most exciting moments in our lives! Just sheer, goddamned—good reporting! [Laughter] I was gonna say "luck." [Laughter] But you know, I knew Penny wasn't out having a cup of coffee, taking a piss or something.[18]

PENNEBAKER: When we came back, we would sort of show each other bits of film that we'd gotten. It would be like the pirates coming back and throwing the jewels on the table, you know. It was that kind of feeling. A tremendous excitement of showing things that you'd got that were incredible.[19]

Robert Drew's recognition of the need for skilled personnel has seldom been better illustrated. *Crisis* has repeated cases of moments that could not be predicted or planned for, except in the most general way. Some no doubt owe as much to luck as to planning, but by investing time, money, and trust in his field personnel, Drew had shown that candid television journalism could take advantage of such opportunities as they arose, or were engineered. The result was an unimagined record of a national crisis, and a film that may be the last of its kind ever made.

The Results—Today, 1

It begins with *Dixie*, played in march tempo, with quick, clipped shots of the Alabama governor's mansion and state capital building, and the governor, George Wallace, looking alert, active, perhaps feisty. It shifts to *Dixie* played slowly, plaintively, over shots of two black students in a car, their facial expressions chosen to convey tension or uncertainty. It shifts again, to *The Battle Hymn of the Republic* in mid-tempo with shots of the Washington Monument, the Department of Justice Building, U.S. Attorney General Robert F. Kennedy looking serious, and finally to the Lincoln Memorial as the opening narration begins.

NARRATOR: Not in the 100 years since Abraham Lincoln had the power of the American presidency been completely committed to the equality of the Negro race in the United States.

Nor had it been on this day, June 10, 1963. In the next thirty hours, John F. Kennedy will have to make a chain of decisions deeply affecting millions of Americans, and the future of his own presidency. His decisions will also affect the immediate actions of four people:

—George Wallace, governor of the state of Alabama, determined to defy a federal court order by personally blocking the entrance of two Negro students to the University of Alabama;

—Robert Kennedy, Attorney General of the United States, responsible for enforcing the federal court order to gain admission of the two
students;
 —Vivian Malone and James Hood, Negro students determined to
enter the University in spite of the governor's opposition.
   Finally, a more far-reaching decision of historic consequence for
the President is whether to commit the presidency, in a speech before
the United States, and the world, behind racial equality as a moral
issue.
   This is the account of a crisis [Title-CRISIS:] and the story behind
a presidential commitment. [Title-BEHIND A PRESIDENTIAL
COMMITMENT][20]

From early morning of 10 June to John Kennedy's televised speech on
the evening of 11 June, *Crisis* switches back and forth from Birmingham
to Washington, from the White House and the Justice Department to the
University of Alabama campus at Tuscaloosa. The Kennedys, and their
efforts to implement the federal court order, are the clear center of the
film's attention; Governor Wallace and the two students are covered less
extensively, and less intimately.
   There are both serious, substantive segments and lighter, more personal
moments. Among the latter: both Robert Kennedy and George Wallace
are seen playing with their children; the two students are seen joking about
the coming confrontation. On a more serious note: Governor Wallace
telling his staff, "be sure not one rock is thrown . . . or any violence in any
manner. . . . We're not gonna let anybody desecrate the University";
the black students being briefed on how to dress and act and how the
confrontation will be managed; Robert Kennedy telling U.S. Army General
Clayton Abrams, "I'm not very much in favor of picking the governor up
and moving him. . . . It would be better if we just . . . push him aside."
   Structurally, *Crisis* pursues two main lines of action: the confrontation
in Tuscaloosa and its micro-management by Robert Kennedy and his
deputies, and the closely-related decision on whether and when to have the
President address the nation on the situation. Confrontation management
has more insightful material to offer, and gets more time and attention; in
spite of Pennebaker and Shuker's best efforts the Oval Office discussion
of a possible presidential speech is diffuse and fragmented.
   At fifty-two minutes in length, *Crisis* is a highly compressed chronicle
of "the next thirty hours" that had, in fact, been filmed over approximately
two weeks. And it succeeds best when detailing human action and interaction, "the story *behind* a presidential commitment." The historical and,
especially, political background necessary for a fuller understanding of the
events and their significance is presented in clipped, almost rudimentary,

fashion, a particularly noticeable feature when seen years later. Both the great strengths and serious weaknesses of Drew's brand of candid television journalism are present in this film.

Roughly the first half of the film is given over to setting the stage for the eventual confrontation. There are segments in which the opposing viewpoints are laid out in almost conventional television reporting fashion: Governor Wallace, being driven to his office, saying to the camera, "This is a moral issue. . . . I believe separation is good for the Negro citizen and the white citizen and in their best interest . . . it is not sinful"; Robert Kennedy, on a TV interview show, saying "President Kennedy has said we're going to do this because it is the right thing to do."

And there are less conventional segments that add an increased human dimension to the coming events, at least for those in the audience attuned to the significance of the informal materials: Robert Kennedy unable to locate an important incoming phone call in the cluster of telephones and call directors in his office; Vivian Malone being photographed for the cover of *Time* magazine; Jimmy Hood softly singing *For He's a Jolly Good Fellow* while reading a newspaper story about George Wallace; and Governor Wallace having an elderly white female visitor to the state capital shake his hand vigorously and say "I'm for you a hundred percent and a thousand percent and I always have been!" There is an ongoing series of alternating substantive and informal segments that lay out, in limited fashion, the continually developing background of the crisis.

Meeting with the President

The most important of the materials, however, is the June 10th meeting in President Kennedy's office. It is presented in two segments, of two-and-a-half minutes and five minutes, separated by eight minutes of other materials. The first segment deals with whether the President should make the television speech; the second concerns the strategies to be used in the next day's confrontation in Alabama.

The first segment from the President's meeting illustrates some of the problems Drew and his associates faced in presenting this unique material, material that, in its enactment, was diffusely structured and informally conducted, a discussion rather than a debate and one not easily condensed into a television documentary covering thirty hours, five principal characters, and two cities almost a thousand miles apart.

After some brief background by the narrator as the participants are entering the Oval Office and arranging themselves, the discussion begins.

THEODORE SORENSON: The next question that we need to take up if you want, Mr. President, is whether you're going to make a nationwide television address in connection with sending up the message.

THE PRESIDENT: I didn't think so. It just really depends on whether we have something—trouble up on the University—then I would. Otherwise, I don't think that we would, at this point.

ROBERT KENNEDY: I think it would be helpful. I think there's a reason to do it; I think you can talk about the legislation and then talk about employment, talk about education. To do it for 15 minutes, I think would alleviate a lot of problems.

THE PRESIDENT: Well, we could do it then—I don't want to do it for a half hour.

ROBERT KENNEDY: I think it would take away a lot of the problems that we're having at the present time.

LAWRENCE O'BRIEN:—helpful to the legislation.

ROBERT KENNEDY: You mean in the legislation?

O'BRIEN:—is it going to be helpful to bring about enactment of this legislation?

ROBERT KENNEDY: Yeah! Because I think you're gonna come across reasonable, and understanding, and—.

RAMSEY CLARK: You're gonna make a speech and nothing's gonna happen—.

ROBERT KENNEDY: No, but he's gonna introduce the legislation and he can say that, that we're going to have some difficulties—and then describe that we're gonna have problems this summer; we hope that the fact that we're making this kind of effort at the federal level, that Negroes would understand their responsibilities and—.

?: I don't—.

O'BRIEN:—legislation's gonna—hurt—.

?: Fine!

O'BRIEN: I think you'll get to the real nub of this thing on the Hill and that's when you may want to do this.

ROBERT KENNEDY: Well—I mean—you're gonna have—that's not gonna be till September or October or November and I don't think you can get by now without saying—having an address on television, at least during that period of time, giving some direction and having it in the hands of the President.

THE PRESIDENT: Okay, alright—anyway—well, let's pass on now. I think we see—we're gonna get something ready anyway cause we may need that tomorrow—.

ROBERT KENNEDY: We have a draft. Now it doesn't fill all these points but it's something to work with. And there's some pretty good sentences and paragraphs.

THE PRESIDENT: Alright, it'll help us get ready, anyway because we may want to do it tomorrow. Okay.

NARRATOR: The President is still undecided, but the speech will be prepared.[21]

This segment takes approximately two-and-one-half minutes in the finished film; it takes much longer to examine carefully, identify the speakers in the flow of conversation, and transcribe their often incomplete and interrupting remarks. Except for the President and his brother, the participants are not identified to the audience nor is there any attempt to indicate who is supporting which action—speech or no-speech—by the President. The picture track sometimes shows the speaker, but more often shows the President or his brother reacting to the voices of others. The Oval Office is large and obviously not designed for sound recording, and the participants, other than the President and the Attorney General, are often speaking at some distance from the microphone.

More significantly, this is a conversation, not a series of concise interview statements; the participants are communicating informally, often in a verbal and nonverbal shorthand that an outsider might never fully comprehend. The process of development of an idea or a strategy at this level of government can be important and interesting; what it cannot be is rushed. To be fully effective, the audience for such a segment has to be given time to settle in to the situation, to get comfortable with the variety of voices and the manner of exchange, to sense the flow of argument and to absorb some of the complex visual information—expressions, gestures, body positions—that accompany and both amplify and modify the bare verbal record.

But two-and-one-half minutes is not much time in which to accomplish all the necessary work of understanding. The weighing of the short-range political considerations involving the effects of a televised speech on the civil rights legislation about to be presented to a probably reluctant congress, and the long-range political-historical effects of invoking the prestige of the presidency in identifying the University of Alabama confrontation as part of a large "moral issue" of equality of civil rights for all citizens cannot be satisfactorily accomplished in so short a time. It is a dilemma faced frequently by producers of any form of reporting, and one that often cannot be resolved with complete satisfaction.

The second segment in the President's office has similar limitations of diffuseness and lack of full intelligibility, but the action being discussed is more linear: "What do we do if—?" Possible actions in Tuscaloosa and responses by the President are considered; Robert Kennedy will pursue several options and the President's actions will await his brother's preparations.

Managing the Crisis

"If you have guns . . . I'd rather not have them visible." Nicholas Katzenbach, Deputy Attorney General of the United States, in shirtsleeves and loosened tie, briefs federal marshalls in Alabama on the afternoon of 10 June. A short segment following the second Oval Office segment, it makes dramatically clear—with the aid of a slow zoom-in and soft cross-lighting on Katzenbach's face—the potential seriousness of the next day's events. Katzenbach says, "Not that I want any shooting or anything of that kind, but if you're in [an] escort of that kind you've got to take whatever force is necessary to protect the lives of those two students. They're our responsibility."[22]

Shortly afterwards, the events of 11 June begin, and *Crisis* presents its best example of the working out of an actual strategy—the managing of the confrontation. Robert Kennedy and General Abrams discuss how rapidly the Alabama National Guard can be placed under federal control and actually brought to the campus. There is a tricky timing problem involved; the President and his brother do not want to nationalize the Guard until a clear defiance of the federal court order by Governor Wallace has taken place, but they also do not want to have to wait until the next day to physically bring the Guard in because of the publicity, at home and abroad.

In a flurry of phone calls and meetings, covered by Drew's teams in Washington and Tuscaloosa, the details are hammered out. A major concern of the Justice Department's side is the public's perception of the events. Katzenbach says to Robert Kennedy: "Well, I have every indication [Wallace is] not going to step aside up there! And I have every indication he will dramatize to that group of reporters and that crowd the fact that he has been forcibly removed!"[23]

Kennedy then suggests a new plan which will allow Katzenbach to be turned back by the Governor, and then nationalize the Guard fast enough to return for a second try that same afternoon.

Katzenbach and Abrams, in Tuscaloosa, discuss the plan. Katzenbach says, "If [the students] could go to their rooms, that would be a good solution, plus that way we wouldn't have retreated and it would be perfectly obvious to every one of those newspaper people." Abrams replies, "It does seem to me that it makes it clearer, the basis for federalizing the troops." And Katzenbach concludes, "And I can simply put that on [Wallace]; I'm gonna say, 'You will not assure me at this point—,' and 'I'm requiring assurance from you at this point—,' . . . 'The ball is with you.'"

What is missing from this brief description of strategy development are the elements that Robert Drew sought to bring to the practice of television journalism—the non-verbal information that candid photography and sound recording could provide. What might appear as over-graphic and hyper-sensitive reporting in print is apparent and natural on the screen.

The plan continues to develop; it will later be carried out almost exactly as Katzenbach and Kennedy have planned.

When Katzenbach phones back to report his and General Abrams's reaction to the plan, one of the more problematic moments in the film occurs. Three of Robert Kennedy's children had been visiting their father's office. As Pennebaker in Washington and Leacock in Alabama filmed both sides of the phone conversation, four-year-old Kerry is at her father's side.

KENNEDY: Do you want to say hello to Kerry?
KATZENBACH, clearly surprised: Yeah!?
KERRY: Hi, Nick.
KATZENBACH: Hi, Kerry. How are you, dear?
KERRY: Are you at our house?
KATZENBACH: No, I'm not out at your house. I'm way down in the Southland. Way down South. And do you know what the temperature is down here? . . . Ninety-eight degrees. You tell your father that. Tell him we're all gonna get hardship pay! [aside to others in the room] It's Kerry![24]

After Kerry says "Good-bye. Good-bye. Good-bye!" with four-year-old abandon, the conversation returns easily to more serious matters. Reviewer reaction differed: one writer found it one of "many memorable intimate glimpses"; another questioned whether a moment of national crisis "was . . . propitious for presenting one's youngster before the TV cameras." That the moment was clearly unplanned, and that the filmmakers were charmed by the interchange between the child and the number-two man in the Justice Department, is evident. In any event, the segment with Kerry remained in the film, a light, human aside in the midst of an important moment in American history.

Refinements to the confrontation plan continued to be developed and carried out. A selection of significant moments from the last third of the film summarizes the flow of the action:

KENNEDY, on the phone to Katzenbach: I'd almost dismiss [Wallace] as being rather a second-rate figure for you; . . . I'd have sort of that tone of voice, don't you think?

KATZENBACH, to Gov. Wallace at the "schoolhouse door": And I've come here to ask you now for an unequivocal assurance . . . that you will step aside, peacefully, and do your constitutional duty, as governor.

WALLACE: I deem it to be my solemn obligation and duty to stand before *you*, representing the right and sovereignty of this state and its people. . . . I do hereby denounce and forbid this illegal action by the central government.

TOM PETTIT, NBC-TV reporter: Governor George Wallace of Alabama has stood in the schoolhouse door.

KENNEDY, on the phone to his brother, the President: Will you issue the proclamation [to nationalize the Alabama National Guard] now, and sign it? The executive order, yeah. Right now?

NARRATOR: The National Guard troops arrive by mid-afternoon.

PETTIT: Governor Wallace has stepped aside. . . . The second confrontation is over. . . . Governor Wallace is . . . going back to Montgomery, the state capitol, to continue a fight, . . . he says, he is winning.

KENNEDY, watching Pettit's comments on an office TV set: Ha!

PETTIT: Here come the Negroes.

KENNEDY, to his brother: But I think as soon as we could would be the best way. . . . Okay. [hangs up] He's gonna make that speech now.

PRESIDENT KENNEDY, speaking on television: We face, therefore, a moral crisis as a country and a people. It cannot be met by repressive police action. It cannot be left to increased demonstrations in the streets. It cannot be quieted by token moves or talk. It is a time to act in the Congress, in your state and local legislative body, and, above all, in all of our daily lives.

WALLACE, to supporters in his office: We had peace and we get troops. No telling what we'd get if we had a little disorder; might get the United Nations![25]

The last half of *Crisis*, detailing the management of the Alabama confrontation, is a vindication of Drew's insights and methods, as it is of Leacock and Pennebaker's shooting, Shuker and Lipscomb's work as correspondents, and Leacock's editing. The outcries of some critics who saw the film as an unprincipled TV sideshow are partially answered by the wealth of detail presented in the film. The detail provides information and understanding unavailable in any other reporting of that event: Robert Kennedy's tone and facial expression when dismissing Governor Wallace as a "second-rate figure"; Nicholas Katzenbach, tall and normally erect, bending over to bring himself more nearly to eye-level with the shorter George Wallace on the "schoolhouse" steps; Robert Kennedy's facial and verbal reaction—"Ha!"—to Wallace's reported claim that this was "a fight . . . he says, he is winning." *Crisis*, especially the second half, is rich in reportable moments and patterns of action that no reporters captured except for Drew and his associates.

Crisis is not without its limitations. It is, first of all, incomplete, as all reporting inevitably is; its principal value is as a complement to more conventional reporting, and vice-versa. Increased length would have added measurably to the level of accuracy of the report, but given the difficulties Drew had in getting even the 52-minute program shown, it is unrealistic to expect that a longer version would have been accepted. The "crisis" structure of the program can be questioned: is *Crisis* a narrative thriller of a Kennedy-Wallace confrontation, or a film providing detailed observations of high-level governmental interactions for the attentive viewer?

Crisis faced, and faces, a problem common to many cinema verite documentaries about events of great public interest and importance: can it be an insightful description of the interactions of individuals executing a complex and uncertain plan of action, or must it be more actively concerned with the broad reasons for and implications of various policy decisions in a time of national political crisis? An interesting contrast can be drawn with *On the Pole*, where there is no great concern with the outcome of the race itself; attention is focused specifically, and acceptably, on Eddie Sachs, and all other information and action is secondary. *Crisis* would have encountered even greater critical difficulties had it attempted a similar structural balance; had attention been focused more completely on Robert Kennedy, or perhaps Nicholas Katzenbach, the howls of critical protest would undoubtedly have been even louder and ABC, accepting the conventional definition of "documentary" as "word-logic"-based, might have refused the program.

In its final, edited form, *Crisis* presented its audience something new, puzzling, and difficult to interpret. Faced with such an enterprising offering, it is not unreasonable to suggest that the program's most powerful critics might have said that the program might have been better. Critics could have explored, at a professional level, how improvements might have been achieved, such as: greater length, alternative structures, and different balances between the various source materials. Unfortunately, for Drew, and for candid television journalism, that level of informed critical reaction was not to be.

The Results—1963, 1

PENNEBAKER: I was just really astonished. Astonished and depressed, because I assumed that when the people saw that, they'd say, wow, you know, that was just a changed look.[26]

LEACOCK: And the *New York Times* wrote a *blistering* editorial attack on the administration for making the Oval Room into a TV studio.[27]

SHUKER: I don't think it was cynical, I just think it was a little hypocritical. If they had had that entre and had that kind of enterprise, I think it would have been a different story.[28]

JACK GOULD, *New York Times*: [Drew's] presentation will surely stand as a prime example of governmental surrender to the ceaseless and often thoughtless demands of the entertainment world.[29]

DREW: I consider [Gould's review] a willful misrepresentation.[30]

The 21 October 1963 broadcast of *Crisis* resulted in sharply divided reviews and criticisms. But the reaction that troubled Drew and his associates the most was the editorial condemnation of their efforts, in advance of the completion or broadcast of the program, by the *New York Times*. It was an indignant public spanking by the most influential, and certainly the most often researched and cited, newspaper in the nation.

The *Times* opened the controversy in late July with a front page story, "TV Filmed Kennedys In Alabama Crisis." Reporter Val Adams described *Crisis* as "a film in which President Kennedy and Attorney General Robert F. Kennedy discuss Gov. George C. Wallace in connection with the desegregation of the University of Alabama," and pictured it as a Kennedy-Wallace confrontation. The story states that the film was "made last month in the Kennedys' offices with their permission."

[Producer Gregory] Shuker visited the Attorney General and asked permission to film him at work at the peak of the crisis.

The producer said his company had long wanted to do "an inside story" during a national crisis, one involving the President but where national security was not involved. The Attorney General approved and obtained the cooperation of the President. . . .

"It is history as it really happened, filmed from the standpoint of drama rather than a lecture," Mr. Shuker said.[31]

Adams had apparently not seen any of the film himself. Using "one source who has seen the rushes," and perhaps information from Shuker, he describes "decision-making conferences" and "the two Kennedys and their aides conferring in the President's office." He also reported that "The White House has not seen the film, now being edited in New York," and that "Mr. Shuker said . . . he would take it to Washington and screen it for the Attorney General."

Two days later, a Saturday, the editorial page of the *Times* declared that the site of governmental decision-making was "Not Macy's Window."

> It is astounding that a documentary film (for TV use) was allowed to be made last month in the offices of the President and the Attorney General while they were engaged in actual decision-making conferences on how to handle Negro registration at the University of Alabama.
>
> Under the circumstances in which this film was taken, the use of cameras could only denigrate the office of the President. How can anyone—even or especially the President—act and talk without some consciousness of the camera and the tape recorder? The process of decision-making is not the occasion for creation of an "image." The propagandistic connotations of this filming are unavoidable.
>
> The "Tour of the White House" with the First Lady was of an entirely different nature. So are TV interviews with the President or the Attorney General in their offices. But to eavesdrop on Executive decisions of serious Government matters while they are in progress is highly inappropriate. The White House isn't Macy's window.[32]

The editorial came three months before the results would be shown, but the stage was set, at least partially, by the *Times*'s initial reaction.

The as-yet-unfinished film was soon encountering serious difficulties. *Newsweek*, apparently reacting to industry rumors, wondered if the program had become "too hot to handle."

> [The opportunity to film the Kennedys] was an extraordinary scoop. . . .
>
> But as sometimes happens in the curious world of TV journalism, ABC [in late July] was acting as though it had been handed not an exclusive but a hot potato. [ABC News] Vice President James Hagerty . . . said that ABC was "interested" in the film, which is being cut, but had not "made any final decisions yet" as to whether to show it.
>
> Cause of all this caution: word of the scoop prematurely leaked out last week—before ABC had a sponsor, and before the White House itself had seen the film and offered its blessings.[33]

Drew Associates had no prior agreement for airtime and, having spent "the rent money" on raw stock and processing, was trying hard to make sure *Crisis* found a national audience. One fact that did help was finding a sponsor for the program.

SHUKER: No thanks to ABC; they weren't interested in financing it going in! [Laughter] We had to find an advertiser, through an ad agency—in this case, it was Xerox through Papert, Koenig and Lois, directly through a man named Fred Papert, who was head of that agency at the time, wonderful guy, who *really did* understand, *totally*, what we were trying to do. He was a great champion.[34]

PENNEBAKER: Pappert saw the stuff and realized that what we were doing was historical, and even though there was a lot of pressure on everybody *not* to do it, in the face of it, he sold them on it. So when I came back to New York, we had a program that was already sold; all we had to do was edit it.[35]

The first rough edit of the material was "schemed" by Shuker. Drew then took over and assigned the second half of the film to Leacock while editing the first half himself. But the publicity given the unfinished film had made Robert Kennedy increasingly wary.

SHUKER: Bob Kennedy was nervous when he screened a cut of it in New York [in late summer, 1963] that there would be some problems there because that [civil rights] legislation was still hanging. And it could offend somebody, like Dirksen or Lyndon Johnson, and therefore we made a compromise version and narrated over most of it.[36]

PENNEBAKER: They demanded that the live dialogue in the White House be taken off. Which I would *never* have given in to. Drew didn't really need to; I think he was strong enough to have told them to fuck off. Because that version—the version with the live dialogue—did play at Lincoln Center [at the New York Film Festival, in September, 1963], and it does exist, and it should *never* have been relinquished on television! With what they put over in the way of narration in the film. Which just was so—was so kind of meaningless that it destroyed that absolutely extraordinary sense of tension in that room. Which was one of the most fantastic things I've ever filmed![37]

DREW: My deal with Kennedy in the beginning was that I would shoot the film and edit it, so the film would not be presented for review in the sense that they would have anything to say about the editing. But if the President in his remarks, verbally, said anything that was thought to be compromising to the office of the Presidency, that I would be willing to obliterate the sound track, or change it. . . .

It was the deal, . . . and I think a chief of state needs some kind of an "out," and that that's a pretty good one. They can't edit the film, but if their remarks are going to get them into some kind of trouble that I can't know about, that's probably fair enough.[38]

LEACOCK: We broke some journalistic rules, too. In *Crisis*, we gave them the right to censor it, and they ultimately exercised it. . . .

. . . But the choice is: You will not allow what you do to be censored! So you're totally censored. "Get out." I don't think that's a great choice.[39]

The choice, between limited censorship in return for limited access, and no censorship resulting in no access, was, and is, a difficult one, about which journalists, critics and viewers will honestly differ. A difficulty in the case of *Crisis* is that Drew's narration does not indicate that any review by the White House has taken place and what, if any, modifications have been made; the audience has no opportunity to judge whether anything unsatsifactory has taken place.

But access to the subject was a fundamental requirement of Drew's candid television journalism; only by having the camera and recorder present could candid observations take place. To what extent that presence changed the situation being reported on, and how the information gained in spite of any changes was to be assessed and valued are still unresolved questions. Drew and his associates, who were repeatedly involved in both gaining access to a variety of subjects and in evaluating the results of that access, hold plausible views. Drew claims, "We start out with somebody and pretty soon, we're not there. There was a [point in *Crisis*] when one of the characters [Nicholas Katzenbach] wants all the press to back away so he can make a confidential phone call. He makes a confidential phone call and we're staring right down his throat, because he's learned we don't exist."[40]

But what Drew and his associates felt they understood quite clearly was questioned—sharply—by others.

JACK GOULD, *New York Times*: The staged quality of the [film] was particularly exemplified in a sequence involving Mr. Katzenbach in Alabama. With a firm display of Federal sternness, he and an aide ordered reporters and other persons away from his radio-equipped car; he must talk in private to the Attorney General—so viewers of last night's managed news film could clearly hear his words, it turned out.

If Mr. Drew promised Federal officials that he could operate discreetly without intruding on the content of the events, then he little knows the human reaction to the presence of cameras. Time after time a viewer could see for himself that the participants were conscious of the lens, which automatically raised the question of what was being done solely for the benefit of the cameras. In a moment of governmental crisis, just such a concern should not be present in the first place.[41]

LEACOCK: I hate the *New York Times*. I've never gotten a good review out of those idiots.[42]

More than the quality of the reviews was in question, however. As the program came to the air on 21 October, fundamental issues in the emerging field of television and film journalism were being debated. New capabilities, not yet fully understood or even explored, were coming into conflict with old conventions created to accommodate the strengths and weaknesses of an earlier era of reporting. The two most visible critics were Jack Gould, of the *New York Times*, and John Horn, of the *New York Herald Tribune*, each a principal television reviewer for his newspaper, and each with radically differing opinions of *Crisis*. The display of viewpoints illustrated the complexities of Drew's task of trying to introduce a revolution in the practice of television journalism. Juxtaposed with each other, the statements of Gould, Horn, Drew and his associates, form an intense and extensive colloquy on *Crisis* and on the journalistic quandaries the program presented to critics, audiences, and filmmakers.

> HORN: On June 10 and 11, there occurred a sequence of events in Alabama and Washington, D. C., which stands as a pinnacle in the American civil rights struggle. . . .
> These events were televised at the time they occurred.
> Now the personal, human story behind the public story of those eventful two days in June has been told in an unprecedented television documentary which is a milestone in film journalism.[43].
> GOULD: The White House decision to permit candid cameras in the offices of President Kennedy and Attorney General Robert F. Kennedy during last June's segregation crisis proved to be as thoroughly ill-advised as many had anticipated. . . .
> The cause of curiosity was served but not history or information. And the price paid was the appearance of the private deliberations of the executive branch of government being turned into a melodramatic peep show, with homespun family touches to lighten the tension between Federal officials and Gov. George Wallace of Alabama.[44]
> HORN: The film is candid, on-the-spot coverage of the major participants during the historic showdown between a defiant state, in the person of Gov. Wallace, and the Federal government.
> . . . [the key figures] are seen as never before—closeup and informal, the way they are out of the public eye.
> Simultaneously filming by as many as four crews has made possible a continuous multi-view narrative of these participant's actions, words and reactions.
> . . . *Crisis* is an extraordinary personal experience. In effect, a viewer is a participant in a group of events one person alone could not have experienced.[45]
> GOULD: Mr. Drew's program offered nothing new of legitimate public concern. One saw the President looking more haggard and worn than he has ever appeared on TV, but one heard only a paraphrase of [his]

conversation in the White House. The deliberations over what should be said in his speech committing the Administration to full equality of all citizens were not related.

Instead, there was primarily only a visual play-by-play account of the Attorney General and Gov. George Wallace preparing for a showdown. By concentrating on the mechanics of ousting the Governor from the doorway of the university the emphasis was on a game of strategy with the good guys winning over the bad guy.[46]

HORN: And the most remarkable aspect of the documentary is everyone's lack of consciousness of the camera and microphone, probably because the mobile equipment, easily carried by a two-man team, requires no special adjustments or lights. Evidently the documentarians became an unobtrusive part of the scenery.[47]

GOULD: When the New Frontier took office it was no particular secret that one of the strongest voices against excesses in broadcasting was that of Attorney General Robert F. Kennedy. . . .

At the same time, however, few men in public life have more keenly appreciated the importance of television in the political arena. The part played by the televised debates in the election of his brother to the Presidency spoke for itself and since taking office the New Frontier has consistently welcomed intensified TV coverage of its activities. . . .

Ironically, it was Attorney General Kennedy who walked straight into the trap, momentarily demeaning government through a careless flirtation with the entertainment business. Robert Drew, documentary producer, and the American Broadcasting Company provided the bait with the suggestion that cameras could be set up in offices and homes of the protagonists without intruding on the substance of events.

Yet the bizzare nature of the venture quickly asserted itself. For the Attorney General to tolerate cameras in the privacy of his home during the height of a national crisis itself borders on the unbelieveable. To a matter of utmost seriousness there was imparted a feeling of play-acting that seemed wholly out of place.[48]

SHUKER: Well, that's the reviewer's problem with the personality of Kennedy; I don't think that's accurate. It's kind of hard to explain the atmosphere of those days and those people. I mean, it was—[the] Kennedy family has a sense of priorities in this life. . . . Life is short, and I don't know, . . . somehow, in a funny way, making the Presidency and these big offices *so* unobtainable is like having a king or something, which is what this country is not about.[49]

DREW: I thought that when the journalists, the word journalists, saw what we had done, that they would stand up and applaud. And what happened is that they rose up in rage. Now I think we made a breakthrough and something new and wonderful, and I don't know why that would make other journalists angry. . . .

No print journalist has ever had this . . . opportunity before. No print journalist has ever sat with the President for a day or through a crisis or whatever, and listened to everything he said. . . .

And if you could talk to somebody who has done what I've done, and had my experience, who disagreed with me, then I would feel that it was something worth talking about. If you are talking to a guy who writes editorials for the *New York Times* or who reviews television shows, or even covers the President at news conferences or rewrites handouts or whatever those guys do—they've never *done* what we do.[50]

HORN: Executive producer Robert Drew, produce Gregory Shuker and their ABC News associates are discovering the hard way—is there any other?—that the path of the pioneer is a tough one.

They are the men who for some 10 years have been working on portable camera and sound equipment for television documentaries so that fixed positions and lights could be eliminated, making a TV cameraman no more obtrusive or annoying to a public figure than a photographer with still camera or a reporter with pad and pencil.[51]

GOULD: Sooner or later, it seems, mere accommodation of the reportorial TV medium gives way to a yearning to participate in the actual production of a program. And always there is the enormously human conceit of non-professionals that they can put on a TV show and still be just themselves.[52]

HORN: Why the charges? It seems here that they stem from a traditional antipathy of print to television in the area of information, a misconception about the mechanics of television (no, Virginia, a television camera is not a huge machine requiring "hot lights" or even "lights" at all), and the touchy topic of politics.[53]

DREW: See, you can't teach a person to smell a rose. And [Gould] just [was] totally hostile to the idea. I mean, if it's—if it isn't narrated and written and said by somebody, preferably on-camera, "it ain't a documentary." I mean, it isn't journalism.[54]

SHUKER: I think that probably, deep down, they did not understand. What we were really, basically, trying to do. I don't think that it was malicious on their part. But I think what we were trying to do— sometimes succeeding, many times not—was as different from regular television journalism or, certainly, print journalism, [as] say, when *Life* magazine started up; it was different from anything that had ever happened before.[55]

PENNEBAKER: I think that Drew was . . . trying to make up for, or show Time-Life, or something—that this was gonna be—I mean, I think he thought it was gonna be a *grandiose* project and people would be struck dumb with astonishment at what we'd done. Well, it turned out [Laughter] that they were struck dumb, but not with astonishment; they were really enraged.[56]

SHUKER: I think that what we did, in a weird way, was we succeeded too well. With that film. And it may have been the last great film like that. Certainly was with any president of the United States, *ever!* Nobody would ever get close to doing something like that now! One, because television has become totally different. And two, because it's not Kennedy, who had a great sense of the dramatic. And of course he was *very* aware of how he was gonna look and what that was gonna do for them. It was controversial because of that, but—.

It was managed, I guess, if you want to say that if the act of letting us in was staging something, letting us observe. But they were going to do all that whether we were there or not. We didn't write a script saying, "Hey, put these two actors—let's paint 'em black and put 'em in the University of Alabama! So that Wallace will get pissed off and therefore the Justice Department will have to confront him, and therefore the president will have to decide whether or not to make a speech on this." I mean, come on![57]

The Results—Today, 2

The Preparations

Unlike the narrow, concentrated intensity of *Crisis*, the news and reporting climate of June 1963, was broad, diffuse, and constantly shifting its many centers of attention. Governor Wallace's pledge to "stand in the schoolhouse door" was well known; Wallace had used it extensively in his election campaign the previous fall, and although he knew that rioting was bad publicity, and was prepared to close off the University of Alabama with state troopers, he also clearly intended to make a personal—and highly public—stand against federal intervention, in defense of states' rights.[58]

President Kennedy, meanwhile, was busy with a number of activities and issues. Four days before the "crisis," he made a major speech in San Francisco supporting greater social equality in education. He made no mention of the situation building in Alabama, but the connections were easily drawn by attentive readers.

Kennedy's West Coast trip also included a day at the U.S. Naval Station in San Diego, a reminder that integration problems were only part of the American president's list of concerns. He also made headlines with a major speech on economic policy.[59] The Sunday, 9 June, edition of the *New York Times*, which reported the economic policy speech, also carried almost thirty race relations stories of varying magnitude. A major analysis story examined the civil rights bill the Kennedy Administration planned to send to Congress that very week, and the roles to be played by Vice President Lyndon Johnson and Senate Minority Leader Everett Dirksen in the voting were the subject of considerable commentary.

And on Monday, 10 June, as Robert Kennedy and George Wallace were finalizing their strategies for the next day, President Kennedy announced a meeting to be held in Moscow to begin negotiations for a possible treaty banning the testing of nuclear weapons and also the unilateral end of U.S. atmospheric tests. Whether this was merely the normal course of presidential activity, or a calculated attempt to draw attention away from the Alabama confrontation, or whether the Alabama affair was, in fact, a minor event in the stream of presidential policy making and problem solving, is difficult to determine. But the range of complex events that made up the world of news in that period of days is clear.

The Event

ALABAMA ADMITS NEGRO STUDENTS;
WALLACE BOWS TO FEDERAL FORCE;
KENNEDY SEES 'MORAL CRISIS' IN U.S.
Tuscaloosa, Ala., June 11—Gov. George C. Wallace stepped aside today when confronted by federalized National Guard troops and permitted two Negroes to enroll in the University of Alabama. There was no violence.
The Governor, flanked by state troopers, had staged a carefully planned show of defying a Federal Court desegregation order.[60]

Governor Wallace fulfilled his campaign promise, the Justice Department avoided the use of physical force against the Governor, and the various reporters told what they had seen and heard. As description, the reporting seems accurate, detailed, and thoughtfully organized; it does, however, reflect the physical point-of-view of the individual reporter, which is that of a privileged spectator to a carefully orchestrated public event. The *New York Times* reported, among other things, that Governor Wallace arrived an hour before the scheduled arrival of the students, that he "was dressed neatly in a light gray suit, a blue shirt, a blue and brown tie with a gold tie clip and black shoes," and that he joked with the 150 newsmen "waiting in the broiling sun" before going to "an air-conditioned office to [wait]."[61] In reporting the president's nationally televised speech, the *Times* noted that "only a few opening sentences" dealt with the events of the day in Alabama and, in an early paragraph carried on page 1, commented: "Mr. Kennedy's address was one of the most emotional speeches yet delivered by a president who has often been criticized as being too 'cool' and intellectual. Near the end of his talk, Mr. Kennedy appeared to be speaking without a text, and there was a fervor in his voice when he talked of the plight of some Americans."[62]
The *Times*'s reports on the Alabama confrontation appeared in a broad

page one context of other presidential activities—"[Averell] Harriman To Lead Test-Ban Mission to Soviet for July," "President Calls Negro-Job Talks . . . With 300 Labor Leaders Tomorrow"—other race-related stories—"U.S. Troops Leave [University of] Mississippi Campus"—and assorted local and regional items. The reportorial style was professional and detached; the most personal item, "Courtesy and Curiosity Mark Campus Reception [of Negro Students]," was based on interviews with unnamed dormitory residents where Vivian Malone and James Hood would be living.

The placement of the confrontation story in the upper right corner of page one, together with its four-column-wide headlines, indicated the special importance (or interest) the editors felt the events possessed. In the complex and crowded world of news presented on the remainder of the page, and on the eighty-seven pages following, readers were free to make alternative choices as they saw fit.

The Aftermath

The next day, the Alabama confrontation and President Kennedy's "moral crisis" speech were swept almost entirely off the front page of the *New York Times* by an event that occurred only a few hours after the president went off the air: the ambush killing of the Mississippi field secretary of the National Association for the Advancement of Colored People, Medgar Evers. That story received a two-column headline; a companion story of Kennedy "continuing to push ahead on the civil rights front" by asking for support from former President Eisenhower failed to mention Alabama or the speech. Beyond that, the page one world of news fragmented into reports on a city official's warnings on union racial bias, "NASA Loses Chief of Moon Project," the Russian government's initial reaction to the test ban proposal, and complaints by New York Republican Governor Rockefeller that his Democratic critics were "inspired by the White House."[63]

By the weekend, the confrontation in Alabama received only part of a column in the Sunday news summary; an extended analysis of the civil rights situation, "Campaign for Desegregation Gains Momentum," referred to the Alabama crisis in a single sentence.[64] The flow of reportable events moved irresistibly, and quickly, on.

Reporters and Reporting

The *New York Times* and its television critic, Jack Gould, may have felt justified in the criticisms made of *Crisis*. "How can anyone—even or especially the President—act and talk without some consciousness of the camera and the tape-recorder? . . . The propagandistic connotations of this filming are unavoidable." The issues are real and serious, and the warning is proper.

But warnings deserve to be measured, and they ought not to slide blindly into condemnations. Television reporting is quite different, in both its capabilities and its limitations, from print and the differences are not all in negative directions. The amount of information available in a television scene is several orders of magnitude greater than the crudely limited descriptive capacity of print, and television is often far more accurate. For example, the "light gray suit" Governor Wallace wore in Tuscaloosa photographed black both in still photographs and on film. In more substantive areas, such as what is said, by whom, and, especially, how, television is a clearly superior medium.

Questions of subject self-consciousness and "propagandistic" manipulation are real. Reporters experienced in cinema verite or candid television journalism are not, however, more naive or venal than their print, or conventional television news, counterparts. Self-consciousness recedes, in most subjects, in proportion to the time the camera and recorder are present. The cinema verite reporter is never invisible, but he becomes less and less a novelty or an intrusion. In addition, the flow of events in a time of intense activity, or crisis, requires the subjects to respond and act; the reporter, if allowed to observe, gains understanding by watching and recording that action. Finally, manipulation of facts or image is frequent, or even constant, on the part of elected officials. Reporters experienced in their medium and method often are sensitive to such manipulation and can eliminate it in their final presentation, or include it, if the manipulation is clearly a factor in the report and if professional conventions and audience awareness permit. The broad confrontation crisis, a sequence of highly visible events that the *New York Times* stated "took place in a circus atmosphere," can easily be seen as the competing manipulations of the public and the attending press by both Governor Wallace and the Kennedys.

A comparison of the *Times*'s Alabama reporting with *Crisis* clearly shows the strengths and limitations of Drew's "micro-reporting." Except for brief summary narration, there is little in *Crisis* of the broad context provided by the *Times*. There is, by way of contrast, almost nothing in the *Times* to compare to the accumulation of detail of how these men performed during a crisis, nor could there be. Written descriptions of complex human activities are always grossly imperfect; they may serve certain needs quite well, but there is an inevitable loss of subtle information in the translation to words. Television does some types of reporting very well; newspapers excel in other areas. The differences should be recognized, understood, and valued.

The questions the *Times* raised are valid *and answerable*. They have been more-or-less satisfactorily answered, by hard experience and resultant editorial policymaking, by the more responsible segment of the print press, and—importantly—the audience is generally aware of the resulting reportorial conventions. At the time of *Crisis*, there was little in the way of experience with candid television journalism outside the Drew group, and neither conventional journalists nor television audiences were familiar with its capacities or limitations. It was a time for caution; it is unfortunate that the result was hyper-sensitive overreaction.

The Results—1963, 2

GOULD: The dilemma of the citizen is that he never will know what may have been said or done for the benefit of the camera. The uncertainty will exist no matter how vehement any denials, which was the original flaw in the program's concept.[65]

HORN: Not less but more such television journalism should be produced and telecast. ABC-TV has a fine example of inside history in this outstanding film. It may also have the prototype of future TV documentaries.[66]

Horn's call for "more" was not to be. *Crisis: Behind a Presidential Commitment* became the final documentary effort with any reasonable chance of precipitating the full-scale revolution in television documentary that Drew had once envisioned. Drew's influence within Time, Inc. and within the profession of journalism was waning. The innovations in production techniques and theory had lost their novelty effect and were either being adapted into more conventional methods by the networks or ignored. Never again would there be serious talk of a 52-weeks-a-year documentary series produced by Drew and a semi-independent Murrow-like unit. Overwhelmingly favorable response to *Crisis* by audience, critics, or journalists might have affected a turn-around, but the television networks and, increasingly, sponsors were not interested in independent productions of a serious nature, and the most powerful journalistic voice in America had condemned Drew's grandest and most sophisticated effort.

And the important questions that *Crisis* raised, and for which satisfactory answers might have been found through continued development of candid television journalism, were pushed abruptly aside only thirty-three days after the film's telecast by events in Dallas, Texas—the assassination of Drew's most illustrious and successful subject, John Fitzgerald Kennedy.

22

Drew Associates, 4

PENNEBAKER: [The correspondent] was obviously the person who was deciding what story. Well, . . . the deciding of the story was everything. And it became clear to me that if you didn't have the ability to really do that—I mean, if your arrangement with Drew wasn't that you got to decide at least one of your stories, you were going to have a hard time. Because otherwise, you just became a cameraman, just like that. . . .

So I could see that that was going to be a problem. As it turned out, [Ricky and I] just didn't stay that long. It collapsed before that. But I was feeling—I mean, I had quit almost a year before I officially left, pretty much because of that.[1]

DREW: Well, there were no disagreements in which people left over editing until there was [an] inability to pay people. I'll point that out. . . . Actually, nobody left Drew Associates until after the Time, Inc. break-up, over that subject. And I don't think Ricky and Pennebaker would say . . . that they left because of editing disagreements. I think they left because they wanted to be their own men.[2]

The initial creative period of Drew Associates was wearing thin. What had been a sometimes uneasy alliance of men with differing backgrounds, attitudes, and goals broke down when two important ingredients disappeared: money and creative opportunity. But while Drew and his associates had exercised the creative freedom and opportunity that had been presented to them, Time, Inc. was not simply handing out money; the organization, too, was watching and learning.

PENNEBAKER: Time-Life sold [the films] short. See, they never

196

thought they were worth anything, anyway. They still don't much. They only distribute them very despondently. . . . Their biggest understanding was, "Don't make the films. Buy them from the BBC. Brokers make money—not filmmakers. Production doesn't make money. Get out of production."

That's what Hollywood found out when Joe Kennedy went out there and looked around. Nicholas Schenk makes the money in New York. Out there, you just make your salaries. So pay salaries, and the money gets made in the distribution. So if you want to make really big money, distribute.

And when [Time-Life] found that out, these were all just a waste of time. . . .[3]

The collaboration of Drew and his associates, under the umbrella of Time, Inc.'s money, had produced a remarkable series of films that developed and explored a wide variety of options in candid television journalism, including news event coverage (*Primary*, *The Chair*, and *Crisis*), social problems (*David*, *The Children Were Watching*, and *Petey and Johnny*), personality studies (*Jane*, *Blackie*, and *Susan Starr*), celebrities (*Nehru* and *The Aga Kahn*) and sports (*Mooney vs. Fowle*), among others.[4] Almost all of the productions attempted some innovations that added to the store of experiences that Drew was assembling; only a few, however, were fully successful in terms of effective storytelling through the "picture logic" Drew was trying to develop. From the management side, the results were disappointing and finally unsupportable by the parent organization. The task Drew had assumed for himself and his associates was probably too large for the available resources, both personal and institutional.

PENNEBAKER: I'm very sympathetic to what happened to Drew. I think he wasn't the guy for the job in the end, but there was nobody else. And he had a vision of something that was incredible. As I say, nobody's had a vision like this. . . .

60 Minutes is a joke—an absolute joke—compared to what Drew envisioned, and really wasn't able to sell it. Nobody could have sold it. Because he was caught in a political trap. There was no solution to it.[5]

DREW: [During the editing of *Crisis*] Ricky and Penny pulled out. And I think that since we'd lost our Time, Inc. backing—I think there'd been some good question on their part about how to proceed.

We had a development that was well under way, that was unique. And I think they felt they'd like to continue with their work, and so they pulled out. And about that time, Drew Associates made a deal with ABC News, and we went on and produced six one-hour specials for them.[6]

Drew Associates did not end with the departure of Leacock and Penne-baker; the contract with ABC was at hand and Drew was soon to enter a period of sustained professional and critical success. But the end of the period of initial innovation can be conveniently marked with the departure of those two individuals in late 1963. From that point forward, the creative viewpoints that they had supplied to the development of Drew's candid television journalism, and to cinema verite, would be exercised in projects of their own choosing.

Drew and ABC

ABC was not an unknown entity to Drew and his associates, but this was the first direct contract between the two organizations. Once again a Drew production, *Crisis*, had attracted the attention of Tom Moore, who was now president of ABC. And, again, the timing of Moore's interest was fortuitous for Drew Associates.

> We made our [contract] deal with Tom Moore verbally, and then with the News Department contractually—the ABC lawyers [in October 1963]. And on the day that it was signed, ABC got a new President of News, and that was an old friend of mine, Elmer Lower, who had been with NBC and with CBS and before that was at *Life* magazine, and was my bureau chief in Los Angeles. So Lower invited me to lunch, and he said, "I know that we've just signed a contract with you for six specials. Now really, what I want you to do is bring your organization into ABC, and you can make films forever. But if you want to stay outside of ABC, I'm telling you right now—you'll finish these films, and that's it. You'll be out of here."
>
> [Elmer] made this clear to me—which I didn't argue with or resent. I could see perfectly that this man who was now going to build an organization where there hadn't been one for a while would want his own organization and so forth. So everything from there on was very correct. I presented ideas. He would assign one or two or three, and we'd go out and shoot them. I would show him a rough cut. If he had comments, I would accommodate them, but I don't think he ever had any editorial comments. And the ABC sales department assigned a man to sell them—sell the specials—and some they sold, and some they didn't. But at the end of the—I think that took about two years. At the end of that period, at any rate, that contract was allowed to lapse.[7]

Drew valued his production ideas, and his independence: "He wanted to run his own show." Despite repeated offers, some backed by substantial

positive inducements, Drew claims to "never" have considered joining a
network news or documentary department.

> See, there was no way to operate within a network the way we did
> outside. That is, the whole way they operated and the equipment they
> used was in the—at that time, their equipment was in the Dark Ages
> compared to ours. And the way they worked. I liked two-man teams.
> They liked five-man teams or something. Their union arrangement.
> Every thing. Almost everything about working with the networks
> made it difficult to operate the way we wanted to. But Elmer [Lower]
> was a good news man and a perfect gentleman and had good judgment
> when it came to assigning stories, and we got along just fine until the
> six films were completed.[8]

The Daring Americans

> In thinking about how to sell these programs with the [ABC] Sales
> Department, we realized that all of these films were [happening]
> outside the United States. The subjects were all Americans, and they
> were all taking risks. And so we came up with a series title called *The
> Daring Americans*. A few years later that title would have occasioned
> a lot of skepticism and laughter, but at that time, and in those specific
> circumstances, it didn't—and in fact, was not a bad description of
> what those people were doing.[9]

The ABC-contract films are widely varied. A young Peace Corps woman
in Malaya assisting a rural doctor became *Mission to Malaya* (1964): "It
almost had overtones of stories out of Africa, medical missionary-type
people." *Letters from Viet Nam* (1964) was the first network news special
on the "advisors war," and featured an Army helicopter pilot photographed
in "actual combat" who then made tape recordings of his experiences for
his wife back in the United States.

Besides the helicopter pilots, there are other echoes of the past in *The
Daring Americans*: a racing driver (*Assault on Le Mans*, 1965), a piano
competition (*In the Contest of the Queen*, 1965), and a "multi-subject hour
. . . It would be called a 'magazine show' today," that was reminiscent of
Key Picture ten years earlier (*The Time of Our Lives*, 1965). And there was
a final film on John Kennedy.

Faces of November

"At the death of Kennedy, Elmer Lower, president of ABC News,
called me up and said, 'Go to Washington and make a film.' And I said,
'What kind of film?' And he said, 'Your kind of film.' I said, 'Thanks,'
and went to Washington."[10]

Drew went to Washington with several camera teams but no idea for what sort of film he might make. The television networks were gearing up for the most massive event coverage in the history of the medium; what could Drew do that would be distinctive? "And it finally struck me, and I sort of announced what we would do. 'We'll look backward. While the country is going through an experience, watching a funeral, we'll watch the people watching the funeral.' "[11]

They would look backward, against the direction of compelling national fascination, and "see into people." In the streets of Washington, in the Capital rotunda, along the route of the funeral cortege, at Arlington Cemetery, shooting backward.

"And that night, Kennedy was lying in state in the rotunda in the Capital . . . and there was a ceremony. And after the ceremony, the public was allowed to file past the coffin. And as people approached the coffin, they began to choke up. And as they got to the coffin, something hit them, and you could see this in their faces. . . . And we just kept shooting and shooting and shooting and shooting."[12]

There is more than faces: a ceremonial cannon firing along a line of barren trees, the floodlighted Capital reflected in rainy streets, limp flags at half-staff, the coffin being carried, people watching, some tears. There are dignitaries, and family—Robert Kennedy, brother-in-law Peter Lawford comforting one of the young cousins, the Kennedy sisters, Jacqueline, Caroline. And there are people, in long lines, day and night, filing past, unidentified, but not faceless. The young, the old, black and white, the sober, the tearful, the horrified. In seemingly endless closeups they pass. Then the caravan down Pennsylvania Avenue, to Arlington, more faces, "Taps," salutes, and again the sound of cannons as the crowds filter away leaving only the bare trees of the cemetery against the gray skies. It is documentary filmmaking at its simplest and best; it is, in an odd way, *Life* magazine with background sound.

> [*Faces of November*, 1964] was about twenty minutes long, and it was sort of a minor event at [Drew Associates], in our own minds. We sent it off to Venice and it won the Venice Television Festival, and then it got put into another festival, which was the Venice Film Festival, and it won that . . . in the Short Subject category. . . . ABC, however, couldn't use it, they said, because it was twenty minutes long, and they didn't have a twenty minute place to put it. However, when it won all these prizes, they ran it on—a few minutes of it on a news show one night, in order to be able to tell the world that they'd won a prize.[13]

Following the Kennedy assasination, there were several reports of a television special being prepared by Drew Associates for ABC "as an historical document" that would draw on the footage Drew had accumulated, "the most voluminous and personal outside the [Kennedy] family's home movies." But that project would take Drew twenty years to bring to fruition (*Being with John F. Kennedy* [1983]), and with the delivery of the final films in *The Daring Americans* series in June of 1965, the contract with ABC was concluded.[14]

Moving On

"In 1965, Xerox asked me what subjects were too tough for networks to assign. I gave them a two-page list. They assigned an hour on drug addiction."[15]

With the end of the ABC contract in 1964, Drew was forced to solicit business where he could. His approaches to Xerox, a major sponsor of television specials at the time, lead to their question, his list, the assignment, and, after many false starts, to Jim and Helen, heroin addicts in New York.

The production, *Storm Signal*, was plagued by familiar problems: a rotating group of producers and cameramen, a complex and frequently unphotographable story, and disagreements over editing. James Lipscomb was the "dominant" filmmaker, and Drew was the "managing editor". "We argued about it, and that was the last film Lipscomb made for Drew Associates."

Storm Signal also proved to be troublesome in the marketplace, where it was rejected by all the networks. Then the sponsor and its agency made a bold and untried move; they set up their own network. "Xerox bought time on stations in the top 50 markets, ran the film several times in each and got back figures proving that it was the most looked at documentary of the year and ranked among the top ten specials of any kind."[16] *Storm Signal* also brought Drew Associates its second Venice Film Festival award.

In 1965, the Bell Telephone Company tired of producing studio performances for *The Bell Telephone Hour* and went looking for new ideas. Drew saw a chance to "reconstitute" Drew Associates to full strength and proposed a dozen "fantastic one-hour specials." However, the executive producer, Henry Jaffee, chose to contract directly with individual producers and Drew found himself competing for assignments with Lipscomb and the firm of Leacock-Pennebaker.

Three of the nine specials went to Drew: *Festival of Two Worlds* (1966),

Drew's first film completely in color, on Gion Carlo Menotti; a Belgian jazz festival with Benny Goodman; and the opening of the Metropolitan Opera House in New York, *The New Met* (1966), which won First Prize in the International Cinema Exhibition in Bilboa, Spain.[17]

The next year, Bell, apparently responding to the quality of Drew's productions, asked him to produce the entire series of twelve specials. "For the first time in my life, I turned down business . . . I wanted more time for hand-making the films." Drew agreed to do six of the twelve, choosing, in effect, to pass up the role of series executive producer for the more involved role he enjoyed.

The films, on Duke Ellington (*On the Road with Duke Ellington*, 1967), Yehudi Menuhin (*Carnival of the Menuhins*, 1967), Edward Villella (*Man Who Dances: Edward Villella*, 1968), Louis Armstrong (*Jazz: The Intimate Art*, 1968), and others, are diverse and apparently dissimilar from earlier films such as *Primary*, *On the Pole*, and *The Chair*. In Drew's mind, however, there is a clearly defined series of connections.

> Each film is a solution to a unique problem. All the characters are different, and the arts are different, but they all have certain things in common, which is that we try to use a man and what he does and what it means to him. And this ranges from traveling on the road with Duke Ellington and coming slowly to realize that at this point in his life, Duke is being looked upon as a man who's repeating himself, and people are feeling sorry for him because he has to keep playing the same songs over and over. And on the road, we find out that he's a giant. He's a much bigger man than all that. He loves playing those songs. They're his songs. But also, every night, he composes. For himself, on the road. And he creates songs and never writes them down. He plays them and they fade away, and nobody—and they're gone. And it's the act of creation that's going on. And we're seeing a genius at work. . . .
>
> On the other hand, you've got Yehudi Menuhin, who started to live up, at age fifty, to his reputation as a child prodigy at the age of ten. . . . A man haunted by a past and struggling, intellectually and in every other way. On the anniversary of that [first] great appearance in New York, to make another great appearance in New York. And the music he plays is soulful and heartbreaking and gorgeous and it's the same music, it's Elgar. And that's his story.
>
> What I'm trying to talk about is a pattern. There are patterns within those [films] that carry out the patterns that were in my mind all the years before and that were woven through the films that proceeded and followed. They're all there.[18]

Drew remained convinced and enthusiastic. *Man Who Dances* won an Emmy. But the nature of televison itself was changing, changing beyond the power of Drew's efforts at journalistic innovation to affect it.

> It was now 1969. . . . The one network that had known it could use independents [ABC] now had a News president who felt that he didn't want any. This closed down our access to public affairs subject matter for network broadcast.
>
> The sponsors who had influenced networks to go after special qualities in documentaries were fading. Bell and Howell and Xerox and other companies had shifted into a less active and more conservative mode of broadcasting. As the costs of network hours increased, fewer sponsors could afford to buy whole programs. The networks gained strength as a buyers' market became a sellers' market. They became less responsive to sponsors' wishes. As network competition for audiences increased, culture disappeared as a regular commodity in prime time. The Bell Telephone Company was denied air time for a continuation of its series. At the same time, a kind of program was becoming fashionable that appeared to be a documentary but entailed none of the risk of dealing with the current real world—the Cousteau Undersea Series and the National Geographic Series. Finally, the cost of film increased, making it so costly to shoot real life uncontrolled that for me it became nearly impossible to continue to make really candid films. A lot of imitations appeared that tarnished a name that had been applied to our films, . . . cinema verite.[19]

In the 1970s, "it became a matter of simply surviving," and Drew Associates made films on science and the arts, films for government agencies and corporations, commercials and campaign films. *The Zapper*, about a machine that drives railroad spikes, placed first in the Industrial Film Festival, but a feature film, *The Sunship Game*, about glider racing and the relationship between a glider pilot and his wife, failed to find a distributor. "I consider it to be the most expensive home movie ever made."

Cinema verite techniques were adapted to make three-minute "documentary commercials" for a major corporation, public and corporate interest in the Bicentennial Celebration led to a series of films on "the tall ships", and astronauts frolicked in slow-motion to the music from *Yellow Submarine* in *Apollo 9: The Space Duet of Spider and Gumdrop*. Drew, if nothing else, proved his versatility, and adaptability.

In the late 1970s, Drew produced a half-dozen short "feature reports" for NBC's *Magazine*, but soon encountered the realities of a report on in-house and out-of-house expenditures. "After a year [the executive producer] called me up and said, 'I spent a half million dollars last year on programs for you, and it looks so bad for me that I have to stop it.' "

> Well, in the '60s, I was the father of cinema verite. . . . But then, after I'd made nine one-hour specials on culture, for that period of time, at least, I was known as "the culture maven." [Laughter] I mean, when something cultural came up, people called me. I was "the culture guy." At the same time, all those years I'd been doing science and aviation and space stuff, so in certain quarters, I was regarded as a science or aviation filmmaker. . . . And finally, I was . . . the documentary commercial maker for five or six years. . . .
> . . . I had different kinds of reputations with different parts of the sponsorship world, I guess.[20]

Moving Back

In 1980, Drew made lengthy presentations at two major gatherings of documentary filmmakers and critics; the Conference on Visual Anthropology (COVA) at Temple University in Philadelphia, and the Robert Flaherty Film Seminar, held that year at Wells College in Aurora, New York. The introductions to the films and the answers to follow-up questions gave Drew an opportunity to retrace his career and restate his production philosophy for a new generation of filmmakers. He recalled his background as a *Life* correspondent and a Nieman Fellow, his meeting with Leacock and the early promotional films for *Life*, the development of the methods used in the making of *Primary* and other films, his working relationships within Time, Inc. and with ABC, his conceptions of the filmmaker and "picture logic" versus "word logic," his role as managing editor and as storyfinder/ storyteller, and his belief that he had developed a new form of screen journalism that would allow audiences to see for themselves what had really happened.

Drew also published an article in the journal *Studies in Visual Communication* and participated in a two-week program of his films at the Whitney Museum of American Art's "New American Filmmakers" series, titled "Early *Cinéma Vérité*.: Robert Drew and Associates."[21] His presentations were motivated, in part, by a desire to re-establish his films and his ideas as a part of the mainstream discussion of documentary film; he felt strongly that "we have a range of ideas that seem new today—even today—and it's really hard to get people to see new ideas." He was acutely aware of the fact that his work had been passed over by younger filmmakers and film journalists as only a part of film history. The increased visibility was motivated primarily by a desire not to be forgotten. Drew's concerns may have been re-enforced when he was introduced to the Conference on Visual Anthropology as "alive and well" and still producing films, and when one member of the audience reported being told that Robert Drew had died several years earlier.

"Why Are Documentaries So Dull?"

"I think we failed. . . . There were shows that in themselves were smashing, but we haven't taken this new concept of journalism and brought it home to a big audience. . . . The films weren't programmed in a regular manner. They appeared at odd times, in odd places. The big audience never knew they existed."[22]

In 1983, Robert Drew was quoted in a *New York Times* preview of *Fire Season*, Drew's first cinema verite documentary on national television in many years. The lengthy story reviewed Drew's dissatisfactions with early television documentaries—" 'Why are documentaries so dull?' "—his accomplishments in developing cinema verite, and traced the ups and downs of Drew's attempts to innovate "this new concept of journalism." But it was mainly concerned with Drew's continuing efforts to have his innovations acknowledged and accepted.

"I really thought I could make a revolution in a few months. Then it stretched out to a few years. It has now been 23 years and I think it may just be getting into a position to take off."[23]

Drew's activities have at least managed to keep his ideas visible—and the questions about them alive. *Fire Season* is a complex story of the Civilian Conservation Corps, a jobs program operated by the State of California, which mingles the forest fire fighting activities of several individual members of "the C's" with comparisons of their varied backgrounds—suburban poolsides to urban gang corners—and the efforts of their state director to maintain funding for the program. The complexity of the story makes *Fire Season* a difficult program to capture fully on a first viewing. But the complexity and difficulty are not accidental or unintended.

"I never would have tackled *Fire Season* twenty years ago; it's not as good a subject for verite development. . . .

"And why did I do it now? I did it now, in a way, because I didn't have to prove anything. That is, I didn't have to prove that verite worked, could work. And I felt liberated and freed to try something really tough. And without any guarantees." [Laughter].[24]

Other films have followed: *Warnings from Gangland* (1984), a personalized story of a Los Angeles street gang; *Marshall High Fights Back* (1984), an attempt to examine "an inter-city high school out of control, plagued by gangs, drugs, and violence"; *Shootout on Imperial Highway* (1985), a two-part follow-up on the characters in *Warnings From Gangland*; and *For Auction: An American Hero* (1986), a sympathetic look at midwestern farmers having to sell their machinery and/or land because of falling prices and mounting debts combined with a broader picture of the crisis in American agriculture. It is a fusion of conventional documentary and cinema verite, an attempt to satisfy "the market" with a story.

> NEW YORK TIMES: Is there anything new to say about the farm crisis? No, not really, but go ahead and watch *For Auction: An American Hero* anyway. It is filmed without anger; it is humane; it is elegiac. Intelligence is at work. . . .
>
> In a documentary like this, there is room for a great deal of sentimentality. Sensibly, Mr. Drew avoids it. The narration is spare. There are patches of silence. The camera roves over the fields in Nebraska and Iowa. It visits a moribund small town. The restaurant, grocery and lumber yard are closed. A point is made without straining to make it: a part of American life is dead.[25]

For Auction: An American Hero, the winner in the independent production category of the 1985 Alfred I. DuPont-Columbia University Awards in Broadcast Journalism, is a combination of informative, "word logic" elements with evocative, "picture logic" segments. Drew is clearly rethinking the details of his innovations, tinkering, adjusting, and developing them to meet the needs of "the market": the funding agencies, executive producers, and network executives that an independent filmmaker must satisfy.

But in the intensity of the bits of unrehearsed human drama that survive in his films—in the face of the black history teacher in *Marshall High Fights Back* telling students that black history is "painful" to study because of the tragic record they will encounter, or in the face of a farm wife in *For Auction; An American Hero* crying at the prospect of losing the lifetime work of her and her husband—it is clear that, for Robert Drew, cinema verite has remained the adventure it once was, has remained the challenge of reporting the lives of people who interest him.

"That's what I do. I shoot film. That is, I take a cameraman and I shoot a film. But, *Fire Season*, you know: what's this middle-aged man doing up in the mountains with all these kids, what's this banker doing at a fire, and so forth. Or *Warnings from Gangland*: what's this white guy doing in this project? But I like to go out and shoot."[26]

23

Drew and Cinema Verite—Today

And now, what of Robert Drew? And what of cinema verite?

Both are alive and, in some measure, well. But neither has achieved the level of professional and theoretical influence that had once been foreseen for, and by, them. Drew is a successful independent producer in New York City, owner of a small but active production company, still making documentaries that appear sporadically on national television. Cinema verite, as Drew envisioned it, has undergone considerable mutation in the hands of filmmakers with sometimes quite different views of its potentials and values, but remains largely story-bound; unable, as yet, to become as completely unfettered by older forms as had once seemed possible.

Both Drew and cinema verite have been fundamentally important forces in the field of documentary, yet neither has been able to bring about a sustainable revolution in basic documentary practice beyond the introduction of easily portable recording equipment (although given the technological state of documentary filmmaking through the 1950s, that alone is a significant achievement). A majority of journalistic documentary productions continue to rely on an orderly "lecture logic," with the camera now presenting predictable materials only in a somewhat more informal fashion than was possible three decades earlier. The camera's capacity to "see" human activities in unhurried detail has been largely neglected. But over that period, Drew and other cinema verite filmmakers have influenced documentary film and television journalism in important and interesting ways. Drew's recognition of the limitations of the traditional documentary, his formulation of an alternative method for reporting human activities, his command of institutional resources, his recognition of the importance of talent, and his determined pursuit of his goals have irrevocably changed the nature of what the audience is able to see: films and videotapes with markedly different content than was thought possible, or felt necessary, a generation-and-a-half ago.

Developments in Cinema Verite

Drew's Associates

Donn Pennebaker has continued with his own production company, an independent filmmaker making films for himself and for whomever will pay—"You know, just a working man." Among Pennebaker's notable productions have been *Don't Look Back* (1966), with singer Bob Dylan on a concert tour, and *Monterey Pop* (1968), the prototype rock concert film. He has also done camera work for CBS, ABC, Norman Mailer, Jean-Luc Godard, and a number of advertising agencies and political candidates.[1] Later, he produced *Rockabye* (1981), an aggressively edited cinema verite-styled film on the production of an original play by Samuel Beckett.

And while Pennebaker can be severely critical of the implementations of Drew's "dream," he is almost always supportive of the basic premises, even in the face of apparent failure.

> I think most people think of it as not working. Maybe even Drew does, and I think—of all the things, I guess, in retrospect, I think, is that what Drew put in motion was unbelieveable!
>
> You know, you'd go into a situation, and see if the situation could make the film rather than you going in with a concept or a script. And that had never been done before! The only person who had really done it was Flaherty, and he kind of talked himself out of it through the years, so that by the end of his life he was making a Hollywood film. With a script and the same old shit.
>
> But the idea of what [Flaherty] started never, it seemed to me, had never been really realized. And I don't think it would have been without [Drew]. So it seems to me it was an extremely worthwhile thing to do.
>
> And it woke me up to what really could be done, and has changed me now totally; I've never gone back. So I saw it as an unbelieveable success! [Laughter] Not as a failure![2]

After leaving Drew Associates, Ricky Leacock went into partnership with Donn Pennebaker as Leacock-Pennebaker Films, making films for the *Saturday Evening Post* (*Happy Mother's Day*, 1963), Norddeutcher Rundfunk (*A Stravinski Portrait*, 1964), and CBS Reports (*Ku Klux Klan:*

The Invisible Empire, awarded an Emmy, 1965), but left in 1968 to become head of a department of film (now the Film/Video Section) at MIT.

"[Leacock-Pennebaker] couldn't cope with me. I made [only] two short films in a period of about three years, *Chiefs* [1969] and *Hickory Hill* [1968], both for television. Everything else I was doing—I was shooting for Norman Mailer [*Maidstone*, 1968], I was shooting for Godard. It didn't make any sense to me. I enjoyed them, but it had nothing to do with me."[3]

Leacock suffered personal problems: "I started to drink too damned much. And I stopped that. Totally."[4] But he remained active with teaching, multi-media productions, and "a high-technology, avant-garde theatrical presentation."[5] Now in semi-retirement from active filmmaking and living in Paris, Leacock's interest in cinema verite remains strong, alongside honest uncertainties about its past, and its future.

> We had—at least I think I had—a sense that we had really opened up a whole new world, and that the horizons were limitless. And somehow—it went on for a few years, and somehow it ran out of steam. I don't know quite—I still don't understand. It seemed to run into a vacuum. Maybe that's my problem.
>
> And then you've got the inevitable backlash, of what I regard as more and more faking. Working more and more to get—the insistence on perfect—you know, good lighting, good sound, get rid of the reporter, having the soundman festooned with radio mikes, putting out mike booms—slowly, intrepidly marching backwards! Stedicam. All this bullshit! Has nothing to do with filmmaking. In my view. With journalism. Has to do with slick results, and if the story doesn't work, invent it.[6]

Greg Shuker has continued to work intermittently with Drew while pursuing his own career as an independent producer; he was associate producer to Drew on *Warnings from Gangland* (1984) and earlier produced *Free at Last* (1968), "a piece of real cinema verite storytelling" on the civil rights activities of Rev. Martin Luther King, Jr., which won the Grand Prize in the Venice Film Festival (1968) and an Emmy (1969).

> SHUKER: I think that what happened with that plan and with that vision was that the marketplace changed. . . . Television just started to grow. . . . And then it became pervasive, as the great advertising medium in history, television.
>   . . . ratings became more and more important in television. One way to achieve ratings was consistency of faces on the screen. The nature of Drew Associates's product was verite, was stories. Bob avoided on-air correspondents, on-air hosts, and so forth. And with

good reason, I think. It was purer film, purer story, purer journalism. It was more verite verite! . . .

So I guess that Bob's instinct was right about being on the air every week, getting people in the habit of watching. I think that the great tragedy of that—the sadness, I guess [soft laughter]—is that he didn't take into account, nor did anybody, I think, that the viewing public wanted a consistency, which was the host, and the on-camera person. . . . And the medium of television is more show business than we would acknowledge, sometimes, and show business means personalities. Therefore, you need a personality. And Bob didn't want that. [long pause] He wanted the story to dominate.[7]

Other Filmmakers

As the "Living Camera" series and *Crisis* were completed in 1963 and Drew's former associates moved off in different directions, critical attention in the field of cinema verite passed on to other filmmakers, most notably the Maysles brothers and Frederick Wiseman. Their productions followed in the technological footsteps of Drew and his associates—lightweight mobile cameras recording actual events with minimal interference—but with considerably different intents and structural strategies.

After Al Maysles declined to join the Drew organization in 1961, he and his brother David produced a variety of notable documentary films independently as Maysles Films, Inc., films made possible by the active commercial and corporate/industrial production schedule the Maysles maintained.[8]

The Maysles diverged from Drew's model of candid television journalism, developing a more personal form of documentary in terms of both their subject matter and their own relationship to the final film product. Individuals would less and less be treated from a journalistic standpoint; narrative conventions of storyline, pacing, and climax would more often give way to detailed observations of an individual's actions and characteristics; the complexities of those actions would be explored rather than ignored.

Salesman (1969) portrayed four bible salesmen, *Gimme Shelter* (1970) followed the Rolling Stones rock group on an American concert tour, and *Grey Gardens* (1975) presented the private world of an aging woman and her old-maid daughter living as recluses, observed in such stark detail that there were bitter charges of "cruelty, exploitation, greed and exhibitionism."[9] But *Grey Gardens* also occasioned more basic considerations of the Maysles' films and the observational goals the filmmakers espoused.

> The Maysles . . . carefully avoid the sort of humanism which informs the documentary tradition from Flaherty to Grierson to [Pare] Lorentz, and is even apparent in the issue-oriented Drew films. . . .

In an important sense, this attitude goes against the grain of American and British documentary tradition, where the filmmaker's role in advancing understanding and, quite often, in bettering social conditions is tacitly assumed as the moral obligation of the documentarist. . . .

. . . The Maysles have . . . consistently employed direct cinema techniques to focus on the complex world of experience—not to reduce this world to a pretty picture or tall tale nor to plead for "understanding" or "progress," but to communicate a sense of the intricacy and inherent ambiguity of human existence. Because it does not *adhere* to the documentary tradition of Flaherty and his disciples, *Grey Gardens adds* to the documentary tradition; in place of unified, "inspiring" works of great power and beauty, the Maysles offer a disjointed, troubling film that intrigues no less that it disturbs.[10]

The viewpoint of the observational, or "naturalistic," novelist and a willingness to deal in unresolveable complexity set the Maysles brothers and their films apart from Drew's affinity for realism and for the story. There is, if the best view of their films and purposes is taken, a genuine disregard for the possible negative reactions of the audience to the film's more bizzare and offensive subject matter, along with a willingness to risk the hazards of ambiguity and a "non-story" in search of a different level of accuracy. The Maysles were moving cinema verite in directions quite different than Drew intended or had foreseen.

Frederick Wiseman has produced, taken sound for, and edited, over twenty films; taken together, they form the largest and most cohesive body of documentary filmmaking on a single theme in existence. And they have provoked widely varying reactions.[11]

Jay Sharbutt, Associated Press television writer wrote: "A 105-minute wretched excess called *Primate* [1974] . . . is the most tasteless, nauseating, misleading and senselessly offensive program ever to hit television."[12] In a TV review of *Hospital* (1970), *Life* magazine's Richard Schickel wrote: "[Wiseman] wants merely to show us the day-to-day quality of our society's institutions, thereby letting us render our own judgments of their quality."[13]

Wiseman's approach is quite different from the Maysles's and from Drew's. All of his films center on institutions, not individuals; all are tightly arranged and edited into a thematic, or mosaic, structure. He departed from the concept of a story that was so important in Drew's approach; together with the fact that individuals are never conventionally identified and that the processes of the institution are never explained, the films created a complexity and seeming lack of direction that Drew's journalistic training and sentiments would not permit. Wiseman's methods can be seen as an attempt to go beyond the restrictions of narrative and present a different, hopefully improved, means of dealing with human complexity on a broad, institutional level.[14]

Another branch of documentary filmmaking that was influenced by Drew and cinema verite was visual anthropology, which soon discovered the merits of the recording system Drew had shepherded into existence. They also discovered the limitations, for ethnographic purposes, of the presentational forms Drew and other cinema verite filmmakers used. Visual ethnographers as diverse in ethnographic method and filmic style as Robert Gardner (*Dead Birds*, 1963; *Rivers of Sand*, 1974), Hillary Harris and George Breidenbach (*The Nuer*, 1970), Napoleon Chagnon and Timothy Asch (the Yanomamo films, 1975), and David and Judith MacDougall (the *Turkana Conversations* trilogy, 1976–77) adapted cinema verite methods for narrower, more scientific purposes. Ethnography was concerned with "the goal of truth," and the attributes of an acceptable ethnographic film were often far removed from both cinema verite and candid television journalism. The resulting discussion has enlarged the range of theoretical problems and possibilities for cinema verite far beyond those which Drew and some of his associates had been able to concern themselves with.[15]

The Profession

In 1987, the *New York Times* wrote, "*60 Minutes* has been an epic hit. The broadcast has finished among the top 10 shows in the ratings for 10 consecutive years. It has made more money for CBS than any other show at the network ever has."[16]

And in 1979, Donn Pennebaker said, "*60 Minutes* is a joke—an absolute joke—compared to what Drew envisioned."[17]

Professionally, it was the audience that rendered the decision. The "commonly shared experience" that Drew envisioned has been provided by executive producer Don Hewitt and correspondents Mike Wallace, Harry Reasoner, Morley Safer, Ed Bradley, and others. And although Hewitt is less formal in presenting it—"it's not that we're so smart, we just stumbled on a formula"—the theory behind his success with *60 Minutes* is not dissimilar to Drew's.

Hewitt said, "If you package reality as attractively as Hollywood packages fiction, I was willing to bet that you could raise the ratings of television documentaries. The typical documentary got a 12 to 18 percent share of the audience, and I thought we could do something like a 22. [In December 1985], we got a 38."[18]

Numbers are an important part of the *60 Minutes* story; they served as an effective foil against professional criticism of the ambush and celebrity interviews as the show tightened its grip on "its educated, money-spending, up-scale audience."

> NEW YORK TIMES: [*60 Minutes*] remains one of the most valuable [shows] to advertisers. Commercials on the broadcast will sell for $225,000 to $250,000 per 30-second spot this [1987–88] season; each episode has 13 30-second commercials; that means that CBS can bring in roughly $3 million per broadcast in advertising revenues, against a per-show cost of less that $800,000.
>
> Those are numbers that even the most devoted adversary can admire.[19]

Drew does, sort of.

> The reason *60 Minutes* works is because it does do what I'm talking about, in a funny way. . . .
>
> One reason, probably the fundamental reason, that *60 Minutes* works, at all, is that there are surprises in it. And to the extent that they waylay people, accuse them, manhandle them, mistreat them, and so forth, they are being dramatic.
>
> Now I don't approve of that kind of drama, but in terms of fulfilling the need for drama, they're doing it, they're doing it. The bastards! You know. If that's journalism, I'll—you know—eat it!! But it is drama.[20]

But commercial and professional success were not the only rewards. "Don Hewitt became a bona fide power broker at CBS, gaining the ear of top company executives." It was a level of corporate influence Drew never attained; in spite of the effort he and his associates expended, and in spite of the changes in documentary filmmaking that can be traced directly to those efforts, a three-volume history of Time, Inc. alloted Drew's "early experiments" less than a page.[21]

Time, Inc. continued its efforts in program production for a time after Drew's departure, but without regular access to network audiences, "the distribution roadblock was insurmountable." The corporation then chose another route into the television age—cable, which became "a major profit center of Time, Inc., as large as magazine publishing."[22] The numbers are impressive: by 1982, "[Home Box Office] and other video enterprises accounted for 24 percent of revenues and 47 percent of profits of the parent company, Time, Inc."[23] In 1986, a Time, Inc. subsidiary, American Television Communication Corporation, the nation's second largest cable television operator, bought third-ranked Group W Cable for $2.1 billion; the value of those combined cable operations, $3.5 billion, contributed to a 30% rise in Time, Inc.'s stock price in only two months.[24] And the corporation reported a 43 percent rise in net income for the first quarter of 1988 "on the strength of subscriber growth for HBO and successful home-video releases from HBO Video."[25] The decision to abandon the production of television journalism and to move in the direction of distribution may have been motivated by a desire to protect the financial stability and, therefore, the editorial independence of the print segments of the organization—or it may have simply been good business.

The journalism profession never understood Robert Drew. This was partly because of suspicions regarding his background with Time, Inc., and partly because of the challenges he presented to traditional journalistic values and methods. There is even some question whether the profession took him seriously; there are few professional critiques in print, most are reviews. Many journalists simply saw that what he presented did not fit their mold; they could not, and did not, see a different future.

The opposition of the *New York Times*, and columnist Jack Gould, to Drew's efforts in producing *Crisis* was particularly unfortunate. Gould and the *Times* did not see increased attention to intimate detail and human complexity but rather the growth of campaign managers and partisan propagandists who would trade on the credibility of documentary to produce a concealing (as opposed to revealing) psuedo-verite. Such a conservative stance may sometimes be required in the broad profession of journalism; the "knife" of cinema verite may be too sharp to be used, except under carefully controlled circumstances. Hard questions remain, however, as to how best to give innovators a proper chance, and the answer lies in more open attitudes and better critical exchanges between professionals. Drew gave journalism the capacity to make real-life material possible in film and television; journalism, and Drew, are still struggling with what to do with that capacity.

The Audience

Audiences, at all levels, are the ultimate arbiters of communicative success. And that fact presents a difficult dilemma to the responsible cinema verite filmmaker: increased accuracy in observing and understanding the subject situation is often unnoticed by the audiences. Drew's choice of the novel as his model made great practical sense. Based firmly in a long storytelling tradition, this comparatively new form had dominated literature and then the feature film; it had not been extended to film journalism.

Drew seized the opportunity, and attempted to balance the audience appeal of dramatic individuals, events, and structures with the informational purposes of the journalist. The result was cinema verite.

But cinema verite has both needs and limits. It needs access and time; access to the individual subject or event, and time to adequately observe, structure, and present the results. Cinema verite, therefore, has raised endless questions about the shrillness required to attract and hold an audience's attention, and whether a successful audience strategy can actually destroy reporting. For all cinema verite filmmakers, whether they are observers or communicators, naturalist or realist, there is always an audience to be reckoned with. And part of that audience's makeup is the narrative heritage.

Narrative is a tradition. From the Homeric epics and *Beowulf* through *Oliver Twist* and Molly Bloom to *Rabbit, Run* and *Apocalypse Now*, narrative has been a principal means of communicating among human beings. It is a prime vehicle for entertainment, education, and history-making.

Documentary, on the other hand, has the potential to be something radically different. Documentary is, potentially, a means of recording, with unappreciated accuracy, close approximations of actual human events for later study and understanding. And it is the traditional force of narrative that is most limiting to a clear view of the documentary film.

Film came into being and grew in a society saturated with narrative creations. Narrative's history exceeds even history's history; early oral narratives became the source materials from which portions of our earliest written history have been developed. Narrative accompanied the development of civilization; narrative was familiar, and culturally accepted. After its brief beginnings as a crude documentary novelty, film quickly adopted narrative forms; it needed an audience in order to survive and thrive, and that audience understood and accepted narrative. Filmmakers became, understandably, narrativemakers.

And for hundreds of generations, the source materials of narrative have been words. Storeable and transportable, words spread their effects historically, geographically, and culturally. Words, and the skills to deal with them, are acceptable and familiar everywhere.

Film, together with its older sibling, photography, is a new and confounding element in human communication. It is not a familiar medium. Almost everyone speaks, and many write, but only a handful of human beings have created any film or photographic communication beyond a family snapshot. Schools teach at least a minimum of word skills, aimed at students as both consumers and originators of words-as-communication, but they almost universally ignore the far greater power and complexity of the visual medium. Filmmakers, faced with both a critical and general audience largely ignorant of the communicative complexities of the film medium, have largely chosen to imitate their predecessors rather than to explore the fundamentally different nature of film as a medium of documentary communication and some of the possibilities which that difference may have opened up.

Documentary critics equally fail to see and understand the true documentary quality of the films they examine; most make little if any effort to inquire into the authenticity and representativeness of the materials used in the finished film, or into the degree of editorial manipulation that has been performed as it relates to the original chronology and context of the material. The most powerful documentary recording resource yet developed is therefore allowed to rest on the communicative intentions of individual producers or production organizations, while allowing producers to divorce their source material from its original meaning and context reduces the material, and the criticisms of it, to the level of an unreferenced rhetorical exercise.

That it would be difficult to devise a different critical and production approach is clear. Critics would have to begin to understand both the recording and editing processes in much deeper ways; research into the processes of individual productions would have to be much more detailed and extensive; audiences would have to be made slowly aware of the implications of narrative editing and structuring; and filmmakers would have to be shown that there are adequately large audiences for less-narrative treatments of documentary materials. That it would be difficult, however, does not mean that it should not be attempted; the value of true documentary material to contemporary understanding and to historical accuracy cannot be underestimated, nor allowed to slide unnoted into the control of filmmakers for whom narrative is simply a powerful and comfortable tradition, unquestioned and unquestionable.

Robert Drew

15 May 1987. Relaxed, coatless, tie loose, hair still dark, face a bit full, step agile, manner often restless, Robert Drew was seated on a short couch in the ground-floor office of the East 70s Manhattan townhouse where he had worked and sometimes lived for over twenty years. The Drews gave up their fifth-floor apartment in 1985 in favor of a home in upstate New York, two hours north of the city. The fourth-floor editing and vault storage areas had also been closed down, and Drew Associates, Inc. main-

tained only minimal facilities on the first level. At 63, Drew was, profession-ally, winding down his operations—a bit.

Over a small desk in the corner, where Drew works busily as his secretary interrupts with this or that business detail, is mounted a full page from *Variety*, an advertisement for *Being with John F. Kennedy* (1983), a two-hour syndicated television special produced for the 20th anniversary of Kennedy's death featuring sequences from *Primary*, *Adventures on the New Frontier*, and *Crisis*.[26] An Emmy statuette rests quietly on the marble top of a fake mantelpiece, *Man Who Dances* the engraved citation; there are prizes from Spoleto, Mannheim, and Venice. A thick scrapbook of reviews and articles extends from "Cuba Fidels as We Burn" (*Yanki, No!*, 1960) through "Whom the Bell Extols" (*Bell Telephone Hour*, 1968); the range of programs, if not the quality of the headlines, is impressive.[27]

Nearby is a copy of *Why Not The Top*, Drew's latest promotional effort on behalf of the "Himalayan Soaring Expedition." "[It] keeps moving back year by year," Drew says matter-of-factly. "We hope to do it now in December 1988." In the eighteen months since Drew initiated the project with scenes of the California Sierras filling in for Mt. Everest, things have changed: there will no longer be cameras aboard the record-challenging glider, video has been dropped in favor of the super-quality IMAX film format, the production will be completely scripted in advance of shooting, and the scenes the glider pilots will have seen on their attempt will be recreated from a special camera plane. Drew has just returned from meet-ings with one major corporate sponsor and is courting another: "We'll see; somebody might tumble."

Another promotional film boosts a twenty-five-year-old idea: Drew's plan for a series of films on chiefs-of-state, with examples from a nearly-completed production on the Nehru/Gandhi family in India, "candidly recorded over three generations." Corazon Aquino in the Philippines, King Juan Carlos of Spain, and Peru's Alan Garcia Perez are among the "daring leaders" projected for inclusion. *Defenders of the Frontier Democracies* may yet prove that tenacity in pursuit of an idea eventually pays off.

Meanwhile, Drew is talking about "my next film."

> It's an airplane that's built on a tube. It's a tube. And on the front of the tube is a seat and on the back is a tail and in the middle is a wing with a pusher engine. And I had it put together last summer so that I could fly with hawks and birds and photograph them from the air. And there's another seat behind mine for the co-pilot.
> So I fly up to the bird, until I'm within range, and feel a good shot coming on, turn the ship over to the co-pilot, who half the time is

Anne [Drew's second wife], lift the camera out of a case on one side, and pick it up to shoot the picture. And I didn't think of this as being anything too strange, until one day I got the feeling that somebody thought I was too old to do that. Well, maybe you could get too old to do *that*, but you don't have to be too old to make films.[28]

"Old." It is a concept Drew views with some amusement, and considerable detachment; it is not, clearly, one he applies to himself.

"I mean, I meet—I go back to my old fighter squadron reunion. Those guys are old! They're all retired! And I found myself talking to them—sort of trying not to reveal it—pitying them a little bit, trying to make them feel better about being retired. And after awhile, I realize that they were talking to me trying to make me feel better about having to work! [Laughter] And there you are."[29]

But even Drew must recognize and anticipate the inevitability of human processes. He promotes, he plans, he hurries off after the details of one or another of his projects. But he cannot, and does not, avoid some consideration of the future.

Joyce Cary wrote *The Horse's Mouth*. I recommend it; it's a wonderful book. But the central character in the book—and I read this book first when I was about 25 or something—the central character is a muralist; he paints pictures on walls. And his great need in life is to find a wall to paint on. And this creates all kinds of wonderful scenes throughout the book, but it ends with the scene where he has found a warehouse on the Thames—he's an English fellow—a warehouse on the Thames with a wall that's about 200 yards long. And it's about three stories high. And he's just painting as fast as he can because (1) it's a wonderful wall, and (2) they're tearing it down. So, as he goes, the wall is being torn down [behind him.]

But it's a beautiful example of a guy who is obsessed with something, and never wants to stop. And so the day I can't find a wall—that is, the money to make films—I'll probably have to retreat to the typewriter. But the fact is that I do stories. So, I'll do them on film as long as I can; then I'll probably do them on paper, as long as anybody will look at them.[30]

24

Afterword

It is a clear, crisp Sunday in New York City, 14 February 1988, Valentine's Day. But inside the recently condensed offices of Drew Associates, Robert Drew is angry, even hurt. His feelings are signalled, not by shouting or bluster, but by a prolonged, awkward silence. Then:

DREW: Tell you what; there's no way for you to deal with this. So why don't you print your book and I'll have to write a book!

And he [Pennebaker] said it, and there's no doubt that you should print it. But—but this is just bullshit! This is just—outrageous. He's taking credit for what I did, and painting a portrait of me wanting to do something I didn't do. And he's getting away with it and it pisses me off because he's lived a lifetime doing what he does. You can see it on the screen. I've lived a lifetime *telling the truth; he's* the guy who's been telling stage performances. And yet, in your book, it looks like Drew's some guy who didn't know what he was doing, and falsifying the world.

O'CONNELL: I'm trying to be attentive to the kinds of institutional problems that come up—.

DREW: What has that got to do with Pennebaker falsifying the history of my work! My life!! It's got nothing to do with institutions; it has to do with this guy building a case, for something that wasn't true.[1]

Drew's anger is momentarily diverted into discussion of the reasons why material critical of his work and motives has been included. But the sometimes anger, sometimes hurt, sometimes puzzlement is real, and frequently undisguised. In a later conversation, in a moment of particular exasperation he says, "You don't know me, after all this time!"

He is right. After four years, eight interviews, the review of dozens of additional interviews and articles and the screening of more than twenty films, after questioning his closest associates and after fashioning the sometimes disparate fragments into a coherent whole, Robert Drew remains distant, complex, and imperfectly understood.

Drew had been invited to review the initial version of this study to point out any inaccuracies, and to offer his comments.[2] The review was intended to give him the opportunity to respond in the same volume, so that corrections and comments could accompany the study and give a reader a more complete and balanced view.

The review had been difficult to arrange: Drew was in Panama, shooting hawks for a *National Geographic Explorer* special; he was in Europe as a special guest at a film conference; he was completing editing on a *Frontline* special on air traffic safety; and the deadline for submission of the study was rapidly approaching.

Finally, Drew's most pressing commitments were satisfied and a review meeting was arranged. Then, two days before the meeting, there was a flurry of phone calls, and the meeting was postponed for a day: Drew's wife, Anne, was seriously ill, in the hospital, the exact nature of her ailment unknown, and her condition uncertain. On Saturday, the problem was resolved with a major operation. Drew chose to go ahead with the rescheduled meeting, but he was clearly feeling the effects of his vigil and was not as fully organized and prepared as he might have wanted to be.

Drew Reviewing O'Connell

After pleasantries, the beginning of the meeting is almost formal, with Drew reading from notes on one of his ever-present yellow pads, the reading sounding almost scripted—and careful.

> I think you've done a fantastic job, but you have explored history— my history—at so many levels and in so many details that some of them have got to be wrong, and some of them have got to be subject to other interpretations. . . . There are factual errors, clear errors of interpretation, there are other things that are less decisive . . . and I wouldn't disagree too much there, but there is a sense in the "music" of the thing that is important and which you've gotten mostly, but some people that you quote in the book are dissonant or tone-deaf or even hostile.[3]

Before getting to questions of "music" and hostility, there are smaller details. Drew is quick to point out a poorly chosen word or phrase. An original sentence reads: "But [*On the Pole*] is certainly not high-level 'journalism'; there is no consideration of the economics of racing—for the drivers or for the city of Indianapolis—there is only passing attention paid to spectacle-vs-safety issues, and Eddie's off-season career as a hair dresser is conveniently overlooked."

The sentence follows a paragraph which summarizes the strengths of *On the Pole* as an early cinema verite film. Drew objects to "high-level," feeling that use of the term implies its opposite, "low-level." "High-level" is changed to "traditional" in the final version of the study.

There are a good number of specific changes: chronologies revised, names corrected, and differing recollections of particular events resolved by the addition of an endnote. Incidents of the author's imprecise understanding or writing are explained more fully. There are broader concerns, however, not so easily answered or corrected.

The Critical Method

> The critical method I found fascinating because it accorded with something in my own critical method, which is not to compare the films with what we were competing with, but to hold them to the same high standards as some of our own finest achievements! [Laughter]
> And I enjoyed that, but . . . the more that we succeeded in any given film, the more we depress the quality of the other films, in a critical view. . . . I don't mind being criticized by my own standards—don't get me wrong—I just wouldn't like to seem less than the people I was competing with because my own standards were higher than theirs.[4]

Drew's point is a valid and important one. In this study, much of his work has been measured against his own films and against his stated purposes and proposals, and not against the work of other major producers of television documentaries of the period. That critical choice has resulted in an unintended, and perhaps unfair, imbalance. For example, the attention given to *On the Pole*, a remarkable film to have appeared so early in the development of cinema verite, has the effect of unintentionally setting a standard for the measurement of later Drew films.

> There were always two lines [of development]. From the very first two films, *Primary*, which was a news film, and [*On the Pole*], which was a human, drama film, there were always the two lines, two ways to go in exploring the use of candid footage.
> And the fact that [*On the Pole*] was a drama helped set the stage for the *Living Camera* dramas. The fact that the news films that we did, for ABC *CloseUp!*, were not living drama films is not the way to

criticize them; from my standpoint, the question was, "What candid footage should we get, and how did that work in comparison with the other documentary films being made on those subjects." And I could tell you that our films were alive and electric and human, on a scale that other films weren't, and had never been. And so I don't see them as a failure in terms of not being an [*On the Pole*]; I see them as a success in terms of not being a—an ABC *Closeup!*, or a *See It Now*, or something like that.[5]

Drew seems satisfied to have made his point and to have it acknowledged; no copy changes are made. But an even more fundamental, and more personal, objection underlies our conversations, one that is far more difficult for author and subject to agree on.

Penny

You start with the story of Drew and the idea and the associates, and then at some point it's my feeling that the story gets turned over to someone else, who is generally *wrong*, in the sense of "music" and interpretation, and often in the facts. . . . You should know, and I should make clear, that the picture of Pennebaker that emerges here is not just a contrasting artistic sensibility, which is what I thought it was, but an active and hostile denigrator, if not fabricator. The piece is littered with a sort of network of negative things, which are not true and should be answered.[6]

Robert Drew, from his opening "script."

There are deep, fundamental differences between Robert Drew and Donn Alan Pennebaker, differences in professional skills (producer-writer, cameraman-editor), in personal outlook (a sense of drama, an attentiveness to interpersonal details), and a far different sense of the "music" of a documentary film. And Drew is offended, even wounded, by the frank expression of so many of those differences by Pennebaker.

Drew's dissatisfactions begin with smaller points.

We're about to start getting into Pennebaker here in detail now. "When they came back from shooting *Yanki No!*, we sat down and started to talk about stories, and Drew . . . started bringing in people, reporters from the magazine, and I could see that he was going to pay them a lot of money." [Laughter]

One theme that I never imagined that Pennebaker was so obsessed with was with money. He's got a whole pattern throughout his comments with money. And you asked me once if we paid them a lot of money, and I showed you some records indicating, I think, that more or less people were getting paid about the same, except Ricky and

Penny were getting paid a little more. That's my recollection. And if Penny wants to say we paid [correspondents] a lot of money, again, I don't see what a historian is gonna do about that, so—he says it, but it isn't true.[7]

Although he declined to release specific figures, Drew provided a payroll record from September 1963, which shows that Pennebaker, Shuker, and James Lipscomb were paid the same amount, with Leacock earning a third more and Hope Ryden and Abbott Mills a third less.

" 'We all had to sit down and think, well, is it gonna be commercially saleable.' Pennebaker was never, ever, was asked that question, or party to such a question. I mean, he can say this, but he's just—baloney. The only questions that Penny could have gotten into were 'Is this a good story?' "[8]

Drew is also offended by Pennebaker's reactions to the presentational forms that Pennebaker saw as being imposed on the highly realistic source material he and others were bringing back from the field.

PENNEBAKER (draft copy): And Drew began to get, I think, split up.
He began to see that he was going to have to deliver to Time-Life, and ABC, programs that fitted in with what they had in mind, but that Ricky and I were speeding very fast in another direction. With which, I think—I mean, I've always felt—that he was fairly sympathetic. And in fact was quite interested.[9]

DREW: "And Drew began to get split up." Well, that's his view.
That I was going to "deliver programs that fitted in with what they had in mind." Bullshit! Time, Inc. and ABC received what I made, and what they had in mind was absolutely no guidance to me! But this is a measure of Pennebaker's distortion; Pennebaker's building a case, and he's full of shit! And I was not "split up" because I had to deliver things Time, Inc. and ABC wanted; I didn't know—they didn't *want* anything! I mean—shit![10]

Drew is almost microscopic in his examination of Pennebaker's criticisms. He is also extensive; almost half of our Valentine's Day conversation is devoted to comments about Pennebaker. Some are spontaneous personal reactions; others are more professional and substantive.

O'CONNELL: But the question that keeps coming back, at least in some discussions, is . . . life is ambiguious, and not very clear, and the story line in most—perhaps the majority of situations—is not very clear, . . . [and] you inevitably get into the situation of trying to simplify the storyline, so that the audience can percieve it.

DREW: Okay. Let's talk about ambiguity and confusion. The guy who was the biggest proponent of chaos is Pennebaker. Pennebaker felt that *Jane* was chaos, ambiguity and chaos, throughout. You quoted him saying that. Talk to [Hope] Ryden. She didn't think it was ambiguous or chaos; she know goddamned well that they were on a tryout, and that the audience either liked it or didn't, and that Jane got along with her co-star or didn't, that they rewrote it better or worse or didn't—there's nothing confusing about that story! And the confusion was is Pennebaker's mind. . . .

Now, Pennebaker's a mystifier, he's a mystical guy. In fact, "ethereal" would almost be—"childlike"—part of his attractiveness, and he was always so attractive, his childlike side.[11]

But the differences between Drew and Pennebaker are not only the differences in "artistic sensibility" that Drew refers to. They also reflect wide differences in interest and professional opportunity, especially Pennebaker's experiences as a cameraman and editor.

PENNEBAKER: It's possible to go to a situation and simply film what you see there, what happens there, what goes on, and let everybody decide whether it tells them any of these things. But you don't have to label them, you don't have to have narration to instruct you so you can be sure and understand that it's good for you to learn. You don't need any of that shit.

Most people look at [*Don't Look Back*, 1966] and say it's documentary. It is not documentary at all by my standards. It throws away almost all its information and becomes purposely abstract and tries to be musical rather than informational. . . . I never felt any reason to be informational because it wasn't something that I should tell you about. What I want to tell you about is the mood, I guess, not the information.[12]

Drew, by contrast, was a reporter, more concerned with communicating a topic than reflecting on it. And although he was greatly influenced by novels, dramas, and fiction films in his treatments of his subject matter, Drew's selection of subject matter has been very much in the reporter's tradition.

DREW: Pennebaker says that I distrusted reality, in effect, and was looking for performances. . . . And my whole effort was to get us into the real life connected with events of importance in the country. And to get us out of these stadiums and shows.

And if you look at what happened after Pennebaker left Drew Associates—I became more and more able, and dedicated, to getting into real life in all kinds of circumstances, and he became more and more dedicated to doing performances. His films are performance films; he's terrific at it, and I don't—but mainly he's rendering some-body else's art; that's his way of doing it.

And to accuse me of being a guy who was for performances is absurd.[13]

Pennebaker's most important films after leaving Drew Associates were *Don't Look Back* (1966), filmed with singer Bob Dylan on tour in England; *Monterey Pop* (1968), filmed at the Monterey International Pop Festival; and *Sweet Toronto* (1970), filmed at the Toronto Rock 'n Roll Revival.

Given these differences, it is small wonder that Pennebaker and Drew could not continue to work together much past the four-year point in their association. The remarkable assemblage of talents—Drew as leader, motivator, and managing editor; Leacock as willing cinematic innovator; Pennebaker as technical manager and contemplator; and Shuker as the most proficient story-finder—would revolutionize documentary filmmak-ing, but could not maintain a singular creative direction.

> DREW: "Drew Associates did not end with the departure of Lea-cock and Pennebaker. The contract—. But the end of the period of initial innovation and experimental development can conveniently be marked with the departure of those two individuals and the creative viewpoints they had supplied." [Long pause]
>
> OK. So Ricky went on and produced *Happy Mother's Day* [1963], and did some filming for the Germans on Stravinski [*A Stravinski Portrait*, 1964]. Penny made the Dylan film [*Don't Look Back*] and the concert film [*Monterey Pop*], did some shooting for other people, on a wonderful film on a rehearsal for—a musical rehearsal [*Original Cast Album*, 1970]. And he produced some films on the Department of Energy guy [James Schlesinger; *The Energy War*, 1979].
>
> I probably made ten times the number of films the *two* of them made, after that. Which pioneered in the shooting and the editing of candid filming in all strata of life. And those films, which were *not* total cinema verite films but which tried to use candid filming to create all kinds of filming, were regarded as fresh, new, different, innovative, creative, and won all the prizes you could win.
>
> So, in a way, the implication that these guys were supplying the innovation, or the vision, or the energy, and that that all stopped twenty years ago or whatever it was, is just *bullshit!*[14]

Drew emphasized that after Leacock and Pennebaker left, Drew Associ-ates signed a very large contract with ABC for six specials, and won "all those prizes, . . . the Venice Film Festival first prize and the other Venice Festival first prize and so forth." It is difficult for him to accept the study as an examination of only the initial productions of Drew Associates.

[You say] "At the end of the Time, Inc. contract, the initial creative impulse of Drew Associates was probably worn out." The "initial creative impulse of Drew Associates" was *mine*. And the fact that Ricky and Penny were gone did not wear out *my* creative impulse.

And the stuff we produced has been ignored or underated here, for some reason. But what we then made for ABC [after 1963] was pioneering! In every sense. That is, taking *verite* into the air in a war, and into third-world countries, and—. Anyway. I'm just saying that that's a judgement you would make with which I would disagree.

"Probably worn out." [Snorts] You don't know me, after all this time! Okay.[15]

I am unable to make clear to Drew that I was referring to "the *initial* creative impulse of Drew Associates," and that while I agreed that many of his later productions had merit, and in some cases explored important areas of cinema verite filmmaking, I also felt that the initial period, 1960-1963, had been the period of the most radical and long-lasting change in the field of documentary film. Drew did not agree.

But, at its most basic, our differences relate to matters of presentation and preconceptions.

DREW: I'm just trying to absorb what this means: "An earlier set of preconceptions have been recognized and resolved, at least in part, by cameramen and field producers as they became able to record what actually happened instead of what they felt should happen." I assume you must be—.

O'CONNELL: What I'm doing is referring back to the pre-verite days when the conception was that you had to make things happen rather than to observe them happening.

DREW: Okay, now I get that. "But they were replaced by another, more powerful, perhaps more accurate set of preconceptions about how an audience expects to have material presented to it. The ability to explore and record—" OK, . . . I guess I take it absolutely for granted that characters in action, in scenes, that have a line of development, is *clearly* the way to tell a story. [Laughter] And when that's called a "preconception", I can hardly—

O'CONNELL: One of the questions he [Pennebaker] seems to be asking, and [which] the people who I deal with in terms of talking about films are dealing with, is the question of: life is not always dramatic; audiences really expect and accept drama, on television; then how do you make that bridge, and what do you give up when you make a story dramatic, and acceptable to an audience?

DREW: Here's what you give up. If you're gonna do this, you give up the freedom to do anything else. You give up the freedom to walk in and talk; you give up the freedom to walk in and direct; you give up the freedom to walk in and pre-ordain, or lecture, or put Roger Mudd in front of the camera. And it's *very hard* to do it without those crutches and things. And most guys can't imagine doing it; if you asked them to do it, they wouldn't *begin* to do it; they wouldn't know how! So, you give up the "tools of the trade," as they now—the networks—use them. And you begin something else. Which is like fishing, and a waiting game, and an observational thing which is more intense than these guys can imagine.

But you don't give up truth.[16]

Drew's objections to the use of the Pennebaker criticisms spotlight an acknowledged limitation of the study. This study is based on the recollections of four individuals who were deeply involved in, and responsible for, much of the initial development of cinema verite. That their views and judgments differ is not surprising, and those varying perspectives are an important part of the developmental record; they are, in fact, "documents" about documentary. It was not the intention of this study to cross-check any of the participants' assertions, nor to insist that any charges be corroborated by other independent sources; this is not a case of investigative reporting, and while an increase in the diversity of information might be desirable, the conditions here are somewhat different. These are recollections of complex and now distant events, and they are sometimes contradictory. They are presented in the interests of providing a broad survey of competing evidences from an important period in documentary history.

But the question of using critical, even damaging, statements that have not been, and probably cannot be, adequately authenticated is troubling, to both author and subject. I felt that a balance was needed to Drew's enthusiasms, and Pennebaker, without prompting, provided a differing but not actively antagonistic view. Leacock, in his comments, is much more cautious in making any criticisms, and Greg Shuker generally agrees with Drew's views, although not without some reservations.

In several cases involving Pennebaker's most critical comments, I have used those comments to provide an alternative and challenging view to Drew that I felt raised important questions that a reader would value. While these most critical comments are not always answered directly by Drew, in part because of a reluctance to create a confrontation in print that may not have existed in fact, they are adequately balanced by the flow of Drew's comments throughout the study.

The basic purpose of this study is analytical, not laudatory, and involves critical judgments by the author and by those most directly involved in the important documentary developments of the past thirty years. It is important to point out to readers that Drew faced, and resolved in necessarily practical ways, both personal and professional obstacles to his goal of candid television journalism, and that some of those resolutions are open to question by others with equally good faith in the practice and future development of documentary film. I hope, and feel, that at some point Robert Drew will agree.

Appendixes
Notes
Bibliography
Index

Appendix A

Comments by Robert Drew
and Richard Leacock

Following completion of the final draft of this study, Robert Drew was invited to review it in the interest of accuracy and to point out any errors and make comments. A number of minor corrections were made as a result of his review, and his comments are presented below. Comments by Richard Leacock on an earlier draft of this study follow Drew's comments.

DREW ON O'CONNELL

In the first half of his book Mr. O'Connell has written an account of the ideas I care about and the sources and development of those ideas and of the young man who came to author them—with a dedication to veracity and detail that are a wonder to me. He has done much to clear up an information trail, for which I am grateful. As if to leave to me something to comment upon, he has all but declared those ideas moribund. For this end note I shall comment on the big ideas and on Part 2 of Mr. O'Connell's book.

The Idea

The central idea is having a greater impact on our world than any of us could have imagined—the idea that candid looking into real people caught up in dramatic situations might become effective through television as a new form of journalism for our time, a new kind of commonly shared experience. If I erred it was in underestimating the profusion and variety and fluidity of forms this idea could take. My "52 hours" of straight verite have taken their place along with Grierson's "theatre in every hamlet," as a groping forecast of a reality that, when it did develop, went far beyond the early imaginings—that became a theatre in every living room and some kind of verite in every theatre. The idea is at work in

231

documentaries, magazine shows, series on nature and culture and sports, national events and the news. The idea brought us Vietnam and helped split a nation, dispense a President and kill a war. In one funeral it knit a nation and in one fourth of July it helped restore a nation's confidence. In hearings it uncovered one presidential cover up and in another it exposed a secret and illegal government.

No theoretician has guided it—certainly not this one. No, it is not pure. It has been used to exploit violence, sex, and tabloidism. Ambulance chasers, frontmen, and narrators have been mixed in with the heroes and artists and honest technicians who have conveyed its impact. The virtues and vices are mixed into a McLuhan-esque stew that ranges from *Cops* to *Crisis*, from *That's Incredible* to bloody images of Lebanon.

The photographic means for capturing experience, which once existed in the hands of only a few of us, are now in the hands of thousands of organizations and millions of home video camera owners and their children.

What all this means for documentarians is that the tools are readily available for realizing our dreams on tape. How each of us does is up to luck as always and to our skill and talent as never before.

For the country what this means is that candid looking into people has become compelling as drama, revealing as journalism, and useful as shared experience.

I have felt myself on a frontier for most of thirty years. It has been a glorious experience and the best, I have good reason to believe, is yet to come.

Part 2 of the Book

The irony of this book is that the author who labored to straighten the historical record and who largely succeeded in doing so in part 1 introduced in part 2 another commentator who was considerably less sure and a critic who managed to tangle again many of the trails of history. The critic, it turns out, is O'Connell himself. In that role O'Connell turns from a graduate student self-described as a local TV station photographer into a world-class film critic ready to straighten out the judgments of cineasts, critics, and juries from Venice to Cannes and Paris to London and New York. His judgments range from detailed criticisms of the films to their place in the world of ideas, film, and journalism. Those judgments are often sweeping, grandiose, and more than a little haywire. I am afraid this book will not spare students and historians trying to judge these matters from the necessity of actually looking at the films.

Sometimes O'Connell's grip on the principles of cinema verite, story and drama, and their relevance to the media slips completely.

On drama. O'Connell quotes from an early book, *Cinema Verite in America* by Stephen Mamber, "Reality does not always coincide with drama and when it does we had better look twice" (p. 132). O'Connell himself writes, "Life is not always dramatic. . . . what do you give up when you make something dramatic?" (p. 226).

Of course there is not and never has been any thought that life is always dramatic. When it is, however, that drama is the quintessential element of real life that the old documentarians could only simulate. Simulate it they did. Documentarians who knew only the ersatz could be forgiven for suspecting the real thing when cinema verite brought it to the screen. One must be less charitable about commentators who years later raise such questions as if they had not been answered long ago.

Drama is accessible to filming in its natural state only from time to time. But when filmmakers succeed in capturing drama, there is no longer any point in trying to deny that they did it or that their achievement has value.

On story. O'Connell writes that cinema verite "remains largely story-bound" (p. 207), as if this were a limitation to be lamented. In reality, of course, the story is the power that liberates film storytelling from the lecture-logic of narration and other deadly limitations of print.

The implication repeated rather often in this book is that story is something imposed on a subject. The verite filmmaker cannot make up a story or conjure up a drama. He or she can only recognize it and render it.

Many good people have put much thought and effort into the concept of story. Richard Leacock on the use of story:

I don't want to tell all about a subject but, by finding a good story within it and telling it well, to reveal a great deal about the subject.

Hope Ryden on where the power lies:

You can come to care about what happens in a story to the degree that your central character is perceived to care about what happens.

Jim Lipscomb on form:

It helps to have a story that builds to a central point but it is not absolutely necessary. You can very well have a 'then-and-then-and-then' story.

Greg Shuker on story-finding:

Read Conrad and read Hemingway and read the papers. Its all out there.

Drew on story and media:

If you cannot find a story within a subject that allows you to use the powers unique to your medium, then leave that subject to a medium that is suited to handle it.

Every medium survives by doing what it does uniquely and best. It would be silly to criticize the *New York Times* for not running picture essays or *Life* for not running all the news fit to print. It is absurd for O'Connell to criticize drama for not being exposition—for instance *On the Pole* for not considering "the economics of auto racing" (p. 82), *Primary* for "being inadequate at the level of analytic generalization" (p. 69), *Crisis* for "failing to set the historical background" of segregation (p. 105). When O'Connell refers to these as failures and serious weaknesses in my theories, I am afraid he is drawing attention to failures in his own understanding of the subject he is writing about.

Film can create interests in ways print cannot. Print can satisfy those interests in ways that film cannot. They are not antagonists but both part of a continuum that stretches from facts on one end to feelings on the other, a range that is beginning to provide the world with a powerful multimedia engine-for-knowing.

On a number of points O'Connell is plain wrong. "Picture logic" has indeed replaced "word logic" in many great documentaries and in much "reality programming"; cinema verite was never intended to "explain vastly complex events"; the structure of *Primary* is anything but "extremely marginal."

O'Connell's grip on facts is not helped by turning over sections of his account to another narrator, D. A. Pennebaker. In those sections the person of Robert Drew changes, the Drew films become one calamity after another and a series of moves and events are described that never took place. Some samples:

—No meeting between the press secretaries of Eisenhower and Kennedy took place to screen *Crisis*. (See p. 270 n. 37. Several of my examples were modified or deleted in later editing.)

—Associates were not excluded but were a part of every finishing mix but one. (See p. 116.)

—Pennebaker was not prevented from making his own films and when presented the opportunity tended to turn the editing over to someone else. (See p. 196.)

—I continued to edit as carefully for truth contained in the candid footage after Chapter 17 as I did before. (See p. 146.)

—I drove us to get out of theatres and arenas into real life, as I do to this day. The former Associate who claims the reverse is Pennebaker (see p. 208), the one who continues to rely most on recording other artists for his art—*Don't Look Back, Monterey Pop, Original Cast Album.*

—Pennebaker never spoke for Leacock at Drew Associates the way he presumes to speak for him in these pages. (See p. 116, 146, 196.)

These are small items in the scheme of things but they abound and their cumulative effect is not small to those of us who were there. One day when Leacock and Pennebaker and I were discussing this book, I asked Pennebaker why he had said some of these things. There was a reason, he said. It was personal, one Leacock and I could understand, and I now know Penny did not intend them to come out the way they did.

O'Connell in these pages tells us that he is using Pennebaker's comments as "a corrective." Corrective to Drew's enthusiasms, he says once. Corrective to his own work, he again implies.

But in part 2, beyond O'Connell's grip on ideas and facts, it is his forays into criticism that might benefit most from correctives. His critique of *Primary* as crude and lacking and *On the Pole* as a summit of achievement, coupled with his assessment that "only a few of the films were fully successful," show the earmarks exhibited by those few viewers who can be called nonintegrators. When presented with a succession of shots cut together in a film, most moviegoers have no trouble integrating them into impressions and stories. The nonintegrator mainly sees just the shots. When O'Connell describes *Primary* as "confusing, meaningless, and a mishmash of inadequacies" (p. 69), I fear he is telling us what it is like to not be able to integrate. When he declares that "in spite of the best efforts of Drew and his associates, *Primary* is not self-explanatory; the details of "dramatic logic" had not yet been worked out" (p. 70), he opposes the judgment of generations of viewers and critics who saw in *Primary* just the opposite. This is the critic O'Connell has turned loose on a body of film he calls important and which, if it were as lacking as he says, one might wonder why he bothered to write about.

It is in part 2 that O'Connell suggests that the initial creative impulse of Drew Associates departed with Leacock and Pennebaker. I valued their creative contributions enormously, but I must say that I was there before their arrival and made more films winning more air time, audiences, and awards—three Venice Festival first prizes in four years, an Emmy, a Peabody, etc.—after their departure. This was in a period when L.P. [Leacock-Pennebaker Films] was declining toward its eventual dissolution. This was also a period of enormous creative contributions by other talented associates—Greg Shuker, Jim Lipscomb, Hope Ryden, Mike Jackson, Tom Bywaters, and others. All of them have continued to this day as have I. I would guess that O'Connell's demarcation of the end of an initial creative period may more accurately mark the end of his own attention span. For the rest of us it was only a beginning.

I admire every one of my former associates. And though the last few pages may not seem to reflect it, I admire Dr. O'Connell for what he has been able to make of the almost impossibly challenging job the rest of us have not found the audacity to tackle.

Robert Drew
February 1992

LEACOCK ON O'CONNELL

Chapter 6

The descriptions of *American Football* and *Bullfight at Malaga* miss the whole point of these exercises in frustration. The equipment did not work. We, not just Drew, were trying to make a new kind of movie and we were learning. I had already had a crucial experience in Israel filming Leonard Bernstein on a conducting tour, for *Omnibus*, in 1958, but it is made to appear in this account that Drew was wrapped up in network deals. I also took the new equipment (very clumsy with cables) to Moscow with Bernstein in 1959 and shot with it, along with Pennebaker and Al Maysles, in Bernstein's dressing room, with Bernstein and Boris Pasternak, also for *Omnibus*.

Chapter 10

What can I say? It was Drew and I who went to Detroit to talk to Kennedy, and then to [Washington] D.C. on his plane, and then to his house in Georgetown. He had a cold and met with us in the drawing room with Caroline. Can you honestly imagine JFK saying "what's in it for me?" He listened attentively. We asked only that I, alone, with no tripod, no lights, and asking no questions of anyone, be in his suite with my "noiseless" camera. His reply was to the effect that this was a very intimate situation and that I could easily make him look very foolish. I replied that I thought it would be rather foolish for me to do such a thing but that he had to trust me, as he would someone that he hired to work with him. He replied that "if you do not hear to the contrary, you can assume that you can do this." I remember those words as if it were yesterday. On the night in question, I slipped alone into that room.

Filming *Primary* there were no written plans on camera positions; these are post facto notes. Drew and I were the only ones with a supposedly synch rig and it had a hundred-foot load [2-1/2 minutes].

I have to say that O'Connell's discussion of *Primary* is stupid. He has no idea how important this film was and is. Henri Langlois of the *Cinemateque Français* called it "the most important documentary since Lumiere." Its technical flaws are minuscule. This film gets better and better precisely because it did not do what documentaries are supposed to do. It did not deal with the issues. Further, this was a unique moment in the history of film; there is no way that this film could be made today. A pox on this pompous crap about the technical and conceptual lapses and about the film being crude and primitive, with sound, camera, editing, and structure of marginal quality.

Chapter 13

Pennebaker tells about me second hand. Drew was there, I was there.

Chapter 15

Sorry, but I made the decision to drop [Gov. G. Mennen] "Soapy" Williams and called Drew later. Check with Shuker if you will.

Chapter 16

What to say about Pennebaker's flights of speculative fancy on Drew's relationship with ABC. As far as I know he had nothing to do with it. You might as well quote Shirley Temple!

There seems to be an assumption that Drew, Pennebaker, and I are after the same thing. We are not. Drew's dream, to put twenty to fifty, whatever, hour-long shows on broadcast TV was our nightmare.

Chapter 17

What Pennebaker thinks is second-, third-, and fourth-hand gossip.

Chapter 18

The "Crisis Structure." The producer-filmer-editor lament. This is classic in the industry and gets nowhere. About the only way to sort it out is to look at the characteristics of their films when not working together.

Shooting Jane. Naturally, I take a dim view of the constant use of "made possible by Drew's innovations"; more accurate to say "Drew Associates' innovations." How's that?

Paul and the Chair. Again, I am sorry but Drew is wrong. Look it up. It was not "judges" in "court"; it was the Parole Board at a hearing, and it was covered by the local TV boys.

Chapter 19

"Free Cinema." Is it possible that O'Connell has not seen *Jazz Dance* (1954) shot by me and Bob Campbell for Roger Tilton long before it was mimicked as *Momma Don't Allow*. Anyway, the Brits had no influence on us and they never ever lost control.

Pre-Verite. Morris Engel had a big influence on me and we tried to get NBC interested in building a sixteen-millimeter camera based on my idea of using the Bulova watch as a synchronizing device. Later, we (Drew Associates) built this with Mitch Bogdanovitch. It was only *Weddings and Babies* that used synch, portable (if you were strong enough to carry it) sound. *Lovers and Lollipops* was shot silent. I wrote of Morris Engle's innovative use of portable equipment in *Harper's* magazine before I ever met Drew.

Callenbach, 1961. Callenbach is talking about what I did with a camera and knows perfectly well what Drew did. This is not an "error."

Marcorelles, 1962. O'Connell doesn't even understand what Marcorelles is saying. Marcorelles is speaking positively of the theoretical implications for both narrative and documentary filmmaking; of a body of work that resulted from the collaboration of a number of people, including Drew, who, he takes care to point out, makes final decisions. Louis Marcorelles is not asking for naive answers to nonquestions, as O'Connell implies.

Lyon, France, 1963. The conference on *cinéma vérité* at Lyon in 1963 is recognized as one of the most important gatherings in the history of film. Not according to O'Connell. Who are Cameron and Shivas? This conference had international repercussions. Ask the Hungarians (Judit Elek for example) or the Poles. This is where we first saw each other's work and got to know each other. These films could not have existed a couple of years before. There were theoretical arguments; must we develop a new grammar? Are we destroying the art of the cinema? Drew was there briefly. In my opinion, the French connection was crucial to our international, intellectual impact. How do you think the Drew films got shown in theatres in France? This account is ludicrous.

Chapter 21

Nurturing a Crisis. It was Lipscomb and I who went and filmed George Wallace in the Governor's Mansion, etc. Later I went over to Katzenbach, with Pat Powell taking sound while Lipscomb did the shooting of George Wallace on the confrontation day.

Managing the Crisis. "In a flurry of phone calls and meetings covered by

Drew's teams . . . " In my view, this is close to psychotic; Drew wasn't even around. This is Shuker and Pennebaker's story. But O'Connell is missing the heart of how we worked. All of us were making decisions, gambling, risking our necks; these were not "personnel" or Drew's "teams." These are filmmakers and journalists. These are people who are making a film together, and the end of the story is that Drew could not hold the group together and join a network. For me it looked more and more like the nightmare, so when Penny and I split there was nothing left of the early group; no more editing your own footage, etc. I guess that's the way Drew wanted it, and he went ahead and made films the way he wanted without a bunch of dogs yapping at his ankles. I haven't even seen those later films, so I have no opinions about what happened after *Crisis*.

The Results—1963, 2. *Crisis* was merely the end of a single period at Drew Associates; a period when funding from Time, Inc. was available to experiment with. . . . I had signed a contract (having read it carefully) with Drew Associates that contained a punitive clause forbiding me to work for American television for one year if I should break this contract. This clause was subsequently enforced and I spent a year attending European film festivals, spreading the gospel according to St. Richard, and making TV commercials in London and Dublin, illegally.

Chapter 23

The Audience. If O'Connell honestly believes that reaching a large audience is the ultimate measure of communicative success, then this and most other worthy books should not be published.

Chapter 24

Unfortunately I have to say that I think O'Connell has again managed to miss the point. Take a look at the series on the civil rights movement, *Eyes on the Prize*, and you can see what happened as the equipment, which we and others pioneered, became available. This is not "Drew's dream"; it is the real world that is ticking along out there [and] doing very well, thank you. Take a look!

In my opinion, it is the nature of broadcast television, that "cultural wasteland," that posed a problem for Bob Drew and there is not a word about that in this book. And don't get me wrong; I love and admire Drew and I loved every minute of the time I spent working with him. It was a gas!

Richard Leacock
October 1989

Filmography: Robert Drew

1954

Key Picture (*Magazine X*). Produced and edited by Robert Drew and Allan Grant. Sponsor: NBC.

1957

American Football. Producer: Robert Drew. Photographer: Richard Leacock. Sponsor: Time, Inc.
The B-52. Producer: Robert Drew. Photographer: Richard Leacock. Sponsor: Time, Inc.

1958

Balloon Ascension. Producer: Robert Drew. Photographers: Richard Leacock, D. A. Pennebaker. Sponsor: Time, Inc.
Weightless (*Zero Gravity*). Producer: Robert Drew. Photographer: Jess Payley. Sponsor: Time, Inc.

1959

Bullfight. Producer: Robert Drew. Photographer: Richard Leacock. Sponsor: Time, Inc.

1960

Primary. Conceived and produced by Robert Drew for Time-Life Broadcasting. Photographers: Richard Leacock, D. A. Pennebaker, Terence McCartney-

Filgate, and Albert Maysles. Managing editor: Robert Drew. Writer: Robert Drew.

On The Pole. Executive producer: Robert Drew. Filmmakers: Richard Leacock, D. A. Pennebaker, William Ray, Abbott Mills, and Albert Maysles. Correspondents: James Lipscomb, and Gregory Shuker. Co-produced by Time, Inc. and Drew Associates.

Yanki No! Producer: Robert Drew. Filmmaker: Richard Leacock, with Albert Maysles and D. A. Pennebaker. Reporters: William Worthy, and Quinera King. Co-produced by Time, Inc., ABC-TV, and Drew Associates.

1961

X-Pilot. Executive producer: Robert Drew. Associate producer: Howard Sochurek. Filmmakers: Terence McCartney-Filgate, and Albert Maysles. Correspondent: Gregory Shuker. Co-produced by Time, Inc., ABC-TV, and Drew Associates.

The Children Were Watching. Executive producer: Robert Drew. Filmmaker-producer: Richard Leacock. Photographer: Kenneth Snelson. Correspondents: Lee Hall, and Gregory Shuker. Co-produced by Time, Inc., ABC-TV, and Drew Associates.

Adventures on the New Frontier. Executive producer: Robert Drew. Filmmakers: Richard Leacock, D. A. Pennebaker, Albert Maysles, and Kenneth Snelson. Correspondents: Lee Hall, Gregory Shuker, and David Maysles. Co-produced by Time, Inc., and Drew Associates.

Kenya (Part I: *Land of the White Ghost*; Part II: *Land of the Black Ghost*). Executive producer: Robert Drew. Filmmaker-producer: Richard Leacock. Filmmaker: Albert Maysles. Correspondent: Gregory Shuker. Co-produced by Time, Inc., ABC News, and Drew Associates.

Eddie (*Drive*) (*On The Pole #2*). Executive producer: Robert Drew. Filmmakers: Richard Leacock, and D. A. Pennebaker. Photographers: Albert Maysles, Abbott Mills, and William Ray. Correspondents: Robert Drew, Gregory Shuker, and James Lipscomb. Co-produced by Time-Life Broadcast, and Drew Associates.

David (*Synanon*). Executive producer: Robert Drew. Filmmakers: Gregory Shuker, D. A. Pennebaker, and William Ray. Correspondent: Nell Cox. Co-produced by Time-Life Broadcast, and Drew Associates.

Petey and Johnny (*Spanish Harlem*). Executive producer: Robert Drew. Producer: Richard Leacock. Filmmakers: James Lipscomb, Abbott Mills, and William Ray. Co-produced by Time-Life Broadcast, and Drew Associates.

Mooney vs. Fowle (*Football*). Executive producer: Robert Drew. Filmmaker: James Lipscomb. Photographers: William Ray, Abbott Mills, Richard Leacock, D. A. Pennebaker, and Claude Fournier. Correspondents: Hope Ryden, and Peter Powell. Co-produced by Time-Life Broadcast, and Drew Associates.

1962

Blackie (Airline Pilot). Executive producer: Robert Drew. Filmmakers: William Ray, and D. A. Pennebaker. Correspondents: Gregory Shuker, and Peter Powell. Co-produced by Time-Life Broadcast, and Drew Associates.

Susan Starr. Executive producer: Robert Drew. Producers: Hope Ryden, and Gregory Shuker. Filmmakers: Hope Ryden, and D. A. Pennebaker. Photographers: D. A. Pennebaker, Claude Fournier, Peter Eco, James Lipscomb, Abbott Mills, and Richard Leacock. Correspondents: Hope Ryden, Patricia Isaacs, James Lencina, and Sam Adams. Co-produced by Time-Life Broadcast and Drew Associates.

Nehru. Executive producer: Robert Drew. Filmmakers: Gregory Shuker, and Richard Leacock. Co-produced by Time-Life Broadcast, and Drew Associates.

The Road to Button Bay (Girl Scouts). Executive producer: Robert Drew. Filmmakers: Stanley Flink, Abbott Mills, Hope Ryden, James Lipscomb, Richard Leacock, and D. A. Pennebaker. Co-produced by Time-Life Broadcast, and Drew Associates.

The Aga Khan. Executive producer: Robert Drew. Filmmakers: Gregory Shuker, D. A. Pennebaker, and James Lipscomb. Co-produced by Time-Life Broadcast, and Drew Associates.

The Chair (Paul). Executive producer: Robert Drew. Filmmakers: Gregory Shuker, Richard Leacock, and D. A. Pennebaker. Correspondents: Gregory Shuker, Robert Drew, John MacDonald, and Sam Adams. Co-produced by Time-Life Broadcast, and Drew Associates.

Jane (The Jane Fonda Story). Executive producer: Robert Drew. Producer: Hope Ryden. Filmmakers: Hope Ryden, D. A. Pennebaker, Richard Leacock, Gregory Shuker, and Abbott Mills. Co-produced by Time-Life Broadcast, and Drew Associates.

1963

Crisis: Behind a Presidential Commitment. Executive producer: Robert Drew. Producer: Gregory Shuker. Filmmakers: Richard Leacock, James Lipscomb, and D. A. Pennebaker. Produced by ABC News in association with Drew Associates.

1964

Faces of November. Executive producer: Robert Drew. Producer: Gregory Shuker. Photographers: James Lipscomb, Sidney Reichman, and Al Wertheimer. Correspondent: Tom Johnston. Produced by ABC News in association with Drew Associates.

Mission to Malaya. Executive producer: Robert Drew. Producer: Hope Ryden.

Photographer: Sidney Reichman. Produced by ABC News in association with Drew Associates.

1965

Letters from Vietnam. Executive producer: Robert Drew. Producer: Gregory Shuker. Photographer: Abbott Mills. Produced by ABC News in association with Drew Associates.

In the Contest of the Queen (Anton Kuerti). Executive producer: Robert Drew. Producer: James Lipscomb. Photographers: James Lipscomb, and Sidney Reichman. Correspondents: Gregory Shuker, Tom Johnston, and James Goode. Produced by ABC News in association with Drew Associates.

Assault on LeMans (Phil Hill). Executive producer: Robert Drew. Producer: James Lipscomb. Photographers: James Lipscomb, and Abbott Mills. Correspondents: Gregory Shuker, Tom Johnston, and James Goode. Produced by ABC News in association with Drew Associates.

The Big Guy (Jim Beattee). Executive producer: Robert Drew. Producer: James Lipscomb. Photographers: James Lipscomb, and Abbott Mills. Correspondents: Dan Fales, James Goode, and Gregory Shuker. Produced by ABC News in association with Drew Associates.

The Time of Our Lives. Executive producer: Robert Drew. Producers: Gregory Shuker, and Hope Ryden. Photographers: Sidney Reichman, and Abbott Mills. Correspondents: James Goode, and Dan Fales. Produced by ABC News in association with Drew Associates.

Men Encounter Mars (Mariner IV). Executive producer: Robert Drew. Producers: Gregory Shuker, and James Lipscomb. Photographers: James Lipscomb, and Frank Simon. Produced by Drew Associates. Sponsor: NASA.

1966

Storm Signal (Drug Addiction). Executive producer: Robert Drew. Producer: James Lipscomb. Photographers: James Lipscomb, and Frank Simon. Correspondents: Mike Jackson, and Tom Johnston. Narrator: James Lipscomb. Produced by Drew Associates. Sponsor: Xerox.

Another Way. Executive producer: Robert Drew. Producer: Hope Ryden. Photographer: Sidney Reichman. Produced by Drew Associates. Sponsor: Peace Corps.

A Man's Dream: Festival of Two Worlds (Spoleto). Executive producer: Barry Wood. Producer: Robert Drew. Photographers: Frank Simon, and Nick Proferes. Correspondent: Mike Jackson. Produced by Henry Jaffe Enterprises. Sponsor: Bell Telephone Company.

International Jazz Festival (Belgium). Executive producer: Barry Wood. Producer: Robert Drew. Photographers: Abbott Mills, and Nick Proferes. Correspondents: Mike Jackson, and Dorothy Tod. Produced by Henry Jaffee Enterprises. Sponsor: Bell Telephone Company.

The New Met: Countdown to Curtain. Executive producer: Barry Wood. Producer: Robert Drew. Photographers: Abbott Mills, Mort Heilig, Al Wertheimer, Robert Hagensen, Darwin Deen, Edward Horton, Frank Calabria, Harold Posner, and Peter Powell. Produced by Henry Jaffee Enterprises. Sponsor: Bell Telephone Company.

1967

On the Road with Duke Ellington. Executive producer: Robert Drew. Producer: Mike Jackson. Photographers: Abbott Mills, and Darwin Deen. Produced by Drew Associates. Sponsor: Bell Telephone Company.

The Virtuoso Teacher (Joseph Fuchs). Executive producer: Robert Drew. Associate producers: Mike Jackson, and Harry Moses. Photographers: Abbott Mills, Darwin Deen, and Walter Helmuth. Produced by Drew Associates. Sponsor: Bell Telephone Company.

Carnival of the Menuhins. Executive producer: Robert Drew. Producer: Mike Jackson. Associate producer: Harry Moses. Photographers: Abbott Mills, Juliana Wang, and Walter Helmuth. Produced by Drew Associates. Sponsor: Bell Telephone Company.

1968

Man Who Dances: Edward Villella. Executive producer: Robert Drew. Producer: Mike Jackson. Photographers: Abbott Mills, Ernest Nukanen, Juliana Wang, Ralph Weisinger, and Walter Helmuth. Produced by Drew Associates. Sponsor: Bell Telephone Company.

Jazz: The Intimate Art. Executive producer: Robert Drew. Producer: Mike Jackson. Associate producer: Harry Moses. Photographers: Abbott Mills, Juliana Wang, and Ralph Weisinger. Produced by Drew Associates. Sponsor: Bell Telephone Company.

Nelson Rockefeller. Executive producer: Robert Drew. Producers: Mike Jackson, and Tom Bywaters. Produced by Drew Associates. Sponsor: Nelson Rockefeller Campaign.

Another World, Another Me. Executive producer: Robert Drew. Producers: Gregory Shuker, and Tom Bywaters. Photographer: Abbott Mills. Produced by Drew Associates. Sponsor: National Park Service.

Confrontation in Color. Executive producer: Robert Drew. Producer: Mike Jackson. Photographers: Abbott Mills, and Walter Helmuth. Produced by Drew Associates. Sponsor: Greater Philadelphia Movement.

1969

The Space Duet of Spider and Gumdrop (Apollo 9). Producer: Robert Drew. Photographer: Walter Helmuth. Sponsor: NASA.

Songs of America (Simon and Garfunkel). Executive producer: Robert Drew.

Producer: Mike Jackson. Photographers: Abbott Mills, and Peter Powell. Produced by Drew Associates. Sponsor: Bell Telephone Company.

1970

The Martian Investigators (Mariner IV). Executive producer: Robert Drew. Producer: Mike Jackson. Photographer: Al Wertheimer. Produced by Drew Associates. Sponsor: NASA.

1971

The Sun Ship Game (Soaring). Producer-director: Robert Drew. Associate producers: Anne Gilbert, and Mike Jackson. Photographers: Peter Powell, and Abbott Mills. Produced by Drew Associates. Sponsor: Drew Associates and Max L. Raub Productions.

1972

Beyond the Limits. Producer: Robert Drew. Associate producer: Anne Drew. Photographers: Dan Drasin, and Thatcher Drew. Produced by Drew Associates. Sponsor: Department of Community Affairs, Commonwealth of Pennsylvania.

1973

Late Start. Producer: Robert Drew. Photographers: Dan Drasin, and Mike Jackson. Produced by Drew Associates. Sponsor: Department of Welfare, Commonwealth of Pennsylvania.

Deal With Disaster. Producer: Robert Drew. Photographers: Mike Jackson, and Dan Drasin. Produced by Drew Associates. Sponsor: Department of Community Affairs, Commonwealth of Pennsylvania.

Mini-documentaries: *Saving the Birds, Helping the Blind,* and *Junior Achievement.* Producer-director: Robert Drew. Produced by Drew Associates. Sponsor: IBM.

Mini-documentaries: *Teaching Reading; Children's Hospital; School Bus; State Legislature; Pittsburg, Kansas; Mississippi; Typewriter; Oceanography.* Producer: Robert Drew. Director: Gregory Shuker. Produced by Drew Associates. Sponsor: IBM.

Who's Out There? (Orson Wells and Carl Sagan). Producer: Robert Drew. Photographers: Gary Graver, Bill Weaver, Mike Jackson, and Dan Drasin. Produced by Drew Associates. Sponsor: NASA.

Life in Outer Space and *The Mind of Man.* Producer: Robert Drew. Director: Gregory Shuker. Produced by Drew Associates. Sponsor: NASA.

1974

Saving Energy, It Begins at Home. Executive producer: Robert Drew. Producer: Thatcher Drew. Photographers: Robert Neil, and Dan Drasin. Produced by Drew Associates. Sponsor: Department of Community Affairs, Commonwealth of Pennsylvania.

Junk Cars. Executive producer: Robert Drew. Producer: Thatcher Drew. Photographer: Nick Proferes. Produced by Drew Associates. Sponsor: Department of Community Affairs, Commonwealth of Pennsylvania.

1975

A Feast of Talent. Executive producer: Robert Drew. Producer: Gregory Shuker. Photographer: Mike Jackson. Produced by Drew Associates. Sponsor: Affiliate Artists.

The Tall Ships Are Coming. Producer: Robert Drew. Associate producer: Anne Drew. Photographer: Bob Elfstrom. Produced by Drew Associates. Sponsor: IBM.

Mini-documentary: *Christmas Birds.* Executive producer: Robert Drew. Producers: Anne Drew, and Mike Jackson. Produced by Drew Associates. Sponsor: IBM.

Mini-documentaries: *Ohio River, Conserving Energy, Apollo Soyez, Children Learn to Write by Dictating, World Food Crisis.* Producer: Robert Drew. Director: Gregory Shuker. Produced by Drew Associates. Sponsor: IBM.

1976

Things Are Changing Around This School. Executive producer: Robert Drew. Producer: Gregory Shuker. Photographer: Dan Drasin. Produced by Drew Associates. Sponsor: IBM.

Mini-documentaries: *Los Neitos, Urban League Training Center, Lodi Lady, Mt. Vernon Distar.* Executive producer: Robert Drew. Director: Gregory Shuker. Produced by Drew Associates. Sponsor: IBM.

Congressman Ruppe. Executive producer: Robert Drew. Producer: Thatcher Drew. Photographer: Thatcher Drew. Produced by Drew Associates. Sponsor: Ruppe Election Committee.

What's In a Name? Executive producer: Robert Drew. Producer: Thatcher Drew. Photographer: Sidney Reichman. Produced by Drew Associates. Sponsor: Wilson Foods-LTV.

Men of the Tall Ships. Producer: Robert Drew. Associate producer: Anne Drew. Photographers: Thatcher Drew, Robert Elfstrom, Stephen Ascher, Peter Sandomire, Robert Drew, James Fitzgerald, Frank Rahr, Denis Maloney, Coulter Watt, Juliana Wang, and Gregory Shuker. Produced by Drew Associates and The American Sail Training Association.

Six Americans on America: Chatham, Massachusetts; Morristown, New Jersey; Sa-

vannah, Georgia; San Antonio, Texas; Freelandville, Indiana; San Francisco, California. Producer: Robert Drew. Director: Gregory Shuker. Photographer: Sidney Reichman. Produced by Drew Associates. Sponsor: Mutual Benefit Life.

Parade of the Tall Ships. Producer: Robert Drew. Photographers: Robert Elfstrom, Thatcher Drew, Robert Drew, and Coulter Watt. Produced by Drew Associates. Sponsor: IBM.

1977

Kathy's Dance. Executive producer: Robert Drew. Producer: Anne Drew. Photographers: Nick Proferes, Juliana Wang, and Coulter Watt. Produced by Drew Associates. Sponsor: Sears-Roebuck Foundation.

1978

Westinghouse commercials. Producer: Robert Drew. Director: Gregory Shuker. Photographers: Nick Proferes, and Juliana Wang. Produced by Drew Associates. Sponsor: Westinghouse Corporation.

A Unique Fit - LTV Merger. Producer: Robert Drew. Produced by Drew Associates. Sponsor: LTV Corporation.

Talent for America. Executive producer: Robert Drew. Producer: Anne Drew. Photographers: Nick Proferes, Adam Gifford, Vic Losick, Sidney Reichman, Thatcher Drew, and Mike Jackson. Produced by Drew Associates. Sponsor: Sears-Roebuck Foundation.

1979

Undersea at Seabrook. Producer: Robert Drew. Associate producer: Anne Drew. Photographers: Bill Sweeney, and Robert Drew. Produced by Drew Associates. Sponsor: Morrison-Knudson.

Images of Einstein. Executive producer: Robert Drew. Producer: Gregory Shuker. Photographer: Nick Proferes. Produced by Drew Associates. Sponsor: IBM.

The Zapper. Producer: Robert Drew. Photographer: Nick Proferes. Produced by Drew Associates. Sponsor: Portec.

The Snowblower. Producer: Robert Drew. Photographer: Robert Drew. Produced by Drew Associates. Sponsor: Portec.

NBC feature reports: *Grasshopper Plague, Maine Winter, One Room Schoolhouse*. Producers: Robert Drew, and Anne Drew. Photographers: Coulter Watt, and Nick Proferes. Produced by Drew Associates. Sponsor: NBC News.

1980

Apex City. Executive producer: Robert Drew. Producer: Gregory Shuker. Photographers: Sidney Reichman, and Thatcher Drew. Produced by Drew Associates. Sponsor: IBM.

LTV '80. Executive producer: Robert Drew. Producer: Thatcher Drew. Photographer: Sidney Reichman. Produced by Drew Associates. Sponsor: LTV Corporation.

Spot Car. Producer: Robert Drew. Photographer: Coulter Watt. Produced by Drew Associates. Sponsor: Portec.

NBC feature reports: *Freeway Phobia, 1980 Census, Durham Diets, Endorphins, Professor Rassias, Alcohol Car*. Producers: Robert Drew, and Anne Drew. Photographer: Coulter Watt. Produced by Drew Associates. Sponsor: NBC News.

1981

Blitz the Cities. Executive producer: Robert Drew. Producer: Thatcher Drew. Produced by Drew Associates. Sponsor: LTV Corporation.

1982

Herself, Indira Gandhi. Executive producer: Robert Drew. Producer: Anne Drew. Photographer: Tom McDonough. Produced by Drew Associates. Sponsor: Corporation for Public Broadcasting.

Fire Season. Producer-director: Robert Drew. Director-cameraman: Sidney Reichman. Photographers: Tim Houlihan, and Carl Gilman. Produced by Drew Associates. Sponsor: Corporation for Public Broadcasting.

784 Days That Changed America: From Watergate to Resignation. Executive producers: Nancy Dickerson, and William Carpenter. Producer: Robert Drew. Writers: Robert Drew, and Nancy Dickerson. Photographers: Sidney Reichman, Joe Rose, Duff Thomas, and David Steward. Sponsor: Television Corporation of America.

1984–1985

Build the Fusion Power Machine. Executive producer: Robert Drew. Producer: Thatcher Drew. Photographers: Sidney Reichman, Carl Kreigeskotte, and Vic Losick. Produced by Drew Associates. Sponsor: Ebasco.

Being with John F. Kennedy. Executive producers: Robert Drew, and Nancy Dickerson. Filmmaker: Robert Drew. Correspondent: Nancy Dickerson. Production facilities: Drew Associates. Sponsor: Golden West Television.

Warnings from Gangland. Producer-director: Robert Drew. Associate producer: Gregory Shuker. Cameraman-director: Sidney Reichman. Photographer: Mark Curtis. Writer: Anne Drew. Produced by Drew Associates for *Frontline*. Sponsor: Corporation for Public Broadcasting and WGBH Educational Foundation.

Marshall High Fights Back. Producer: Robert Drew. Directors: Robert Drew, and Sidney Reichman. Photographer: Sidney Reichman. Writer: Anne

Drew. Produced by Drew Associates. Sponsor: Corporation for Public Broadcasting.

Shootout on Imperial Highway. Producer: Robert Drew. Photographer: Marc Curtis. Produced by Drew Associates for *Frontline.* Sponsor: WGBH Educational Foundation.

1985–1986

The Transformation of Rajiv Gandhi. Producer: Robert Drew.

For Auction: An American Hero. Producer: Robert Drew. Associate producer: David Steward. Correspondent: Thatcher Drew. Photographers: Mark Curtis, and Sidney Reichman. Produced by Drew Associates. Sponsor: Corporation for Public Broadcasting.

OK Heart. Executive producer: Dr. John E. Walsh. Producer: Robert Drew. Field producer: Thatcher Drew. Producer for WVIA: Ed Finn. Photographers: Justis Taylor, Peter Schnall, and Sidney Reichman. Produced for WVIA by Drew Associates. Sponsor: State Farm Insurance; Nabisco, Inc.

1987–1988

Your Flight is Cancelled. Producers: Robert Drew, and Anne Drew. Photographers: Marc Curtis, James Jernigan, and Robert Drew. Produced by Drew Associates for *Frontline.* Sponsor: WGBH Educational Foundation.

Messages from the Birds. Executive producer: Christopher Palmer. Producers: Robert Drew, and Anne Drew. Photographers: Robert Drew, and Coulter Watt. Produced by Drew Associates. Co-produced by National Audubon Society, Turner Broadcasting, and WETA-TV.

River of Hawks. Executive producer: Robert Drew. Photographer: Robert Drew. Produced by Drew Associates. Sponsor: National Geographic Society.

1988—1989

Kennedy versus Wallace. Executive producer: Robert Drew. Producer: Gregory Shuker. Co-producer: Anne Drew. Photographer: Stephen Ward. Narrator: Clarke Bittner. *Crisis* segments. Filmmakers: Richard Leacock, James Lipscomb, D. A. Pennebaker, and Hope Ryden. Narrator: James Lipscomb. Produced by Drew Associates.

1989–1990

London to Peking: The Great Motoring Challenge. Executive producer: Robert Drew. Field producers: Gregory Shuker, and Coulter Watt. Photographers: Coulter Watt, Vic Losick, Gregory Shuker, David Cunningham, Craid MacNab, and Robert Drew. Writers: Cliff Robertson, and Robert Drew. Produced by Drew Associates.

1990–1991

Life and Death of a Dynasty. Executive producer: Robert Drew. Producers: Anne Drew, and Robert Drew. Photographers: Coulter Watt, J. N. Sharma, Sidney Reichman, Robert Drew, M. K. Rao, Tom McDonough, Mark Shelley, and Richard Leacock. Field producer: Gregory Shuker. Sponsor: The William Benton Foundation. Executive producer-director: Lewis Freedman.

Appendix C

Summary of Awards: Drew Associates

American Bar Association

1983—Silver Gavel Award—*784 Days That Changed America*

American Film Festival

1961—Blue Ribbon Award—*Primary*
1978—Blue Ribbon Award—*Kathy's Dance*

Cannes Film Festival

1962—First Prize—*The Chair*

Chicago Film Festival

1978—Silver Hugo—*Kathy's Dance*

Council on International Non-Theatrical Events (CINE)

1964—Cine Golden Eagle—*Crisis: Behind a Presidential Commitment*
1965—Cine Golden Eagle—*In the Contest of the Queen*
1967—Cine Golden Eagle—*A Man's Dream*
1968—Cine Golden Eagle—*The New Met*
1968—Cine Golden Eagle—*Duke Ellington*
1968—Cine Golden Eagle—*Man Who Dances*
1969—Cine Golden Eagle—*Jazz: The Intimate Art*
1969—Cine Golden Eagle—*The Space Duet of Spider and Gumdrop*
1970—Cine Golden Eagle—*Martian Investigators*

1975—Cine Golden Eagle—*Who's Out There*
1976—Cine Golden Eagle—*The Tall Ships Are Coming*
1977—Cine Golden Eagle—*What Do We Do Now?*
1977—Cine Golden Eagle—*Parade of the Tall Ships*
1978—Cine Golden Eagle—*Kathy's Dance*
1980—Cine Golden Eagle—*Apex City*
1982—Cine Golden Eagle—*Herself, Indira Gandhi*
1985—Cine Golden Eagle—*Marshall High Fights Back*
1986—Cine Golden Eagle—*For Auction: An American Hero*
1991—Cine Golden Eagle—*Life and Death of a Dynasty*

DuPont-Columbia Award

1985–1986—Best Documentary—*For Auction: An American Hero*

Education Writers Association

1985—First Prize—*Marshall High Fights Back*

Flaherty Award

1961—Best Documentary—*Primary*

International Cinema Exhibition, Bilboa

1967—First Prize—*The New Met*
1968—First Prize—*Man Who Dances*

International Documentary Film Festival, Bilboa

1967—First Prize—*Crisis: Behind a Presidential Commitment*

International Film and TV Festival of New York

1983—Gold Award—*784 Days That Changed America*

London Film Festival

1961—Outstanding Film—*Primary*
1962—Outstanding Film—*Petey and Johnny*, shared with *Mooney vs. Fowle*

National Academy of Television Arts and Sciences

1969—Emmy Award—*Man Who Dances*
1980—Emmy Nomination—*Alcohol Car*

1985—Emmy Nomination—*Marshall High Fights Back*
1986—Emmy Nomination—*For Auction: An American Hero*

New York Film Festival

1963—Invited Participant—*The Chair* and *Crisis: Behind a Presidential Commitment*

George Foster Peabody Broadcasting Award

1982—Peabody Award—*784 Days That Changed America*

Venice Film Festival

1964—First Prize—*Crisis: Behind a Presidential Commitment*
1965—First Prize—*Faces of November*
1966—First Prize—*Storm Signal*

Notes

Preface

1. Richard Barsam, *Nonfiction Film: A Critical History* (New York: Dutton, 1973).
2. For a fuller explanation of these terms, see Thomas W. Benson and Carolyn Andersen, *Reality Fictions: The Films of Frederick Wiseman* (Carbondale: Southern Illinois University Press, 1989), 325.

2. Beginnings

1. Robert Drew, "The Reminiscences of Robert Drew." Seven interviews by Barbara Hogenson (Oral History Research Office, Butler Library, Columbia University, New York, 4 October 1979–23 April 1980, Mimeographed), pp. 4–5, 7. In subsequent references, page numbers refer to the typed transcript in the library's files.
2. Drew's brother, Frank, was seven years younger. Frank Drew later went to the United States Military Academy at West Point, became a general in the Air Force, and is now retired. Drew's sister Nancy married an Air Force pilot; after he died, she remarried. And Drew's second sister, Way, also married an Air Force pilot, who flew for the Strategic Air Command and later retired to work for Rockwell International, an aircraft corporation. Robert Drew, interview by author, 15 May 1987. In subsequent references to my interviews with Drew, only the date is specified.
3. Drew, interview by Barbara Hogenson, 2 August 1979, p. 11.
4. Drew, interview by Barbara Hogenson, 2 August 1979, p. 15.
5. Drew, interview by Barbara Hogenson, 2 August 1979, pp. 19, 20.
6. Drew, interview by Barbara Hogenson, 2 August 1979, p. 22.
7. Drew, interview by Barbara Hogenson, 2 August 1979, p. 24. A portion of the report is reprinted in Ernie Pyle, *Brave Men* (New York: Henry Holt and Co.,

1944), 166. Pyle cites Drew as being "the youngest pilot in the Squadron" and, as a First Lieutenant, outranking his father. He also notes that Drew's father had served in the Navy in World War I.

8. Drew, interview by Barbara Hogenson, 2 August 1979, pp. 26–27.
9. Drew, interview by Barbara Hogenson, 2 August 1979, pp. 45–46.
10. Drew, interview by Barbara Hogenson, 2 August 1979, p. 47.
11. Drew, interview by Barbara Hogenson, 2 August 1979, p. 43.

3. Discovering *Life*

1. "P-80s," *Life*, 9 December 1946, 99.
2. Robert Drew, "The Fliers," *Life*, 9 December 1946, 104.
3. Drew, "The Fliers."
4. "Jets Are Different," *Time*, 23 September 1946, 97-98. The style and a number of the phrases and sentences of the *Time* article are very similar to the later version Drew wrote for *Life*.
5. Drew, interview by Barbara Hogenson, 2 August 1979, p. 64.
6. Drew, 6 October 1984.
7. Drew, 30 April 1984.
8. Drew, 30 April 1984.
9. Memo from Robert Drew to Robert Givrin, 2 October 1948. The copy is from the files of Robert Drew.
10. "City Against Auto," *Life*, 11 July 1949, 78-85.
11. Drew, 30 April 1984.
12. Drew, 30 April 1984, and Drew, interview by Barbara Hogenson, 2 August 1979, p. 67.
13. Drew, interview by Barbara Hogenson, 2 August 1979, pp. 96–97.
14. Caroline Dow Dykhouse, "Robert Drew and the Detroit Workshop, 1949–1951" (Master's Thesis, University of Michigan, 1980), 34–35.
15. Dykhouse, 37–38.
16. Dykhouse, 64–65.
17. Howard Sochurek, interviewed by Caroline Dykhouse, New York City, 11 May 1974.
18. Drew, interview by Barbara Hogenson, 4 October 1979, p. 158.
19. Dykhouse, 78–81.
20. Drew, interview by Barbara Hogenson, 2 August 1979, p. 70.
21. Drew, interview by Barbara Hogenson, 2 August 1979, p. 71.

4. The Seeds of Revolution

1. "Legal Log Jam in Chicago," *Life*, 10 November 1952, 126–33.
2. Drew, 30 April 1984.
3. Drew, 30 April 1984.
4. "Legal Log Jam in Chicago," 130.

5. Drew, 30 April 1984.

6. Drew, interview by Barbara Hogenson, 4 September 1979, p. 107.

7. Drew, interview by Barbara Hogenson, 4 September 1979, pp. 86–88.

8. "Three Prosecutors Engage the DuPonts," *Life*, 8 December 1952, 40–43.

9. Drew, interview by Barbara Hogenson, 4 September 1979, pp. 88–89.

10. "Three Prosecutors Engage the DuPonts," 42.

11. Drew, interview by Barbara Hogenson, 4 September 1979, p. 89 and Drew, 30 April 1984.

12. Drew, interview by Barbara Hogenson, 4 September 1979, p. 71.

13. Drew, interview by Barbara Hogenson, 2 August 1979, pp. 71–72.

14. Robert Drew, "An Independent with the Networks," *Studies in Visual Communication* 8 (Winter 1982):16.

15. Drew, interview by Barbara Hogenson, 2 August 1979, p. 72.

16. "An Independent with the Networks," 16.

17. An "extreme speed" film in 1954 had an A.S.A. rating of 100 Tungsten, about one-half the speed of the films Drew would first use in making his "breakthrough" films and one-tenth the speed of high-speed films of today. (Jackson J. Rose, *American Cinematographer Hand Book and Reference Guide*, 8th ed. [Hollywood: American Society of Cinematographers, 1953], 46.

18. "An Independent with the Networks," 16.

19. Drew, 30 April 1984.

20. Drew, 30 April 1984.

21. Robert Drew to author, 9 June 1987, attachment 1, "pieces of the speech." Drew has not been able to provide a complete copy of his memo for examination: "It was a speech I read to them. What I've been able to find are pieces of the speech plus a letter to Heiskell that summarized the challenge I saw for *Life*. [It] is close to word for word what I said to the group about the future of *Life* and TV."

22. Drew to author, attachment 2. Drew provided only pages 2 and 3 of his letter to Heiskell. No reason was given why page 1 was not included. The copy I received was undated, but from internal references, it was written following Drew's presentation to Time, Inc.'s managers in 1954 and before he departed *Life* for a Nieman Fellowship later that year.

23. Drew to author, attachment 2.

24. Drew, 30 April 1984.

25. Drew, 30 April 1984.

26. The Special Award citation read: "For its significance to motion pictures and for having revolutionized one of the most important branches of the industry—the newsreel." The series received nominations for Best Documentary in 1941 and 1943 and won the award for Documentary Short Subject in 1949.

27. Raymond Fielding, *The March of Time: 1935–1951* (New York: Oxford University Press, 1978), 133–34.

28. Fielding, 11.

29. Fielding, 208–9.

30. Drew, 6 October 1984.

31. Drew, interview by Barbara Hogenson, 4 September 1979, pp. 115–16.
32. Robert Timberg, "Nieman Fellows: Choosing Harvard's Divine Dozen," *Washington Journalism Review*, November 1985, 19.
33. Drew, 30 April 1984.
34. Drew, interview by Barbara Hogenson, 4 September 1979, p. 122.

5. At Harvard

1. Drew, interview by Barbara Hogenson, 4 September 1979, p. 118. Drew spent the 1954–55 academic year at Harvard.
2. Drew, interview by Barbara Hogenson, 2 August 1979, pp. 89–90.
3. Drew, "Notes to a Starting Photographer." Memo to Sidney Reichman, November–December, 1963, part 2, p. 3 (copy in the files of the Oral History Research Office, Columbia University).
4. Drew, 30 April 1984.
5. Drew, 20 November 1983.
6. Drew, "Notes to a Starting Photographer," part 2, p. 6, and Drew, 20 November 1983.
7. Drew, 30 April 1984.
8. Josiah Royce, *The Philosophy of Loyalty* (New York: Macmillan, 1908), 42, 43–44.
9. Drew, "An Independent with the Networks," 16.
10. Drew, "An Independent with the Networks," 17. Erik Barnouw writes that after seeing an early *See It Now* that contrasted, without narration, the campaign behavior of Senators Robert A. Taft and Leverett Saltonstall toward a group of young autograph seekers, "Drew went to Murrow and offered himself 'body and soul' to work in the Murrow unit. Not finding a place with Murrow, Drew badgered Time, Inc. for funds for 'candid' motion picture experiments." Barnouw, *Tube of Plenty: The Evolution of American Television*, rev. ed. (New York: Oxford University Press, 1975), 266.
11. Drew, interview by Barbara Hogenson, 5 January 1980, pp. 233–34.
12. Drew, 20 November 1983. "I have no interest in film as such. . . . I look on cinema as a pulpit, and use it as a propagandist" (John Grierson, quoted in Forsyth Hardy, ed., *Grierson on Documentary* [Berkeley, University of California Press, 1966], 15).
13. Drew, "Notes to a Starting Photographer," part 2, p. 6, and Drew, 20 November 1983.
14. Drew, "Notes to a Starting Photographer," part 2, p. 3.
15. Drew, "Notes to a Starting Photographer," part 2, p. 5.
16. Drew, "Notes to a Starting Photographer," part 2, p. 6.
17. Drew, 20 November 1983.
18. Drew, interview by Barbara Hogenson, 2 August 1979, p. 74.
19. Drew, 20 November 1983.
20. Drew, "See It Then: Notes on Television Journalism," *Nieman Reports* 9 (April 1955): 35.

21. Arthur Zegart, quoted in Drew, "See It Then," 36.
22. Drew, interview by Barbara Hogenson, 4 September 1979, p. 126.
23. Drew, "See It Then," 36–37.
24. Drew, interview by Barbara Hogenson, 5 January 1980, p. 243.
25. Drew, interview by Barbara Hogenson, 23 April 1980, p. 390. For a brief historical perspective on early developments leading to "cinema verite," see Jonas Mekas, "Notes on the New American Cinema," *Film Culture* 24 (Spring 1962): 6–16.
26. Drew, interview by Barbara Hogenson, 4 September 1979, p. 127.
27. Drew, interviews by Barbara Hogenson, 4 September 1979, p. 129 and 5 January 1980, p. 243.
28. Drew, 20 November 1983.
29. Drew, 20 November 1983.
30. Drew, "See It Then," 2.
31. Drew, "See It Then," 37–38.
32. Drew, interview by Barbara Hogenson, 4 September 1979, pp. 122–23, and Drew, 6 October 1984. Taylor's correct title was vice-president in charge of public affairs.
33. Robert Drew to Davidson Taylor, 8 November 1956 (copy from the files of Robert Drew).
34. Drew to Taylor.
35. Drew, "An Independent with the Networks," 18.

6. Returning to *Life*

1. Robert Drew, interview by Barbara Hogenson, 4 September 1979, pp. 133, 131–32.
2. Drew, 20 November 1983.
3. Drew, 20 November 1983.
4. Drew's twenty-minute film follows the University of Colorado Buffaloes and coach Darrel Ward through their "last chance to make good" against the Air Force Academy in the final game of the season. *Life*'s coverage of the game was focused on the Air Force team, which had attained top-10 ranking nationally in only its fourth season. "Air Force Falcons Soar Into Big Time," *Life*, 8 December 1958, 41–44.
5. Drew, interview by Barbara Hogenson, 4 September 1979, p. 136.
6. Drew, interview by Barbara Hogenson, 4 September 1979, pp. 138–39. Magazine story: W. R. Young, "What It's Like to Fly Into Space", *Life*, 13 April 1959, 132–48 and cover.
7. Maj. David G. Simons, "A Journey No Man Had Taken", *Life*, 2 September 1957, 19–27 and cover.
8. Drew, interview by Barbara Hogenson, 4 September 1979, p. 141. Magazine story: "Stirring Drama in Spain", *Life*, 7 September 1959, 22–31.
9. Drew, 20 November 1983.

7. Other Voices—Richard Leacock

1. Richard Leacock, interview by author, 22 September 1984. In subsequent references to my interview with Leacock, only the date is specified.
2. A brief biography of Leacock, together with a filmography, is included in G. Roy Levin, *Documentary Explorations: 15 Interviews with Film-makers* (Garden City, New York: Doubleday, 1971), 195–99.
3. Leacock, 22 September 1984.
4. Ulrich Gregor, "Leacock Oder das Kino der Physiker," *Film*, 4. Jahrgang, Helft 1 (January 1966), 14, quoted in M. Ali Issari, *Cinema-Verite* (Ann Arbor: University of Michigan Press, 1971), p. 82.
5. Stephen Mamber, *Cinema Verite in America: Studies in Uncontrolled Documentary* (Cambridge: MIT Press, 1974), 11.
6. Leacock, in Levin, 210–11.
7. Leacock, in Levin, 211–12.
8. Leacock, in Gideon Bachmann, "The Frontiers of Realist Cinema: The Work of Ricky Leacock," *Film Culture* no. 22–23 (Summer 1961): 13.
9. Leacock, 22 September 1984.
10. Leacock, 22 September 1984.
11. Leacock, interviewed by Mark Shivas, "Interviews: Richard Leacock," *Movie*, April 1963, 16, and Leacock, 22 September 1984.
12. Leacock, 22 September 1984.
13. Leacock, 22 September 1984. The Auricon camera Leacock used in 1958 was the large Super–1200 model that had been designed, in part, to shoot half-hour programs in the early days of television, before videotape was developed; the 1200-foot magazine held thirty-three-minutes of film.
14. Leacock, 22 September 1984. The Auricon camera mentioned here is not the Super–1200 model Leacock used attempting to film Leonard Bernstein in Israel but a much smaller model, the Cine-Voice, that Auricon had originally designed for sound home-movie use. The camera used 100-foot rolls of film and had to be reloaded after two-and-a-half minutes of filming.
15. Leacock, 22 September 1984.

8. Getting Equipped

1. Drew, 30 April 1984.
2. Drew, 20 November 1983.
3. Drew, interview by Barbara Hogenson, 4 October 1979, p. 162.
4. Time-Life Broadcasting's stations were KLZ-TV, Denver (CBS); WFBM-TV, Indianapolis (NBC); WTCN-TV, Minneapolis (ABC); WOOD-TV, Grand Rapids (NBC); and KOGO-TV, San Diego (NBC). Weston C. Pullen, Jr. became a Time, Inc. vice-president in 1960, and president of Time-Life Broadcasting in 1965.

9. Other Voices—Donn Alan Pennebaker

1. Donn Pennebaker, interview by author, 25 October 1984. In subsequent references to my interview with Pennebaker, only the date is specified. For a brief biography and filmography of Pennebaker, see G. Roy Levin, *Documentary Explorations: 15 Interviews with Filmmakers* (Garden City, New York: Doubleday, 1971), 223–33.
2. Pennebaker, 25 October 1984.
3. Pennebaker, 25 October 1984.
4. Pennebaker, 25 October 1984.

10. The Primary Experience

1. Robert Drew, interview by Barbara Hogenson, 4 October 1979, p. 164.
2. Drew, 20 November 1983.
3. Drew, interview by Barbara Hogenson, 4 October 1979, p. 165.
4. The most common cameras for news work in 1960 were the silent, spring-driven Bell and Howell 70-DL and 70-DR models, with an occasional Bolex or Beaulieu in use. Lenses were mostly fixed focal lengths, with 12mm, 25mm, and 50mm the most used compliment, and wide apertures—f/2.0, f/1.4, and f/1.2—were much in demand. The 100-foot-capacity (about two-and-a-half minutes) Auricon Cine-Voice camera was the most widely used sound-on-film camera; it also commonly used fixed focal length lenses and a poorly parallax-corrected optical viewfinder, although the Pan-Cinor 17–68mm zoom lens was beginning to be used.

Sound tracks were almost entirely single-system optical, a process in which the sound track was exposed directly on the original camera film along with the picture; since the development processing was designed for the picture track, the sound track development was almost always of poor quality. Tripods were used with the sound cameras, since the Auricon camera, sound amplifier, camera and amplifier batteries, and power converter necessary for off-tripod operation resulted in an unmanageably heavy and unwieldy combination for all but the most physically sturdy cameraman.

The most common films—Eastman Plus-X Reversal (ASA 50), Eastman Tri-X Reversal (ASA 160), DuPont 930A (ASA 64), and DuPont 931A (ASA 160), all black-and-white—were comparatively insensitive, so artificial lighting was required for most interior shooting; reflector photofloods were commonly used for interviews where AC was available, while many stations used battery-operated "sun guns" for filming night exteriors.

Film was commonly processed in the TV station's own small processing machine, usually by a cameraman, although some larger stations had a laboratory assistant. Editing was often done on a small editing bench equipped with rewinds, a viewer, an optical sound reader as needed, and a hot splicer. The camera original film was projected during the broadcast, and then filed or discarded, depending on the procedures at the individual station.

5. Drew, 20 November 1983. The "directional microphone" shown in still pictures taken during the making of *Primary* is a public-address system microphone only slightly more directional than the general-use omnidirectional microphones of the day.

6. Drew, 20 November 1983.

7. Handwritten notes from Drew's files, p. 2. The notes are numbered in what seems to be a chronological order.

8. Drew's notes, p. 4.

9. Theodore H. White, *The Making Of the President, 1960* (New York: Atheneum, 1961), 79. White's book was the first in a series of intimately detailed records of American presidential election strategy and activity. It makes no mention of any television coverage of the Wisconsin primary campaign and it makes no mention of Robert Drew.

10. Drew, 20 November 1983.

11. Drew, interview by Barbara Hogenson, 4 October 1979, pp. 169–70.

12. Drew, 6 October 1984.

13. Leacock, 22 September 1984.

14. Drew, 20 November 1983.

15. Drew, 20 November 1983.

16. Drew, interview by Barbara Hogenson, 4 October 1979, p. 172.

17. Pennebaker, 25 October 1984.

18. Drew, 20 November 1983.

19. Drew's notes, p. 10.

20. Drew, "An Independent with the Networks," 21.

21. Drew, interview by Barbara Hogenson, 4 October 1979, p. 182.

22. The version currently available in audio-visual distribution is the fifty-two-minute one Drew favors and considers representative of his team's efforts.

23. Drew, 20 November 1983. The *New York Times* saw in *Breathless*, and in Jean-Luc Godard's direction, "an eccentric photographic style that sharply conveys the nervous tempo and emotional erraticalness of the story it tells." A "roaring deer hunt with the camera handheld and pitching wildly in the midst of the huntsmen" was a feature of director Tony Richardson's *Tom Jones*. Each film was included in the *Times*'s Best Films of their respective years. See "Breathless" [review], 8 February 1961, p. 26; "The Best Films of 1961", 31 December 1961, sec. 2, p. 1; "Tom Jones" [review], 8 October 1963, p. 48; "Top Films of 1963," 29 December 1963, sec. 2, p. 1.

24. Drew, 6 October 1984, 20 November 1983.

25. Drew, 6 October 1984. The film *Eddie* (1961) that Drew refers to is a second version of *On the Pole* (1960); both are discussed later in this study.

26. Drew, interview by Barbara Hogenson, 4 October 1979, pp. 172–73.

11. Discovering Eddie

1. Robert Drew, interview by Barbara Hogenson, 4 October 1979, p. 188.

2. Drew, interview by Barbara Hogenson, 4 October 1979, pp. 188–89.

3. Drew, interview by Barbara Hogenson, 4 October 1979, p. 189.
4. Soundtrack, *On the Pole*, Drew Associates, 1960.
5. Drew, interview by Barbara Hogenson, 4 October 1979, pp. 190–91.
6. Drew, 15 May 1987. See "Speedway Documentary," *New York Times*, 23 May 1961, 79 and "On the Air," *New York Post*, 23 May 1961, 75: "A CBS source said the Drew auto-racing package was purchased by CBS Sports. He said CBS News could not buy outside packages."
7. Drew, "Notes To A Starting Photographer," personal memo, November–December 1963, part 3, pp. 6–7. (Mimeographed.)
8. Drew, 6 October 1984.

12. Other Voices—Gregory Shuker

1. "Russia's Wintry Look," *Life*, 26 April 1954, pp. 104–9. Shuker also received a two-line quote of a visitor's impression of the Russian countryside.
2. Gregory Shuker, interview by author, 16 November 1984. In subsequent references to my interviews with Shuker, only the date is specified.
3. Shuker, 16 November 1984.
4. Shuker, 16 November 1984.
5. Shuker, 16 November 1984.

13. The ABC Connection, 1

1. Drew, interview by Barbara Hogenson, 4 October 1979, p. 191.
2. Drew, interview by Barbara Hogenson, 4 October 1979, pp. 191–92.
3. Drew, interview by Barbara Hogenson, 4 October 1979, p. 193.
4. Donn Alan Pennebaker, "The Reminiscences of Donn A. Pennebaker." Ten interviews conducted by Barbara Hogenson (Oral History Research Office, Butler Library, Columbia University, New York, 14 November 1979–29 June 1981, mimeographed), p. 240. In subsequent references, page numbers refer to the typed manuscript in the library's files.
    Drew's recollection of the event is somewhat different. "There weren't any newsreel cameras there. We were the only cameras inside the place at San Jose. . . . Ricky and I were sitting there with hand-held cameras and moving around the way still cameramen would, and there were no other motion-picture cameras." A review of the film shows no other tripod-mounted cameras in the room, although there is a cameraman shooting Roa's walkout with a spring-driven silent camera.
5. Drew, 14 February 1988.
6. Drew, "An Independent with the Networks," 21.
7. Jack Gould, "Television: Yanki No!—A.B.C. Documentary on Castro's Effect on Latin America Produced by Time, Inc.," *New York Times*, 8 December 1960, 71.
8. Lawrence Laurent, "ABC Issues a Film Editorial Tonight Offering 'Close Up!' of Latin America," *Washington Post*, 7 December 1960, sec. C. p. 22.
9. "Television: Two Men And a Camera," *Time*, 19 December 1960, 54.

10. Val Adams, "Daly Quits ABC in Policy Battle; Vice President Was Long at Odds With Network Over Control of News Shows," *New York Times*, 17 November 1960, 75.

11. Laurent, sec. c, p. 22. Also see "Hagerty ABC News-Pubaffairs Deal is Finalized," *Variety*, 23 November 1960, 24.

12. "Time-Life Films Takes New Course for Pitch to Webs," *Variety*, 16 July 1975, 39.

13. "Time Marches On—Right Into ABC's Bell and Howell Pubaffairs Production," *Variety*, 16 November 1960, 29. Art Woodstone, "ABC-TV and Bob Drew (Time, Inc.) Expand Program Vistas as Newest Success Story in Pubaffairs Area," *Variety*, 14 December 1960, 21. Woodstone, "ABC-TV's 'Contiguous Twosome' (Treyz and Moore) Riding Herd on Sports-Pubaffairs-Entertainment," *Variety*, 23 November 1960, 24.

14. Drew, interview by Barbara Hogenson, 5 January 1980, pp. 229–30.

15. Drew, 20 November 1983. The preliminary production agreement between Time Inc. and Drew Associates was dated 1 December 1960. (Drew to author, 9 June 1987.)

16. Drew, 20 November 1983.

14. Drew Associates, 1

1. Drew, 6 October 1984. Drew has listed Leacock, Shuker, Pennebaker, Hope Ryden, and James Lipscomb as the "first generation" of associates. Drew, "An Independent with the Networks," 21. Also listed are Lee Hall, Howard Sochurek, John MacDonald, Stanley Flink, and Sam Adams. Drew, interview by Barbara Hogenson, 4 October 1979, 201. He has also listed the following "fine filmmakers" who have worked for Drew Associates at various times: Mike Jackson, Nick Proferes, Tom Bywaters, Anne Drew, Tom Johnson, Harry Moses, Peter Powell, Phil Burton, and Sidney Reichman. Drew, "An Independent with the Networks," 21.

2. Drew, "An Explanation of the Credits," in "Early *Cinema Verite*: Robert Drew and Associates," program notes from the Whitney Museum of American Art's New American Filmmaker Series, 30 March–11 April 1982, p. 9. Typescript from the files of Robert Drew.

3. Drew, "An Explanation of the Credits," 9. "Filmmaker" was a term Drew utilized in his early productions; when it became apparent that serious film critics applied a quite different meaning to the word and assigned creative responsibility for a film on that basis, Drew stopped using the term. *Crisis: Behind A Presidential Commitment* (1963) is the last Drew film to use "filmmaker" in the credits; "photographers" and "correspondents" are now credited instead.

4. Drew, interview by Barbara Hogenson, 26 March 1980, p. 348.

5. Drew, 6 October 1984. *Football* is more formally known as *Mooney vs. Fowle*. It was apparently common to have working titles that were different from the final titles, and those working titles have become the more familiar to the individuals who worked on the films. *On the Pole* is often referred to as *Eddie Sachs*, for

example, which causes additional confusion because a later adaptation of *On the Pole* used in *The Living Camera* series was titled *Eddie*.

6. Pennebaker, 25 October 1984.
7. Pennebaker, October 1984. Al Maysles left Drew Associates and formed his own film production company with his brother David. The Maysles brothers were successful producers of documentary and industrial films with such notable productions as *Salesman, Gimme Shelter, Grey Gardens*, and several films on the artist Cristo. David Maysles died in New York City on January 3, 1987, at age 54. (*New York Times*, 4 January 1987, 86.)

15. The ABC Connection, 2

1. Drew, 30 April 1984.
2. *X-Pilot*, text from film. 6 February 1961, ABC Television Network. Executive producer, Robert Drew.
3. Stephen Mamber, *Cinema-Verite in America: Studies in Uncontrolled Documentary* (Cambridge: MIT Press, 1974), 49.
4. Although a system for synchronizing the camera and recorder without using a wire connection had been devised, it had not yet been perfected: "some rolls would sync up well, other rolls would float, and other rolls would have intermittent dropouts. There were all kinds of problems." The "cordless" system that Leacock and Pennebaker had developed was initially based on the use of Bulova's "Accutron" wristwatches. The watches, one on the camera and the other on the recorder, used a tuning fork circuit to provide an extremely stable timing pulse to synchronize of the camera and recorder involved. An important feature of this equipment development was that almost all the Drew-Leacock-Pennebaker equipment was based on pre-existing equipment—Auricon cameras, Uher and Perfectone recorders, and the watches. By adapting equipment, rather than designing it, Drew and his associates had cut months, probably years, off the development process and saved significant sums of money. To have designed a portable sync sound system completely from scratch would have been a difficult technical and financial burden and much more time consuming.
5. Leacock, 22 September 1984.
6. Drew, 15 May 1987.
7. *The Children Were Watching*, text from film. 6 March 1961, ABC Television Network. Executive producer, Robert Drew.
8. Drew, interview by Barbara Hogenson, 5 January 1980, p. 225.
9. "Television's School of Storm and Stress: Robert Drew's Documentaries Aim at Photographic Realism," *Broadcasting*, 6 March 1961, 82.
10. A. William Bluem, *Documentary in American Television: Form-Function-Method* (New York: Hastings House, 1965), 123. Bluem died 18 April 1974; see *New York Times*, 19 April 1974, 40.
11. Bluem, 123.
12. Bluem, 128.
13. Bluem, 128.

14. Bluem, 128–29.
15. Bluem, 130.
16. Leacock, 22 September 1984.
17. Drew, telephone interview with author, 15 June 1987. Given the force and long-term effect of Bluem's criticisms and the sharpness of Drew's response, it is interesting that although Drew was somewhat aware of Bluem's views, he had never examined them in any detailed way and, in fact, had to obtain a copy of Bluem's book before responding to questions about it.
18. *Adventures on the New Frontier*, text from film. 28 March 1961, ABC Television Network. Executive producer, Robert Drew.
19. Drew, interview by Barbara Hogenson, 4 October 1979, pp. 211–12.
20. Drew, 14 February 1988.
21. Drew, interview by Barbara Hogenson, 4 October 1979, pp. 197–98.
22. Drew, interview by Barbara Hogenson, 4 October 1979, pp. 212–13.
23. Leacock, 22 September 1984. Drew later commented that "this idea that Leacock did this independently is interesting, but that did not get done without my agreement. . . . Leacock did not drop an assignment and begin another one without an assignment from me to do so. . . . We weren't that haphazard. Nothing got assigned, or shot, unless it was assigned by me. That just did not happen." (Drew, 14 February 1988.)

16. Drew Associates, 2

1. Pennebaker, interview by Barbara Hogenson, 25 March 1980, p. 247.
2. Drew had provided some additional insights on the relationship between the correspondent and photographer during actual field production: "The idea that the cameraman had the responsibility on him of when to roll and when not to roll and what to shoot and so forth and that the correspondent had no responsibility for that is not true. . . . There is a constant eye communication on everything. . . . It is a very intense, two-man, two-brain process. . . . Especially in those days, it was a fishing game, with limited bait, limited time, limited energy, and we were always making these decisions about when to roll and not. The guy who got the other guy up to bat doesn't suddenly stop thinking! or being aware; he goes right on doing it. And in a way, the photographer is operating within *his* decision apparatus, not independently or without it." (Drew, 14 February 1988.)
3. Pennebaker, 25 October 1984.
4. Pennebaker, 25 October 1984.
5. Pennebaker, 25 October 1984.
6. Leacock, 22 September 1984.
7. Drew, 30 April 1984.
8. Drew, 20 November 1983.
9. Shuker, 16 November 1984.
10. Leacock, 22 September 1984.
11. Shuker, 16 November 1984.
12. Pennebaker, interview by Barbara Hogenson, 25 March 1980, pp. 244–45.

17. Breaking the Connection

1. Drew, "An Independent with the Networks," 21.
2. Drew, 30 April 1984.
3. Pennebaker, interview by Barbara Hogenson, 20 May 1980, p. 418.
4. Drew, interview by Barbara Hogenson, 4 October 1979, p. 217.
5. Drew, interview by Barbara Hogenson, 6 March 1980, pp. 356–57.

18. The Living Camera

1. Drew, "An Independent with the Networks," 22.
2. Drew, 14 February 1988.
3. Drew, interview by Barbara Hogenson, 5 January 1980, pp. 233–34.
4. *Eddie*, text from film. Co-produced by Time-Life Broadcasting and Drew Associates, 1961. Executive producer, Robert Drew.
5. The credits for *Eddie* list Richard Leacock, D. A. Pennebaker, Bill Ray, Abbott Mills, and Albert Maysles as filmmakers, and James Lipscomb and Greg Shuker as correspondents. Identical credits are used for *On the Pole*.
6. *David*, text from film. Co-produced by Time-Life Broadcasting and Drew Associates, 1961. Executive producer, Robert Drew.
7. *David*, text from film.
8. Pennebaker, 25 October 1984.
9. Drew, interview by Barbara Hogenson, 18 February 1980, p. 251.
10. *David*, text from film.
11. Drew, interview by Barbara Hogenson, 18 February 1980, p. 259.
12. Stephen Mamber, *Cinema Verite in America: Studies in Uncontrolled Documentary* (Cambridge: MIT Press, 1974), 80. A description of the "Living Camera" films is on p. 62–105.
13. Drew, interview by Barbara Hogenson, 18 February 1980, p. 261.
14. Leacock, 22 September 1984.
15. *Petey and Johnny*. Producer: Richard Leacock. Filmmakers: James Lipscomb, Abbott Mills, William Ray. In Mamber, p. 267.
16. Leacock, 22 September 1984.
17. Drew, interview by Barbara Hogenson, 2 August 1979, p. 262.
18. Patricia Jaffee, "Editing Cinema Verite," *Film Comment* 3 (Summer 1965): 45.
19. Jaffee, "Editing Cinema Verite," 45–46.
20. Pennebaker, interview by Barbara Hogenson, 25 March 1980, pp. 259–60.
21. Drew, 20 November 1983.
22. Drew, interview by Barbara Hogenson, 18 February 1980, p. 263. Drew's principal revision was to cut Lipscomb's eighty-five-minute version down to a more marketable length. The version screened for this study was sixty-six minutes, indicating that it may have been a festival version rather than a broadcast version.
23. *Mooney vs. Fowle*, text from film. Co-produced by Time-Life Broadcasting and Drew Associates, 1962. Executive producer, Robert Drew.
24. Leacock, 22 September 1984.

25. Drew, 6 October 1984.
26. Drew, interview by Barbara Hogenson, 18 February 1980, p. 266. John Bainbridge, "Profile: Like A Homesick Angel," *The New Yorker*, 10 November 1962, 61.
27. Drew, interview by Barbara Hogenson, 18 February 1980, pp. 266–67. Filmmakers on *Blackie* were Bill Ray and D. A. Pennebaker; correspondents were Gregory Shuker and Peter Powell.
28. Mamber, 115.
29. Mamber, 115–16.
30. Drew, 6 October 1984.
31. Drew, 6 October 1984. Stephen Mamber's criticisms of Drew's work are qualified by the following statement: "I'm rather embarrassed to admit it, but the entire time Drew allowed me for an interview was about twenty minutes. He did allow me to see some films in his office (after ignoring a number of letters, and only when I almost literally camped on his door step begging to see some of the movies). I sent him a copy of the book after it came out, and as he has never acknowledged receiving it, I imagine that some of my discussion of his work did not please him very much." (Mamber to author, 5 November 1984.)
32. Mamber, 127.
33. Drew, 8 June 1984.
34. Pennebaker, 25 October 1984.
35. Drew, 15 May 1987.
36. Shuker, 16 November 1984.
37. Drew, interview by Barbara Hogenson, 5 January 1980, p. 264.
38. *Susan Starr*, text from film. Produced by Time-Life Broadcasting and Drew Associates, 1962. Executive producer, Robert Drew.
39. Drew, interview by Barbara Hogenson, 5 January 1980, p. 270.
40. Drew, interview by Barbara Hogenson, 18 February 1980, p. 276.
41. Drew, interview by Barbara Hogenson, 18 February 1980, p. 274–75.
42. Drew, interview by Barbara Hogenson, 18 February 1980, pp. 276–77.
43. Drew, interview by Barbara Hogenson, 18 February 1980, p. 276.
44. Pennebaker, interview by Barbara Hogenson, 6 May 1980, p. 378.
45. Drew, interview by Barbara Hogenson, 5 January 1980, pp. 252–53.
46. Pennebaker, interview by Barbara Hogenson, 6 May 1980, pp. 346–48.
47. Pennebaker, interview by Barbara Hogenson, 6 May 1980, pp. 371–72.
48. Pennebaker, 25 October 1984.
49. Leacock, 22 September 1984.
50. Pennebaker, 25 October 1984.
51. Drew, 15 May 1987.
52. Drew, 15 May 1987.
53. Drew, 6 October 1984.
54. Drew, 6 October 1984.
55. Leacock, 22 September 1984.
56. Leacock, 22 September 1984.
57. Pennebaker, interview by Barbara Hogenson, 6 May 1980, pp. 378–79.

58. Drew, interview by Barbara Hogenson, 18 February 1980, p. 289.
59. Leacock, 22 September 1984.
60. Drew, interview by Barbara Hogenson, 18 February 1980, pp. 284–85.
61. Leacock, 22 September 1984.
62. Drew, 6 October 1984.
63. Leacock, 22 September 1984.
64. Pennebaker, 25 October 1984.
65. *The Chair*, text from film. Co-produced by Time-Life Broadcast and Drew Associates, 1962. Filmmaker, Gregory Shuker; executive producer, Robert Drew.
66. Drew, interview by Barbara Hogenson, 18 February 1980, p. 29.
67. James Blue, "One Man's Truth: An Interview with Richard Leacock," *Film Comment* 3 (Spring 1963): 19.
68. Drew, 6 October 1984.
69. Drew, 14 February 1988.
70. Drew, interview by Barbara Hogenson, 18 February 1980, pp. 287–88.
71. Drew, interview by Barbara Hogenson, 18 February 1980, p. 293.

19. The Critics

1. Drew, 8 June 1984.
2. See John Grierson, "Flaherty's Poetic *Moana*," in Lewis Jacobs, ed., *The Documentary Tradition*, 2d ed. (New York: W. W. Norton, 1979), 25–26. Originally published anonymously in the *New York Sun*, 8 Feburary 1926.
3. Lewis Jacobs, "Free Cinema—I," *Film Culture* no. 4 (February 1958): 9.
4. Colin Young and A. Martin Zweiback, "Going Out to the Subject," *Film Quarterly* 13 (Winter 1959): 39–49.
5. Young and Zweiback, 41.
6. Ernest Callenbach, "Going Out to the Subject: II," *Film Quarterly* 14 (Spring 1961): 39.
7. Callenbach, 40.
8. Louis Marcorelles, "American Diary," *Sight and Sound* 32 (Winter 1962–63): 5.
9. Marcorelles, "American Diary," 6.
10. See the following list, taken from Stephen Mamber, *Cinema Verite in America: Studies in Uncontrolled Documentary* (Cambridge: MIT Press, 1974), 256–61: Louis Marcorelles, "L'Experience Leacock," *Cahiers du Cinema* 24 (February 1963): 17; Louis Marcorelles and Andrew S. Labarthe, "Entretien avec Robert Drew et Richard Leacock," *Cahiers du Cinema* 24 (February 1963): 19; Louis Marcorelles, "Le Cinema Direct Nord Americain," *Image et Son*, no. 183 (April 1963), 52; Louis Marcorelles, "La Fiore aux Verites," *Cahiers du Cinema* 24 (May 1963): 30; Claude Julien, "Un Homme dans la Foule," *Artsept*, no. 2 (April–June 1963), 46; Jean-Claude Bringuier, "Libres Propos sur le Cinema-Verite," *Cahiers du Cinema* 25 (July 1963):16; Jean-Luc Godard, "Richard Leacock," in "Dictionaire de 121 Metteurs en Scene," *Cahiers du Cinema* 25 (December 1963–January 1964): 140; Jane Fonda, "Jane," *Cahiers du Cinema* 25 (December 1963–January 1964): 187;

Ulrich Gregor, "Leacock Oder das Kino der Physiker," *Film* (Munich) 4 (January 1966): 14–15.

11. Ian Cameron and Mark Shivas, "Cinema Verite," *Movie*, April 1963, 13.

12. Cameron and Shivas, 15.

13. Cameron and Shivas, 15.

14. Louis Marcorelles, "Nothing but the Truth," *Sight and Sound* 32 (Summer 1963): 115.

15. Marcorelles, "Nothing but the Truth," 115.

16. Marcorelles, "Nothing but the Truth," 115.

17. Marcorelles, "Nothing but the Truth," 115.

18. See Alan Rosenthal, *The Documentary Conscience* (Berkeley: University of California Press, 1980).

19. Colin Young, "Cinema of Common Sense," *Film Quarterly* 17 (Summer 1964): 26.

20. Young, "Cinema of Common Sense," 27–28.

21. Young, "Cinema of Common Sense," 40. Young's reference is to Siegfried Kracauer, *Theory of Film: The Redemption of Physical Reality* (New York: Oxford University Press, 1960).

22. Peter Graham, *"Cinéma Vérité* in France," *Film Quarterly* 17 (Summer 1964): 31.

23. Graham, 36.

24. Henry Breitrose, "On the Search for the Real Nitty-Gritty: Problems and Possibilities in *Cinéma-Vérité*," *Film Quarterly* 17 (Summer 1964): 36–40.

25. Breitrose, 39.

26. Breitrose, 40.

27. James C. Lipscomb, "Correspondence and Controversy," *Film Quarterly* 18 (Winter 1964/65): 62.

28. Lipscomb, 63.

29. Leacock, 22 September 1984.

30. Drew, 8 June 1984.

31. Drew, interview by Barbara Hogenson, 4 October 1979, p. 220.

32. Leacock, 22 September 1984.

33. Shuker, 23 November 1984.

20. Drew Associates, 3

1. Drew, interview by Barbara Hogenson, 5 January 1980, p. 240.

2. Drew, interview by Barbara Hogenson, 4 October 1979, p. 219.

3. Drew, interview by Barbara Hogenson, 18 February 1980, p. 304.

4. Pennebaker, interview by Barbara Hogenson, 20 May 1980, pp. 413–15.

5. Shuker, 16 November 1984.

6. Pennebaker, 25 October 1984.

7. Leacock, 22 September 1984.

8. Drew, interview by Barbara Hogenson, 18 February 1980, p. 305.

21. The Crisis

1. Drew, "An Independent with the Networks," 22.
2. Shuker, 23 November 1984.
3. Shuker, 16 November 1984.
4. Shuker, 16 November 1984.
5. Drew, 28 February 1988.
6. Shuker, 16 November 1984.
7. Shuker, 16 November 1984.
8. Shuker, 16 November 1984.
9. Shuker, 16 November 1984.
10. Shuker, 16 November 1984.
11. Pennebaker, interview by Barbara Hogenson, 6 May 1980, pp. 399–400.
12. Theodore Sorensen, Special Counsel to the President; Lawrence O'Brien, Special Assistant to the President; Ramsey Clark, Assistant Attorney General, Lands Division; Burke Marshall, Assistant Attorney General, Civil Rights Division; Kenneth O'Donnell, Special Assistant to the President. U.S., Office of the Federal Register. *U.S. Government Organization Manual, 1963–64*, p. 63.
13. Pennebaker, 25 October 1984.
14. Pennebaker, interview by Barbara Hogenson, 6 May 1980, pp. 398–99.
15. Pennebaker, interview by Barbara Hogenson, 6 May 1980, p. 408.
16. Leacock, 22 September 1984.
17. Pennebaker, 25 October 1984.
18. Leacock, 22 September 1984.
19. Pennebaker, 25 October 1984.
20. *Crisis: Behind a Presidential Commitment*, text from film. ABC Television Network, 21 October 1963. Producer, Gregory Shuker; executive producer, Robert Drew.
21. *Crisis: Behind a Presidential Commitment*, text from film.
22. *Crisis: Behind a Presidential Commitment*, text from film.
23. *Crisis: Behind a Presidential Commitment*, text from film.
24. *Crisis: Behind a Presidential Commitment*, text from film.
25. *Crisis: Behind a Presidential Commitment*, text from film.
26. Pennebaker, interview by Barbara Hogenson, 6 May 1980, p. 409.
27. Leacock, 22 September 1984.
28. Shuker, 23 November 1984.
29. Jack Gould, "TV: Too Many Cameras: Documentary on the Segregation Crisis Termed Just a Peep Show," *New York Times*, 22 October 1963, 75.
30. Drew, 8 June 1984.
31. Val Adams, "TV Filmed Kennedys in Alabama Crisis," *New York Times*, 25 July 1963, 49.
32. "Not Macy's Window," *New York Times*, 27 July 1963, 16.
33. "Too Hot to Handle?" *Newsweek*, 5 August 1963, 67–68.
34. Shuker, 16 November 1984.
35. Pennebaker, 25 October 1984.

36. Shuker, 16 November 1984.
37. Pennebaker, 25 October 1984. Pennebaker recalls that one review of the edited material was by Kennedy's press secretary Pierre Salinger and ABC News vice-president James Hagerty, press secretary to former President Dwight Eisenhower. "Hagerty came and sat in one [chair] and Pierre sat in another. And they watched the film." Drew insists that "No such meeting ever took place. . . . The matter was handled completely by myself and Shuker" in conversations with Robert Kennedy and Katzenbach. Shuker reportedly agrees with Drew's version.
38. Drew, 6 October 1984. Drew later reworked *Crisis* as *Kennedy vs. Wallace: A Crisis Up Close* for *The American Experience* series on PBS (15 November 1988), which included a somewhat shortened version of *Crisis* interspersed with present-day interview segments by Vivian Malone and Nicholas Katzenbach. Host David McCullough explained the differences: "Then some of the dialogue in the Oval Office was covered with narration, as it is not here. What was happening, what was said, are what you will see and hear." A review of segments from the Oval Office from a print of *Crisis* supplied by Robert Drew and *Kennedy vs. Wallace* shows that they are identical, except for a short voice-over-and-sync-sound segment of Nicholas Katzenbach explaining Lawrence O'Brien's concerns that a speech might damage efforts to pass pending civil rights legislation. *Kennedy vs. Wallace* therefore contains more narration (in the form of Katzenbach's statements) and somewhat less of the Oval Office meeting than the original *Crisis*. The rumored comments about "nut-cutting on [Capital] Hill," which Robert Kennedy reportedly objected to, appear in neither version.
39. Leacock, 22 September 1984.
40. Drew, interview by Barbara Hogenson, 4 October 1979, p. 178.
41. Gould, "Too Many Cameras."
42. Leacock, 22 September 1984.
43. John Horn, "A TV Milestone in Candid History," *New York Herald Tribune*, 16 September 1963, 21.
44. Gould, "Too Many Cameras."
45. Horn, "A TV Milestone in Candid History."
46. Jack Gould, "Behind Closed Doors: Television Coverage of Matters Involving Executive Decision Can Tarnish National Dignity," *New York Times*, 27 October 1963, sec. 2, p. 13.
47. Horn, "A TV Milestone in Candid History."
48. Gould, "Behind Closed Doors."
49. Shuker, 23 November 1984.
50. Drew, 15 May 1987.
51. Horn, "A Criticism of 'Crisis' Program's Critics," *New York Herald Tribune*, 25 October 1963, 19.
52. Gould, "Behind Closed Doors."
53. Horn, "A Criticism of 'Crisis' Program's Critics."
54. Drew, 6 October 1984.
55. Shuker, 23 November 1984.
56. Pennebaker, 25 October 1984.

57. Shuker, 16 November 1984.
58. "State Seals Off Alabama Campus," *New York Times*, 9 June 1963, 50.
59. "Kennedy Renews Plea For Tax Cut to Bar Recession," *New York Times*, 9 June 1963, 1.
60. Claude Sitton, "Governor Leaves; But Fulfills Promises to Stand in Door and to Avoid Violence," *New York Times*, 12 June 1963, 1.
61. Sitton, 20.
62. Tom Wicker, "President in Plea; Asks Help of Citizens to Assure Equality of Rights to All," *New York Times*, 12 June 1963, 1.
63. *New York Times*, 13 June 1963.
64. *New York Times*, 16 June 1963, sec. 5. p. 1.
65. Gould, "Behind Closed Doors."
66. Horn, "A TV Milestone in Candid History."

22. Drew Associates, 4

1. Pennebaker, interview by Barbara Hogenson, New York, 25 March 1980, pp. 249–50.
2. Drew, interview by Barbara Hogenson, 6 March 1980, p. 353.
3. Pennebaker, interview by Barbara Hogenson, 10 December 1979, pp. 204–5. An in-house history of Time, Inc. notes that the rights to the films were sold to Drew in 1981. Curtis Pendergast, *The World of Time, Inc.: An Intimate History of a Changing Enterprise, 1960–1980* (New York: Atheneum, 1986), 3:137.
4. For a complete listing of the films of Drew and his associates, see Appendix B, "Filmography".
5. Pennebaker, interview by Barbara Hogenson, 10 December 1979, pp. 173, 202.
6. Drew, interview by Barbara Hogenson, 18 February 1980, pp. 298–99.
7. Drew, interview by Barbara Hogenson, 18 February 1980, p. 310.
8. Drew, interview by Barbara Hogenson, 18 February 1980, p. 311.
9. Drew, interview by Barbara Hogenson, 6 March 1980, pp. 322–23.
10. Drew, interview by Barbara Hogenson, 6 March 1980, p. 323.
11. Drew, interview by Barbara Hogenson, 6 March 1980, p. 324.
12. Drew, interview by Barbara Hogenson, 6 March 1980, pp. 328–29.
13. Drew, interview by Barbara Hogenson, 6 March 1980, pp. 329–30.
14. John Horn, "Kennedy Documentary," *New York Herald Tribune*, 28 November 1963, 19; Horn, "Danger on Screen," *New York Herald Tribune*, 22 January 1964, 17; Horn, "Close-Ups," *New York Herald Tribune*, 22 June 1965, 17.
15. Drew, "An Independent with the Networks," 22.
16. Drew, "An Independent with the Networks," 22.
17. The *Bell Telephone Hour* retitled *Festival of Two Worlds* as *Spoleto: A Man's Dream*. See Appendix C for a list of awards given to Drew films.
18. Drew, interview by Barbara Hogenson, 23 April 1980, pp. 368–69.
19. Drew, "An Independent with the Networks," pp. 22–23. Drew's productions since 1980 have been videotape. The development of reliable lightweight video equipment has again made candid television journalism practical, and Drew, while

having little to do with the development of the equipment, was among the early major cinema verite producers to embrace it.

20. Drew, interview by Barbara Hogenson, 23 April 1980, pp. 397–98.

21. Drew, "An Independent with the Networks," 22.

22. Richard Lacayo, " 'Why Are Documentaries So Dull?' " *New York Times*, 20 February 1983, sec. 2, p. 29.

23. Lacayo, 37.

24. Drew, 6 October 1984.

25. John Corry, "A Farm-Crisis Documentary, on [Channel] 13," *New York Times*, 22 July 1986, sec. C, p. 18.

26. Drew, 6 October 1984.

23. Drew and Cinema Verite—Today

1. See Pennebaker's filmography in Levin, pp. 225–33.

2. Pennebaker, 25 October 1984.

3. Leacock, interview in Levin, pp. 218–19.

4. Leacock, 22 September 1984.

5. Scott Campbell, "Media Messages," *[Boston] Globe Magazine*, 15 March 1987, 18.

6. Leacock, 22 September 1984.

7. Shuker, 16 November 1984.

8. See *Showman* (1962), *What's Happening!: The Beatles in the U.S.A.* (1964), *Salesman* (1969), *Gimme Shelter* (1970), *Cristo's Valley Curtain* (1974), *Grey Gardens* (1975), *Running Fence* (1978), and others.

9. Unattributed quotation, in Calvin Pryluck, "Seeking to Take the Longest Journey: A Conversation with Albert Maysles," *Journal of the University Film Association* 28 (Spring 1976): 9.

10. David Davidson, "Direct Cinema and Modernism: The Long Journey to *Grey Gardens*," *Journal of the University Film Association* 38 (Winter 1981): 5, 10, 12–13.

11. For a detailed filmography of Wiseman, see Thomas W. Benson and Carolyn Anderson, *Reality Fictions: The Films of Frederick Wiseman* (Carbondale: Southern Illinois University Press, 1990), 317–23.

12. Jay Sharbutt, "PBS 'Primate' Show 'Most Nauseating'," Associated Press, in *Centre Daily Times* (State College, Pa.), 5 December 1974, sec. 2, p. 11.

13. Richard Schickel, "Where Misery Must Be Confronted," *Life*, 6 February 1970, 9.

14. An abundance of references exist on the career of Frederick Wiseman. For a detailed listing of early references, see Liz Ellsworth, *Frederick Wiseman: A Guide to References and Resources* (Boston: G. K. Hall, 1979). A useful introductory work is Thomas R. Atkins *Frederick Wiseman* (New York: Monarch, 1976). "Frederick Wiseman's Documentaries: Theory and Structure," in Bill Nichols, *Ideology and the Image: Social Representation in the Cinema and Other Media* (Bloomington:

Indiana University Press, 1981), looks carefully at Wiseman's structural strategies. The most detailed analysis of Wiseman's films and methods is Thomas R. Benson and Carolyn Anderson, *Reality Fictions: The Films of Frederick Wiseman* (Carbondale: Southern Illinois University Press, 1989.)

15. Useful references in visual anthropology include Paul Hockings, ed., *Principles of Visual Anthropology* (The Hague: Mouton, 1975), Colin Young, "Observational Cinema," and David MacDougall, "Beyond Observational Cinema"; Karl G. Heider, *Ethnographic Film* (Austin: University of Texas Press, 1976); Napoleon Chagnon, *Studying the Yanomamo* (New York: Holt, Rinehart and Winston, 1974); Napoleon Chagnon and Timothy Asch, producers, *A Man Called 'Bee': Studying the Yanomamo* [motion picture] (Watertown, MA: Documentary Educational Resources, 1975); and Robert Gardner and Karl G. Heider, *Gardens of War: Life and Death in the New Guinea Stone Age* (New York: Random House, 1969).

16. Peter J. Boyer, " '60 Minutes': A Hit Confronts the Odds," *New York Times*, 13 September 1987, sec. 2, p. 1.

17. Pennebaker, interview by Barbara Hogenson, New York, 10 December 1979, p. 202.

18. Don Hewitt, quoted by Tom McNichol in "And the Winners Are . . .," *Washington Journalism Review*, February 1986, 32. In a poll of the magazine's readers, *60 Minutes* was chosen "Best Network TV Magazine Show."

19. Boyer, 38.

20. Drew, 30 April 1984.

21. Curtis Pendergast, *The World of Time, Inc.: The Intimate History of a Changing Empire, 1960–1980* (New York: Antheneum, 1986), 3: 136–137.

22. Pendergast, 141. Four of the Time-Life television stations were sold in 1972; the fifth, in Grand Rapids, Mich., was sold a decade later. The corporation's move into cable "reflected the feeling that Time, Inc. had already missed its chance in conventional broadcasting." Pendergast, 489.

23. John J. O'Connor, "Where's That Promised New World of Cable?" *New York Times*, 25 November 1984, sec. 2, p. 1.

24. Earl Bohn, "Westinghouse to get $2.1 Billion for Cable Network," Associated Press, in *Johnstown Tribune-Democrat* (Johnstown, Pa.), 26 December 1985, 13B; "Time Will Sell a Piece of ATC to the Public," *Broadcasting*, 5 May 1986, 46.

25. "Time, Inc. Net Income Up 43%," *Electronic Media*, 2 May 1988, 31.

26. *Being with John F. Kennedy*, 1983, coproduced by Nancy Dickerson and Drew Associates. Producer and writer, Robert Drew. Distributed by Golden West Television.

27. Jack O'Brian, "Cuba Fidels as We Burn," *New York Journal-American*, 8 December 1960, 17. "Whom The Bell Extols," *Newsweek*, 1 January 1968, 54.

28. Drew, 15 May 1987.

29. Drew, 15 May 1987.

30. Joyce Cary, *The Horse's Mouth* (New York: Grosset and Dunlap, 1944). Drew, 15 May 1987.

24. Afterword

1. Drew, 14 February 1988.
2. P. J. O'Connell, "Robert Drew and the Development of Cinema-Verite in America: An Innovation in Television Journalism" (Ph.D. dissertation, The Pennsylvania State University, 1988). Drew's comments are included as an appendix to both the dissertation and this work. His comments are somewhat different in each case.
3. Drew, 14 February 1988.
4. Drew, 14 February 1988.
5. Drew, 14 February 1988.
6. Drew, 14 February 1988.
7. Drew, 14 February 1988.
8. Drew, 14 February 1988.
9. Pennebaker, 25 October 1984.
10. Drew, 14 February 1988.
11. Drew, 14 February 1988.
12. Pennebaker, quoted by G. Roy Levin, in *Documentary Explorations* (Garden City, NY: Doubleday, 1971), 235, 243.
13. Drew, 14 February 1988.
14. Drew, 14 February 1988.
15. Drew, 14 February 1988.
16. Drew, 14 February 1988.

Bibliography

Adams, Henry. *The Education of Henry Adams*. New York: Houghton Mifflin, 1918.

Adams, Val. "Daly Quits ABC in Policy Battle; Vice President Was Long at Odds With Network Over Control of News Shows." *New York Times*, 17 November 1960, 75.

——. "TV Filmed Kennedys in Alabama Crisis." *New York Times*, 25 July 1963, 1.

"Air Force Falcons Soar Into Big Time." *Life*, 8 December 1958, 41–44.

Angell, Carrie. "Early *Cinema-Verite*: Robert Drew and Associates." Whitney Museum of American Art, March 1982. Mimeo.

Atkins, Thomas R., ed. *Frederick Wiseman*. New York: Monarch Press, 1976.

Bachmann, Gideon. "The Frontiers of Realist Cinema: The Work of Ricky Leacock." *Film Culture*, no. 22–23 (Summer 1961): 12–33. (Also in *Film: A Montage of Theories*, edited by Richard Dyer MacCann, 289–300, New York: E. P. Dutton, 1966.)

Bainbridge, John. "Profile: Like a Homesick Angel," *New Yorker*, 10 November 1962, 61.

Barnouw, Erik. *Documentary: A History of the Non-Fiction Film*. Rev. ed. New York: Oxford University Press, 1983.

——. *Tube of Plenty: The Evolution of American Television*. Rev. ed. New York: Oxford University Press, 1975.

Barsam, Richard. *Non-Fiction Film: A Critical History*. New York: Dutton, 1973.

Benson, Thomas W., and Carolyn Anderson. *Reality Fictions: The Films of Frederick Wiseman*. Carbondale: Southern Illinois University Press, 1989.

Blue, James. "One Man's Truth: An Interview with Richard Leacock." *Film*

Comment 3 (Spring 1965): 16–22. (Also in *The Documentary Tradition*, 2d. ed. Edited by Lewis Jacobs, 406–19. New York: W. W. Norton, 1979.)

Bluem, A. William. *Documentary in American Television: Form-Function-Method.* New York: Hastings House, 1965.

Bohn, Earl. "Westinghouse to Get $2.1 Billion for Cable Network." Associated Press, in *Johnstown Tribune-Democrat* (Johnstown, Pa.), 26 December 1985, 13B.

Boyer, Peter J. " '60 Minutes': A Hit Confronts the Odds." *New York Times*, 13 September 1987, sec. 2, 1.

Breitrose, Henry. "On the Search for the Real Nitty-Gritty: Problems and Possibilities In *Cinema-Verite*." *Film Quarterly* 17 (Summer 1964): 36–40.

Bringuier, Jean-Claude. "Libres Propos sur le Cinema-Verite." *Cahiers du Cinema* 25 (July 1963): 16.

Callenbach, Ernest. "Going Out to the Subject: II." *Film Quarterly* 14 (Spring 1961): 38–40.

Cameron, Ian, and Mark Shivas. "Cinema Verite," *Movie*, April 1963, 12–25.

Campbell, Scott. "Media Messages." *[Boston] Globe Magazine*, 15 March 1987, 18.

Cary, Joyce. *The Horse's Mouth.* New York: Grosset and Dunlap, 1944.

Chagnon, Napoleon. *Studying the Yanomamo.* New York: Holt, Rinehart and Winston, 1974.

"City Against Auto." *Life*, 11 July 1949, 78–85.

Corry, John. "A Farm-Crisis Documentary, On [Channel] 13." *New York Times*, 22 July 1986, C18.

Davidson, David. "Direct Cinema and Modernism: The Long Journey to *Grey Gardens*." *Journal of the University Film Association* 33 (Winter 1981): 5–13.

Drew, Robert. Eight interviews conducted by author, November 1983–28 February 1988. Drew Associates, New York.

———. "The Fliers." *Life*, 9 December 1946, 104.

———. "An Independent with the Networks." *Studies In Visual Communication* 8 (Winter 1982): 15–23.

———. "Notes to a Starting Photographer." Memo to Sidney Reichman, November, December, 1963. Copy in the files of the Oral History Research Office, Butler Library, Columbia University. Mimeo.

———. "The Reminiscences of Robert Drew." Ten interviews conducted by Barbara Hogenson. Oral History Research Office, Butler Library, Columbia University, New York, 4 October 1979–23 April 1980. Mimeo.

———. "See It Then: Notes on Television Journalism." *Nieman Reports* 9 (April 1955): 2.

Dykhouse, Caroline Dow. "Robert Drew and the Detroit Workshop, 1949–1951." Master's thesis, University of Michigan, 1980.

Ellsworth, Liz. *Frederick Wiseman: A Guide to References and Resources.* Boston: G. K. Hall, 1979.

Fielding, Raymond. *The March of Time: 1935–1951.* New York: Oxford University Press, 1978.

Gardner, Robert, and Karl Heider. *Gardens of War: Life and Death in the New Guinea Stone Age.* New York: Random House, 1969.

Godard, Jean-Luc. "Richard Leacock," in "Dictionaire de 121 Metteurs en Scene", *Cahiers du Cinema* 25 (December 1963–January 1964): 140.

Gould, Jack. "Behind Closed Doors: Television Coverage of Matters Involving Executive Decision Can Tarnish National Dignity." *New York Times*, 27 October 1963, sec. 2, 13.

————. "Television: Yanki No!—A.B.C. Documentary on Castro's Effect on Latin America Produced by Time, Inc." *New York Times*, 8 December 1960, 71.

————. "TV: Too Many Cameras: Documentary on the Segregation Crisis Termed Just a Peep Show." *New York Times*, 22 October 1963, 75.

Graham, Peter. "*Cinema-Verite* in France." *Film Quarterly* 17 (Summer 1964): 30.

Gregor, Ulrich. "Leacock Oder das Kino der Physiker." *Film* (Munich), 4 (January 1966): 14–15.

Grierson, John. *Grierson on Documentary.* Edited by Forsyth Hardy. Berkeley: University of California Press, 1966.

"Hagerty ABC News-Pubaffairs Deal Is Finalized." *Variety*, 23 November 1960, 24.

Heider, Karl. *Ethnographic Film.* Austin: University of Texas Press, 1976.

Hockings, Paul, ed. *Principles of Visual Anthropology.* The Hague: Mouton Publishers, 1975.

Horn, John. "Close-Ups." *New York Herald Tribune.* 22 June 1965, 17.

————. "A Criticism of 'Crisis' Program's Critics." *New York Herald Tribune*, 25 October 1963, 21.

————. "Danger on the Screen." *New York Herald Tribune*, 22 January 1964, 17.

————. "Kennedy Documentary." *New York Herald Tribune*, 28 November 1963, 19.

————. "A TV Milestone in Candid History." *New York Herald Tribune*, 16 September 1963, 21.

Inaugural Special. New York: Time, Inc., 1961.

Issari, M. Ali. *Cinema-Verite.* East Lansing: Michigan State University Press, 1971.

Jacobs, Lewis, ed. *The Documentary Tradition.* 2d. ed. New York: W. W. Norton, 1979.

————. "Free Cinema—I." *Film Culture*, no. 4 (February 1958): 9.

Jaffe, Patricia. "Editing Cinema Verite." *Film Comment* 3 (Summer 1965): 43–47.

"Jane," *Cahiers du Cinema* 25 (December 1963–January 1964): 187.

"Jets Are Different." *Time*, 23 September 1946, 97–98.

Julien, Claude. "Un Homme dans la Foule." *Artsept* 2 (April–June 1963): 46.

"Kennedy Renews Plea for Tax Cut to Bar Recession." *New York Times*, 9 June 1963, 1.

Kracauer, Siegfried. *Theory of Film: The Redemption of Physical Reality*. New York: Oxford University Press, 1960.

Lacayo, Richard. " 'Why Are Documentaries So Dull?' " *New York Times*, 20 February 1983, sec. 2, 29.

Laurent, Lawrence. "Radio and Television: ABC Issues a Film Editorial Tonight Offering 'Close Up!' of Latin America." *Washington Post*, 7 December 60, C22.

Leacock, Richard. Interview conducted by author, 22 September 1984. Film and TV Section, MIT, Cambridge.

————. Interview conducted by Mark Shivas. "Interviews: Richard Leacock," *Movie*, April 1963, 16.

"Legal Log Jam in Chicago." *Life*, 10 November 1952, 126–133.

Levin, G. Roy. *Documentary Explorations: 15 Interviews with Film-makers*. Garden City, N. Y.: Doubleday, 1971.

Lipscomb, James C. "Correspondence and Controversy." *Film Quarterly* 18 (Winter 1964–65): 62.

McNichol, Tom. "And the Winners Are . . ." *Washington Journalism Review*, February 1986, 32.

MacDougall, David. "Beyond Observational Cinema." In *Principles of Visual Anthropology*, edited by Paul Hockings, 109–24. The Hague: Mouton Publishers, 1975.

Mamber, Stephen. *Cinema-Verite in America: Studies in Uncontrolled Documentary*. Cambridge: MIT Press, 1974.

Marcorelles, Louis. "American Diary." *Sight and Sound* 32 (Winter 1962–63): 5.

————. "Le Cinema Direct Nord Americain." *Image et Son*, no. 183 (April 1963), 52.

————. "L'Experience Leacock." *Cahiers du Cinema* 24 (February 1963): 17.

————. "La Fiore aux Verites." *Cahiers du Cinema* 24 (May 1963): 30.

————. "Leacock at MIT." *Sight and Sound* 44 (Spring 1974):104–7.

————. *Living Cinema: New Directions in Contemporary Film-making*. Translated by Isabel Quigly. New York: Praeger, 1973.

————. "Nothing but the Truth." *Sight And Sound* 32 (Summer 1963): 115.

Marcorelles, Louis, and Andrew S. Labarthe. "Entretien avec Robert Drew et Richard Leacock." *Cahiers du Cinema* 24 (February 1963): 19.

Mekas, Jonas. "Notes on the New American Cinema." *Film Culture*, no. 24 (Spring 1962): 6–16.

Nichols, Bill. *Ideology and the Image: Social Representation in the Cinema and Other Media*. Bloomington: Indiana University Press, 1981.

"Not Macy's Window." *New York Times*, 27 July 1963, 16.

O'Brian, Jack. "Cuba Fidels as We Burn." *New York Journal-American*, 8 December 1960, 17.

O'Connell, P. J. *Robert Drew and the Development of Cinema-Verite in America: An Innovation in Television Journalism*, Ph. D. diss. Pennsylvania State University, 1988.

O'Connor, John J. "Where's That Promised New World of Cable?" *New York Times*, 25 November 1984, sec. 2, 1.

"On The Air." *New York Post*, 23 May 1961, 75.

Pendergast, Curtis. *The World of Time, Inc.: The Intimate History of a Changing Empire, 1960–1980*. Vol. 3. New York: Atheneum, 1986.

Pennebaker, Donn A. Interview conducted by author, 25 October 1984. Pennebaker Films, Inc., New York.

————. "The Reminiscences of Donn Alan Pennebaker." Ten interviews conducted by Barbara Hogenson. Oral History Research Office, Butler Library, Columbia University, New York, 14 November 1979–29 June 1981. Mimeo.

Pryluck, Calvin. "Seeking to Take the Longest Journey: A Conversation with Albert Maysles." *Journal of the University Film Association* 28 (Spring 1976): 9–16.

Pyle, Ernie. *Brave Men*. New York: Henry Holt and Co., 1944.

"P–80s." *Life*, 9 December 1946, 99.

Rose, Jackson J. *American Cinematographer Hand Book and Reference Guide*, 8th ed. Hollywood: American Society of Cinematographers, 1953.

Rosenthal, Alan. *The Documentary Conscience*. Berkeley: University of California Press, 1980.

Royce, Josiah. *The Philosophy of Loyalty*. New York: Macmillan, 1908.

"Russia's Wintry Look." *Life*, 26 April 1954, 104–9.

Schickel, Richard. "Where Misery Must Be Confronted." *Life*, 6 February 1970, 9.

Sharbutt, Jay. "PBS 'Primate' Show 'Most Nauseating'." Associated Press, in *Centre Daily Times* (State College, Pa.), 5 December 1974, sec. 2, 11.

Shuker, Gregory. Interviews conducted by author, 16 and 23 November 1984. Bronxville, N.Y.

Simons, Maj. David G., "A Journey No Man Had Taken." *Life*, 2 September 1957, 19–27.

Sitton, Claude. "Governor Leaves; But Fulfills Promises to Stand in Door and to Avoid Violence." *New York Times*, 12 June 1963, 1.

"Speedway Documentary." *New York Times*, 23 May 1961, 79.

"State Seals Off Alabama Campus." *New York Times*, 9 June 1963, 50.

"Stirring Drama in Spain." *Life*, 7 September 1959, 22–31.

"Television's School of Storm and Stress: Robert Drew's Documentaries Aim at Photographic Realism." *Broadcasting*, 6 March 1961, 82–84.

"Television: Two Men and a Camera." *Time*, 19 December 1960, 54.

"Three Prosecutors Engage the DuPonts." *Life*, 8 December 1952, 40–43.

Timberg, Robert. "Nieman Fellows: Choosing Harvard's Divine Dozen." *Washington Journalism Review*, November 1985, 19.

"Time, Inc. Net Income Up 43%." *Electronic Media*, 2 May 1988, 31.

"Time-Life Films Takes New Course for Pitch to Webs." *Variety*, 16 July 1975, 39.

"Time Marches On—Right Into ABC's Bell and Howell Pubaffairs Production." *Variety*, 16 November 1960, 29.

"Time Will Sell a Piece of ATC to the Public." *Broadcasting*, 5 May 1986, 46.

"Too Hot to Handle." *Newsweek*, 5 August 1963, 67.

White, Theodore H. *The Making of the President, 1960*. New York: Atheneum, 1961.

"Whom The Bell Extols." *Newsweek*, 1 January 1968, 54.

Wicker, Tom. "President in Plea; Asks Help of Citizens to Assure Equality of Rights to All." *New York Times*, 12 June 1963, 1.

Woodstone, Art. "ABC-TV and Bob Drew (Time, Inc.) Expand Program Vistas as Newest Success Story in Pubaffairs Area." *Variety*, 14 December 1960, 21.

———. "ABC-TV's 'Contiguous Twosome' (Treyz and Moore) Riding Herd on Sports-Pubaffairs-Entertainment." *Variety*, 23 November 1960, 24.

Young, Colin. "Cinema of Common Sense." *Film Quarterly* 17 (Summer 1964): 26.

———. "Observational Cinema." In *Principles of Visual Anthropology*, edited by Paul Hockings, 65–80. The Hague: Mouton Publishers, 1975.

Young, Colin, and A. Martin Zweiback. "Going Out to the Subject." *Film Quarterly* 13 (Winter 1959): 39–49.

Young, W. R. "What It's Like to Fly in Space." *Life*, 13 April 1959, 132–48.

Index

281

P. J. O'Connell is executive producer for public affairs at Penn State Television (WPSX-TV, University Park, Pennsylvania) and an affiliate assistant professor in the School of Communications at Penn State, where he teaches documentary history and criticism.

He is also director of the Rural America Documentary Project, a twenty-five-year effort by Penn State Television to document a representative cross-section of contemporary life in rural American over the last quarter of the twentieth century.

O'Connell's background is in television news and documentary at commercial stations in Iowa, Minneapolis, and Pittsburgh and at public stations in Pittsburgh and Penn State. His credits include over two-hundred documentary productions as camerman, editor, director, producer, and executive producer. He has received awards from NET, PBS, CPB, and Sigma Delta Chi; a George Foster Peabody Award; and a CLIO from the American TV Commercials Festival.

O'Connell holds a Bachelor of Science from Iowa State in TV production (1956), a Master of Arts from Penn State in Journalism (1974), and a Ph.D. from Penn State in Speech Communication (1988).